Data Management

John Owrey

Costing Human Resources:
The Financial Impact of Behavior in Organizations

*W*ayne F. Cascio
University of Colorado

Kent Human Resource Management Series

Richard W. Beatty, University of Colorado at Boulder
Series Consulting Editor

 VAN NOSTRAND REINHOLD COMPANY
NEW YORK CINCINNATI TORONTO LONDON MELBOURNE

To Dorothy and Joey,
my most valued assets

Hardbound edition by Van Nostrand Reinhold Company Inc.
135 West 50th Street, New York, N.Y. 10020
by arrangement with Kent Publishing Company,
a division of Wadsworth, Inc.

Manufactured in the United States of America

ISBN: 0-442-21501-0
Library of Congress Catalog Card Number: 82-11030

Van Nostrand Reinhold Publishing
1410 Birchmount Road
Scarborough, Ontario M1P 2E7, Canada

Van Nostrand Reinhold
480 Latrobe Street
Melbourne, Victoria 3000, Australia

Van Nostrand Reinhold Company Limited
Molly Millars Lane
Wokingham, Berkshire, England

15 14 13 12 11 10 9 8 7 6 5 4 3 2 1

Library of Congress Cataloging in Publication Data

Cascio, Wayne F.
    Costing human resources.

    (Kent human resource management series)
    Includes index.
    1. Labor costs.   I. Title.   II. Series.
HD4906.C37 1982b   658.1'553   82-11030
ISBN 0-442-21501-0

Series Preface

Historically, the personnel/human resources (P/HR) field has received little attention academically as well as within organizations. Organizations have assumed, incorrectly, that P/HR cannot benefit them because of a dearth of technical information and skills. Colleges of business, reflecting this attitude, often hid P/HR in the teaching of management, seldom including the subject as a course requirement.

Thankfully, much of this is changing. First, the passage of Title VII of the 1964 Civil Rights Act generated interest in human resource planning, selection validation, and performance appraisal. Economic decline, the growth of Teaganomics, and the loss of competitiveness in international markets have also focused attention on the contribution that P/HR can make to organizations.

The books in this series address these issues. The first concerns federal regulation in P/HR management in EEO, job health and safety, and employee benefit plans. The second explores the costing of human resources by measuring the financial impact of behavior in organizations. The volume on performance appraisal became required because of the onus that EEO has placed on criterion measures in organizations for test validation and P/HR decision making. The fourth book, on compensation, address the critical issues of internal, external, and individual equity and how compensation systems may be effectively and efficiently administered. Clearly, fifteen years ago these books could not have been written, but with the growth of technical information in P/HR and the significance of P/HR problems within organizations, these important contributions are now possible. What is most exciting is to see the results of recent research in these important areas being disseminated to students and practitioners. This is a major objective of this series, and it gives me great pleasure to see that plan coming to life. The books in this series are designed to be adopted in university level courses in human resource management and personnel administration. Practitioners, too, will find much valuable information in these books.

For the appearance of this important series, I would like to thank Keith Nave, Wayne Barcomb, and Jack McHugh of Kent Publishing Company, and also the many reviewers who have encouraged the development of this series and provided feedback. The authors included in this series represent the best research in this growing field, and I am proud to be associated with them.

Richard W. Beatty

Preface

Over the past 30 years or so, a large amount of literature on the general subject of costing human resources has accumulated. Much of this literature has developed in three fields—accounting, economics, and psychology—and much of it is unknown to academics and practicing managers alike.

For some time now, I have had the uneasy feeling that a lot of what we do in the personnel or human resource management field is largely misunderstood and underestimated by the organizations we serve. In part, we in the field are responsible for this state of affairs because much of what we do is evaluated only in statistical or behavioral terms. Like it or not, *the language of business is dollars, not correlation coefficients.*

Consider a familiar example. An organization hires a consultant to develop a new selection program because its current program is producing high adverse effects against protected groups, and the organization fears a lawsuit. The consultant develops a more valid selection procedure that eliminates the problem. The organization is now happy because it can stay out of court. However, it would be even happier if it knew that the more valid procedure would save it $100,000 per year in bad personnel decisions.

Methods are now available for estimating the dollar value of personnel programs, and *Costing Human Resources* examines available methods in a number of key areas. No attempt is made to be comprehensive, to cover all possible areas, but some of the methods in this book are versatile enough to be applied in areas that the book does not specifically address.

I have thoroughly enjoyed writing this book—in no small part because the more I researched applicable methods for costing human resources, the more comfortable I felt about the ability of members of the field to assign accurate dollar amounts to their activities. Indeed, I am fully confident, now, that personnel can stand right alongside the other functional areas of business when it comes to vying for resources based on results achieved, results that are measured in dollars.

This book can be used in university level courses in personnel and human resource management, either as a supplementary text or in conjunction with other textbooks in Kent's *Human Resource Management* series. Professionals and human resource managers will also find this book to be valuable.

Wayne F. Cascio
Denver, Colorado

Contents

1

The Costs—and Benefits—of Human Resources

Human resource management activities—those associated with the attraction, selection, retention, development, and utilization of people in organizations—are commonly evaluated in behavioral or statistical terms. Behavioral measures include measures of the reactions of various groups (top management, personnel specialists, applicants, or trainees), what individuals have learned, or how their behavior has changed on the job. Statistical measures include various ratios (for example, accident frequency or severity); percentages (for example, labor turnover); measures of central tendency and variability (for example, mean and standard deviation of cash register shortages and surpluses); and measures of correlation (for example, validity coefficients for selection programs). More and more, however, the need to evaluate human resource management activities in *economic* terms is becoming apparent. In the current climate of rising personnel costs and rising costs for energy and raw materials, operating executives justifiably demand estimates of expected costs and benefits of personnel programs. Methods for estimating these costs and benefits have been available for years (Brogden, 1949; Cronbach and Gleser, 1965), but it was not until the mid 1970s that behavioral scientists began to concentrate on describing and measuring employee behavior in economic terms. Such measurement requires an interdisciplinary approach, a collaboration between accounting and behavioral science. This collaboration should be encouraged; personnel specialists have been accused of not contributing to their organizations, of being so isolated and parochial that they really do not understand how business works, of being incapable of reading a financial statement (Foulkes and Morgan, 1977). Consider a comment by Fitz-Enz (1980):

> Few human resource managers—even the most energetic—take the time to analyze the return on the corporation's personnel dollar. We feel we aren't valued in our own organizations, that we can't get the resources we need. We complain that management won't buy our proposals and wonder why our advice is so often ignored until the crisis stage. But the human resources manager seldom stands back to look at the total business and ask: Why am I at the bottom looking up? The answer is painfully apparent. We don't act like business managers—like entrepreneurs whose business happens to be people. (p. 41)

To be sure, carefully designed, valid personnel programs do contribute to bottom-line success, and it is to the personnel manager's benefit to take advantage of methods now available for demonstrating this contribution. In this chapter, we shall outline some of the key areas to consider in demonstrating the costs and benefits of personnel programs, but first let us distinguish the current approach to costing human resources from its predecessor, human resource accounting.

Human Resource Accounting

At the outset, it is important to point out that there are no generally accepted accounting procedures for employee valuation. The first major attempt at employee valuation was made by the R. G. Barry Corporation of Columbus, Ohio. Barry's 1967 annual report described the inauguration of human resource accounting (HRA) procedures as a first step in the development of sophisticated measurement and accounting procedures that would enable the company to report accurate estimates of the worth of the human assets of the organization. Costs were accumulated in individual subsidiary accounts for each manager under five categories: recruiting, acquisition; formal training and familiarization; informal training, informal familiarization; experience; and development. A full description of the nature of expenses analyzed is given by Woodruff (1970). Costs were amortized over the expected working lives of individuals (or sometimes shorter periods), and unamortized costs (for example, when an individual left the company) were written off.

This is the *historical cost* (i.e., expenses actually incurred) approach to employee valuation. It is an *asset model* of accounting; that is, it measures the organization's investment in employees. For the purpose of external reporting (to inform interested parties of the financial position and of the results of operations of a company, with emphasis on performance measurement), it is widely viewed as most appropriate (Tsay, 1977). The historical cost approach is relatively objective, it facilitates comparisons of levels of human resource investment on a basis consistent with accounting treatment of other assets, and it seems a fair matching of benefits exhaustion with expense in particular time periods (Brummet, Flamholtz, and Pyle, 1968).

The method is not without its disadvantages, however, as Baker (1974) has noted. First, historical cost valuation is based on the false assumption that the dollar is stable. Second, there is a great degree of subjectivity in the detection and write-off of abortive expenditures. Third, since the assets valued are not saleable, there is no independent check of valuation. Finally, this approach only measures costs to the organization; it ignores completely any measure of the value of the employee to the organization. Hence, there is no direct indication of the soundness of the investment in human resources.

In view of the shortcomings of the historical cost approach, it seems prudent to examine other bases of valuation that might provide supplemental information. These fall broadly into three categories: replacement cost, present value of future earnings, and present value to the organization (that is, profit contribution).

Replacement Cost

One alternative to measuring the historical cost of an employee is to measure the cost of replacing that employee. According to Likert (1967), replacement costs include recruitment, training, and development expenditures, together with the income foregone during the training period. Flamholtz (1971) pointed out that it is easier in practice to estimate replacement cost than market value, and the former might therefore be adopted as a surrogate measure of the latter.

On the other hand, it might be argued just as plausibly that the substitution of replacement for historical cost does little more than update the valuation, at the expense of importing considerably more subjectivity into the measure (Baker, 1974). One might also question the usefulness of such a measure. The principal context in which these data would be relevant would be that of dismissal and replacement of staff. In most organizations, such decisions occur too infrequently to make it worthwhile to build into the accounting system the regular production of replacement cost data on all employees.

Present Value of Future Earnings

Lev and Schwartz (1971) proposed an economic valuation of employees based on the present value of future earnings, adjusted for the probability of employees' deaths. That is, the organization determines what the contribution an employee will make in the future is worth to it today. That contribution can be measured by its cost, or the salary wages the organization will pay to the employee. The measure is an objective one because it uses widely based statistics such as census income returns and mortality tables. However, the measure is severely limited because it assigns a value to the *average* rather than to any specific group or individual. There is therefore no benefit in monitoring the efficiency of an individual firm's investment in employee development, since the investment would have little or no impact on the present valuation of future earnings.

Baker (1974) pointed out three other faulty assumptions underlying this method. If the present value of future earnings is regarded as a fair appraisal of the individual's economic worth to an organization, then (1) subject to any profit expectancy built into the discount rate applied, because worth is equal to future cost, the employing organization is indifferent to whether it pays the cost to obtain the value or not (that is whether the employee is retained or not); in either case it comes out even. (2) Insofar as earnings exclude fringe costs, the organization is indeed better off without this resource. (3) Consequently, the value of past recruitment and development of the employee is zero in (1) or negative assuming (2).

Value to the Organization

In professional sports, the value of an athlete's services is often determined by how much money a particular team, acting in an open competitive market (the free agent draft), is willing to pay him or her. An analogous approach might also be taken in other types of organizations. Hekimian and Jones (1967) proposed that where an organization had several divisions seeking the same employee, he or she should be allocated to the highest bidder and the bid price incorporated into that division's investment base. On the surface this approach has merit, but in practice the opportunities to use it are relatively rare. If the objective is to evaluate opportunity costs (that is, the potential profit lost by failing to take the optimal course of action in a given situation), then the appropriate inclusion in the investment base is the highest unsuccessful bid. Moreover, the soundness of the valuation depends wholly on the information, judgment, and impartiality of the bidding divisions.

An alternative aggregate valuation approach has been proposed by Hermanson (1964). It involves establishing the net present value of expected wage payments (discounted at the economy rate of return on owned assets for the latest year) and applying to this a weighted efficiency ratio (the rate of income on owned assets for the current year against the average rate of income on owned assets for all firms in the economy). As we noted earlier, use of such broadly based statistics appears to diminish the precision of the calculations in general. It also incorporates unrelated risk factors into the efficiency ratio calculation. Moreover, human resources so valued would apparently subsume all other intangible assets of a goodwill nature.

Advocates of human resource accounting make a strong and compelling case for the need for this kind of measurement, but they tend to ignore the fact that dollar values cannot always be attached to the information that is collected. Thus, HRA may be of much more limited application than is commonly supposed (Baker, 1974). Perhaps the major limitation of these early approaches to HRA is that they reflect only inputs and not effectiveness. They are *human asset accounting* models that focus exclusively on investments in people (inputs); they ignore completely information about the output those resources produce.

In view of the conceptual and methodological limitations of human asset models, Pyle (1970) suggested that HRA be extended to compute returns on assets and returns on investments. This approach properly compares input and output measures but still fails to distinguish between individual and group effects that produce variability in output. The search continues for a single, limited criterion measure for HRA, but it is unrealistic to expect that such a measure will be developed (Tsay, 1977).

A new approach focuses on attaching dollar estimates to the behavioral outcomes produced by working in an organization. Criteria such as absenteeism, turnover, and job performance are measured using traditional organizational tools, and then costs are estimated for each criterion. For example, in costing labor turnover, dollar figures must be attached to separation costs, replacement costs, and training costs. This method, which measures not the value of the individual but the economic consequences of his or her behavior, measures behavior in terms that are taken seriously by most decision makers—those of dollars. This approach is termed an *expense* model of HRA (Mirvis and Macy, 1976). It is the approach taken in this book to costing human resources, and we shall develop it further in the next section.

Let us summarize our presentation so far. Human resource accounting *asset models* are used to reflect an organization's investment in employees. They are directed toward assessing the value of employees, treating them as capitalized resources (i.e., the economic concept of human capital). In contrast, human resource accounting *expense models* are oriented toward measuring the economic effects of employees' behavior.

Costing Employee Behaviors

The general idea of costing human resources is not a new one. A classic article by Brogden and Taylor (1950) addressed the potential for developing on-the-job performance criteria expressed in dollars. They noted,

> The criterion should measure the contribution of the individual to the overall efficiency of the organization. It centers on the quantity, quality, and cost of the finished product. Such factors as skill are latent—their effect is realized in the end product. (p. 90)

The contribution each employee makes is not related to the size of a firm's investment in an employee, but it is directly related to how each person works and what is produced.

What is different in the general costing approach is the quantification in financial terms of a set of common behavioral and performance outcomes. Standard cost accounting procedures are applied to employee behavior. To do this, the cost elements associated with each behavior must be identified and their separate and mutually exclusive dollar values computed. Costs can be conceptualized in two ways. One reflects *outlay costs* (for example, materials used in training new employees) versus *time costs* (for example, supervisors' time spent orienting the new employees).

A second distinguishes between *variable, fixed,* and *opportunity costs.* Fixed costs are costs that are independent of production rate; variable costs are costs that rise as the production rate rises. Opportunity costs reflect what the organization might have earned had it put the resources in question to another use. An example of a variable cost would be the overtime cost incurred because of absenteeism; a fixed cost would be the salary and fringe benefits for personnel who replace the absentees; and an opportunity cost would be the profit lost during the replacement process. These distinctions are important because only variable costs are directly related to behavior. Fixed costs are incurred regardless of behavioral occurrences, and opportunity costs are realized only if some employees put their free time to productive use while others do not (Macy and Mirvis, 1976).

Each behavior has associated with it distinct costs to an organization, but in most organizations these costs are unknown. Consider four reasons why this is so (Fitz-Enz, 1980):

1. *Personnel people do not know how to measure the costs of behavior.* Many practitioners have little or no background in statistics or psychometrics (the application of mathematics and statistics to mental measurement). Few publicly offered personnel workshops focus on quantitative techniques, and some masters degree programs in the behavioral sciences do not even require courses on statistics. Finally, organizations in the past generally did not train their personnel managers to measure their results. Given these quantitative gaps, the lack of emphasis on measurement of human resource activities is not surprising.

2. *Top management has accepted the myth that personnel activities cannot be evaluated in quantitative terms.* Since most personnel or human resource departments do not measure the results of their efforts in quantitative terms, management remains unaware that it can be done and therefore doesn't request it.

3. *Some personnel managers do not want to be measured.* Clearly this type of manager is a dying breed, yet we still encounter some who truly do not want to have their departments assessed by quantitative measures— and almost without exception, their position in the organization is not one of importance.

4. *A number of human resource managers would like to apply some measures to their function, but they haven't been able to do so.* Those individuals should rest assured of four things: it can be done; it does not take a great

deal of extra work; there is a valid business reason for doing it; and they can expect to be recognized and rewarded for their efforts.

Contrary to common belief, *all* aspects of human resource management (including morale) can be measured and quantified in the same manner as any operational function (Driessnack, 1979). In fact, the measurement of personnel performance encompasses all facets of the business. Let us consider briefly just six important functions where carefully conceived, enlightened personnel policies can pay off:

compensation policies and procedures

benefits programs and insurance premiums

personnel taxes

recruiting, training, and management development

affirmative action

turnover and outplacement

These are some of the major areas where cost savings are easily demonstrated, productivity most rapidly increased, and turnover reductions effected most quickly. For maximum efficiency, all of the areas must work in conjunction with each other, but for purposes of illustration we will discuss each one separately.

Compensation Policies and Procedures

Organizations that do not fully understand what a position is worth often either overpay or underpay their employees. The result is that incompetent overpaid employees do not leave and competent underpaid employees do not stay. Of course, the key to avoiding this situation is a properly structured compensation plan that provides ranges accurately reflecting market worth in that geographic area. The compensation structure need not be complicated or costly. A billion-dollar electrical wholesale distributor operating in over one hundred fifty locations in forty-nine states retained a major consulting firm to develop a compensation structure; the consulting fees were $490,000. Later a personnel manager, with the help of three college students during the summer, developed a program whose midpoints were within one dollar per week of the consultants' ranges for nonexempt personnel and within ten dollars per month for exempt personnel (Driessnack, 1979).

Benefits Administration

Human resource managers usually strive to obtain the most benefits for the dollar, but they do not always monitor the administration of benefits programs to insure that dividends, refunds, or increased benefits are obtained when the premiums exceed the benefit payout. When benefits exceed premiums, insurance carriers are quick to notify an organization of the need for increased premiums the following year. They will usually *not* inform an organization that there will be a dividend available for overpayment; the organization must ask for it.

The benefits chosen must be competitive with other organizations in the same industry and geographic area. While many organizations offer competitive benefits, often they do not enforce their own policies, to their disadvantage. For example, sometimes employees are absent more than the sick-leave policy allows but are still paid for excessive absences. Or worse, sometimes there is no limit on paid sick days, yet no one is criticized in performance appraisals for excessive absence. As we shall see in Chapter 3, attendance and punctuality are measurable costs and are an integral part of performance.

Personnel Tax Management

Some personnel taxes are controllable to the same degree as insurance costs. For example, federal and state unemployment taxes are usually based on work force turnover. In other words, an organization builds up an account in these funds and its account is charged when one of its employees collects unemployment insurance. These payroll taxes are usually levied on the first $6,000 of each employee's salary, and the rates vary from about 1.4 to over 4 percent of the payroll. It is the responsibility of the personnel director to insure that the organization is not paying a higher rate than necessary. Whatever the state rate is, it is deductible up to a maximum of 2.7 percent against the Federal Unemployment Tax Assessment (FUTA). As turnover is controlled, these rates can often be reduced. The same is true for social security taxes—6.65 percent (paid by the employer and matched by the employee) of the first $29,700 in earnings in 1981. As we shall see in Chapter 2, turnover again plays an important role in this area, since three people filling a $60,000 per year position during the course of a year could cost twice the normal social security tax deduction for one employee in that position.

Recruiting, Training, and Management Development

No single area provides a greater opportunity to waste (or save) organizational financial resources than recruiting, training, and management development. No area requires greater expertise, yet recruiting is often one of the first functions assigned to a personnel trainee.

An effective recruiter thoroughly understands the compensation structure of the organization, job requirements, political conditions in the various departments for which he or she is recruiting, and the temperament of the managers who will be interviewing and selecting the new candidates. All too often recruiters lack such thorough understanding. To make matters worse, unrealistically high job specifications lead to hiring overqualified personnel. The Equal Employment Opportunity Commission (EEOC), in evaluating positions in government and industry, found that more than 65 percent of the positions that required a college degree could easily be handled by a high school graduate (Driessnack, 1979). The effect is that a higher starting salary must be paid for the high-potential recruit. Lack of a challenging work environment for overqualified workers leads to the deterioration of morale, increased absenteeism, and high turnover. A department responsible for this situation would be forced to explain, in detail, the reason for an unwise $100 purchase, yet when purchasing $5,000 or more of inappropriate employee, the department is not questioned.

Poor selection and training methods are even more insidious. Consider as an example the selection and training of a police officer. The complete process (recruitment, physical and mental testing, interviewing, background check, and twelve to eighteen weeks at a police academy) may cost as much as $15,000 or more per officer. At a regional police training academy in the southeastern United States, 300 recruits per year were trained at an annual cost of $4,500,000 (300 × $15,000). Of the 300 recruits, an average of 45, or 15 percent per year, dropped out. At an average cost of $10,000 per dropout, the academy was losing $450,000 per year. When a more extensive test battery to select trainees was implemented, the validity of the selection process (i.e., the correlation between test scores and academy performance) improved from 0.20 to 0.30 (a gain of 50 percent). This cut the number of academy dropouts from an average of 45 to 36, for an annual savings of $90,000. As we shall see in Chapters 9 and 10, the potential savings from carefully developed selection and training programs can even be greater in some situations.

Affirmative Action Control

Most organizations recognize that the provision of equal employment opportunity for women, minorities, and older workers makes good business sense. However, human resource management executives have the financial responsibility to see that affirmative action does not result in declining productivity or become an expensive social exercise. There is simply no good reason to lower bona fide occupational qualifications in order to select minorities or women when with a little more effort and a wider search, qualified minorities and women can be recruited. It also makes little sense not to train older, competent, experienced minorities and women for challenging positions. Instead, many companies recruit young, inexperienced minority and female MBAs and place them in positions that require a far higher level of managerial competence than usually expected from a recent graduate. When these employees don't measure up, the companies are stuck with token minorities or women whom they are afraid to fire, and so they downgrade the positions and bear the financial loss. This is an unnecessary expense for any company, it retards the minorities' and women's future growth, and it has undesirable side effects on other employees.

Perhaps personnel mismanagement's most damaging and costly effect on industry and society is in the area of age discrimination. With society's emphasis on youth, it is often the older manager who is fired in a corporate reorganization. Sometimes this is a thinly disguised subterfuge to avoid paying pensions. The odds are 5 to 1 that a recent college graduate will leave within the first three years of employment. The odds of a fifty-year-old recruit staying with an organization for fifteen productive years are far greater (Driessnack, 1979). A comparative turnover analysis (accompanied by turnover cost data) between new college graduates and older workers may well stimulate decision makers to question the wisdom of hiring only young applicants.

Turnover and Outplacement

The control of turnover costs is the direct responsibility of the personnel executive. In Chapter 2, we will show how to compute these costs. When turnover costs become excessive, the cause of the turnover can usually be identified by division, department, manager, and even individual supervisor. Then corrective action (for example, retraining, work redesign, changes in the compensation structure) must be taken, for the cost savings can be large.

One of the more unpleasant aspects of human resource management is layoffs, yet even here money can be saved through sensible outplacement policies. Nonexempt workers can be handled internally by personnel staff, but for executives a consulting firm that specializes in outplacement may be a wise investment. Terminated executives are taught how to develop and market their assets: how to construct a resume, write letters, interview, and negotiate salary. They are taught how to develop the "hidden market," the estimated 80 percent of management jobs that are never advertised. As a result of outplacement counseling, the executive may well find a new position quickly and at a higher salary. More important, he or she maintains a good rapport with the old company, and often becomes a supplier or a customer. Finally, bridging pay rather than severance pay allows the executive to seek new employment while maintaining the image and status essential to him or her. When new employment is secured, the bridging pay stops. Often the difference between the bridging pay and large severance allowances saves more than the fees charged by the consultant.

This is just a brief look into the potential contributions to the bottom line that can be made by effective human resource management practices in these six areas. Although we have examined each one separately, our ultimate objective should be to develop a uniform financial reporting system for the personnel function as a whole. As time and resources permit, the design should phase in several aspects of each personnel function, including employment, compensation, employee relations, and training. As each new area is added to the measurement system, a synergistic effect takes place. Previously unrecognized relationships between functions become visible. The staff begins to recognize how its work is interconnected, and in time, the systems approach to financial measurement of the total human resource management function can be a very powerful tool indeed.

Plan of the Book

The intent of this book is to examine some important areas in which costs can be attached to personnel activities, to identify important cost elements, and to show how they may be combined to yield valid cost estimates. A great deal has been written on these topics, and it is important to integrate this information to develop practical costing procedures. The payoff from doing so may be enormous.

In Part I, we consider procedures for costing personnel decisions to quit, to be absent, and to smoke. The high costs of turnover and absenteeism have been recognized for some time, but few managers are aware of the cost of smoking at the work place. As we shall demonstrate in Chapter 4, this cost is approaching $5,000 per smoker per year.

In Part II, we examine the financial impact of employee attitudes and collectively bargained agreements. It is well known that employee attitudes may affect job behaviors, but it is not well known that the financial impact of attitudes on job behaviors can be measured and dollar estimates assigned to targeted improvements in job attitudes. Such figures can lend strong support to arguments for the adoption of a training or development program.

Labor contract costing is an extremely important area, since failure to estimate accurately the real cost of improvements in wages, hours, or conditions of employment can be disastrous. In Chapter 6, we will show how these costs can be estimated properly.

In Part III, we direct considerable attention to the concept of utility or overall worth, so that managers of human resources can adopt a return on investment perspective with respect to personnel selection, job performance measurement, and training and development efforts. Wise decisions about personnel programs demand a knowledge of their costs and benefits. Such a view encompasses issues of program design, implementation, and evaluation in both tangible (dollar) and intangible terms, but such a view is essential, for the best results are achieved when a system is viewed in total.

Exercises

1. Discuss the advantages and disadvantages of the historical cost, replacement cost, and present value of future earnings approaches to employee valuation.

2. How are human resource accounting expense models different from human resource accounting asset models?

3. Explain how effective human resource management activities can yield financial benefits in the following areas: compensation; benefits; personnel taxes; recruitment, selection, and training; affirmative action; and turnover and outplacement.

References

BAKER, G. M. N. "The Feasibility and Utility of Human Resource Accounting." *California Management Review,* 1974, 16 (4):17–23.

BROGDEN, H. E. "When Testing Pays Off." *Personnel Psychology,* 1949, 2:171–183.

BROGDEN, H. E., and TAYLOR, E. "The Dollar Criterion—Applying the Cost Accounting Concept to Criterion Construction." *Personnel Psychology,* 1950, 3:133–154.

BRUMMET, R. L., FLAMHOLTZ, E., and PYLE, W. "Human Resource Accounting— A Challenge for Accountants." *Accounting Review,* 1968, 43:217–224.

CRONBACH, L. J., and GLESER, G. C. *Psychological Tests and Personnel Decisions.* 2nd ed. Urbana, Ill.: University of Illinois Press, 1965.

DRIESSNACK, C. H. "Financial Impact of Effective Human Resources Management." *The Personnel Administrator,* 1979, 23:62–66.

FITZ2NZ, J. "Quantifying the Human Resources Function." *Personnel,* 1980, 57 (3):41–52.

FLAMHOLTZ, E. G. "A Model for Human Resource Valuation: A Stochastic Process with Service Rewards." *Accounting Review,* 1971, 46:253–267.

FOULKES, F. K., and MORGAN, H. M. "Organizing and Staffing the Personnel Function." *Harvard Business Review,* 1977, 55 (May-June):142–154.

HEKIMIAN, J. S., and JONES, C. H. "Put People on Your Balance Sheet." *Harvard Business Review,* 1967, 45 (January-February):107–113.

HERMANSON, R. H. *Accounting for Human Assets.* East Lansing, Mich.: Bureau of Business and Economic Research, 1964.

LEV, B., and SCHWARTZ, A. "On the Use of the Economic Concept of Human Capital in Financial Statements." *Accounting Review,* 1971, 46: 103–112.

LIKERT, R. *The Human Organization, Its Management and Value.* New York: McGraw-Hill, 1967.

MACY, B. A., and MIRVIS, P. H. "A Methodology for Assessment of Quality of Work Life and Organizational Effectiveness in Behavioral-Economic Terms." *Administrative Science Quarterly,* 1976, 21:212–226.

MIRVIS, P. H., and MACY, B. A. "Human Resource Accounting: A Measurement Perspective." *Academy of Management Review,* 1976, 1:74–83.

PYLE, W. C. "Human Resource Accounting." *Financial Analysts Journal,* 1970, 10 (September):68–78.

TSAY, J. J. "Human Resource Accounting: A Need for Relevance." *Management Accounting,* 1977, 58:33–36.

WOODRUFF, R. C., Jr. "Human Resources Accounting." *Canadian Chartered Accountant,* 1970, 97:156–161.

I

Costing Employee Turnover, Absenteeism, and Smoking

2

The High Cost
of Employee Turnover

Turnover rates and costs for many organizations are unacceptably high. Turnover rates are widely available and easily calculated. For example, a monthly turnover rate may be computed by the formula

$$\frac{\Sigma \text{ turnover incidents}}{\text{average work force size}} \times 100$$

where Σ means "sum of." Typical monthly turnover rates, as reported by the Bureau of National Affairs, are shown in Exhibit 2.1. As the table indicates, the average monthly rates by year are approximately 1.8 percent. This represents an average annual turnover rate of almost 22 percent of the work force for all companies. As you will see in this chapter, turnover can represent a substantial cost of doing business. As an example, consider the following replacement costs for various insurance company personnel as reported by Flamholtz (1972), and the equivalent costs in 1982, assuming an average yearly inflation rate of 8 percent.

Exhibit 2.1   Typical Monthly Turnover Rates

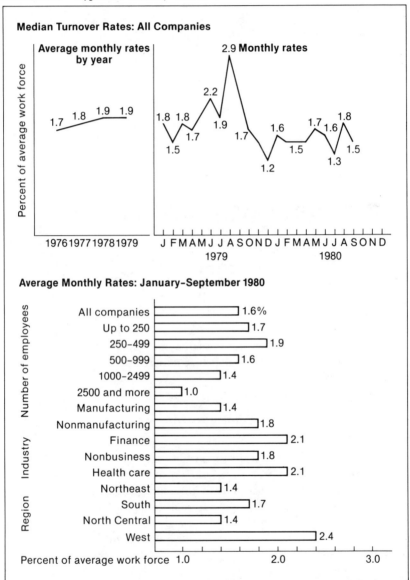

Source: "BNA's Job Absence and Turnover Report—3rd quarter 1980." *Bulletin to Management*, Bureau of National Affairs, Washington, D.C., December 11, 1980, p. 1.

Job	1972	1982
Claims investigator	$ 6,000	$ 12,950
Field examiner	24,000	51,800
Sales person	31,600	68,200
Sales manager	185,100	399,600

In 1977 the U.S. Navy estimated a cost of $30,000 to obtain a naval officer through ROTC, $86,000 for one through the Naval Academy, and $1,500,000 for a competent fighter pilot (Wanous, 1980).

Unfortunately many organizations are unaware of the actual cost of turnover. And unless this cost is known, management may be unaware of the need for action to prevent controllable turnover and may not develop a basis for choosing among alternative programs designed to reduce turnover. A practical procedure for measuring and analyzing the costs of personnel turnover is needed, especially since the costs of hiring, training, and developing personnel are now viewed as investments that must be evaluated just like other corporate resources. Our objective in costing human resources is not only to *measure* the relevant costs, but also to develop methods and programs to *reduce* the costs of human resources by managing the more controllable aspects of these costs.

Turnover is defined as any departure beyond organizational boundaries (Macy and Mirvis, 1976). Turnover may be voluntary on the part of the employee (for example, resignation) or involuntary (for example, requested resignation, permanent layoff, retirement, death). Some reasons for leaving, such as "another job that offers more responsibility," "returning to school full-time," or "improved salary and benefits," are more controllable than other reasons, such as employee death, chronic illness, or spouse transfer. Once the costs of employee turnover are known, therefore, an organization must determine which of these costs are reasonably controllable and focus attention on reducing them.

We hasten to add, however, that all turnover is not bad, and it is unrealistic to expect that any program will eliminate turnover completely. Some mistakes in selection are unavoidable, and employee turnover, to the extent that it is concentrated on erroneous acceptances into the organization, can have a cleansing effect, for it makes room for new employees whose abilities and temperaments better fit the organization's needs. Other employees may have burned out, reached a plateau of substandard performance, or have developed such negative attitudes toward the organization that their continued presence is likely to have harmful effects on the motivation and productivity of their co-workers. Here again, turnover can be beneficial. In contrast to these passive noncontributors, there may be a few active noncontributors who willfully violate organizational rules concerning, for example, drug abuse or intoxication at work, fighting, or stealing company property. Turnover among these individuals is also likely to have a salutary effect on organizational health and productivity.

Thus, it is up to the organization to determine what kinds of turnover are harmful and then attempt to reduce these. This reduction may be accomplished by redesigning jobs to enhance opportunities for responsibility and decision making, providing better working conditions, improving salaries and benefits, or by clarifying and opening up promotional opportunities. We will have more to say on these issues later, but first we need to develop procedures for identifying and measuring turnover costs.

Identifying and Measuring Turnover Costs

The general procedure for identifying and measuring employee turnover costs follows that originally developed by Smith and Watkins (1978). It is founded on the premise that in measuring turnover three major, separate cost categories must be considered: separation costs, replacement costs, and training costs. For each category we shall first present the relevant cost elements and formulas and then give numerical examples to illustrate how the formulas are used.

Separation Costs

Exhibit 2.2 presents the key cost elements, together with appropriate formulas for each, that apply to separation costs. These include exit interviews (S_1); administrative functions related to termination, such as deletion of the employee from payroll, personnel, and benefits files (S_2); separation pay, if any (S_3); and unemployment tax, if applicable (S_4). Thus:

$$\text{total separation costs } (S_T) = S_1 + S_2 + S_3 + S_4$$

The cost of exit interviews is composed of two factors, the cost of the interviewer's time (preparation plus actual interview time) and the cost of the terminating employee's time (time required for the interview ×

Exhibit 2.3 Measuring Replacement Costs

Cost Element	Formula
Communicating job availability (R_1)	$=$ [advertising and employment agency fees per termination $+$ (time required for communicating job availability $\times$ personnel department employee's pay rate)] $\times$ number of turnovers replaced during period
Preemployment administrative functions (R_2)	$=$ time required by personnel department for preemployment administrative functions $\times$ average personnel department employee's pay rate $\times$ number of turnovers replaced during period
Entrance interview (R_3)	$=$ time required for interview $\times$ interviewer's rate $\times$ number of interviews during period
Staff meeting (R_4)	$=$ time required for meeting $\times$ (personnel department employees' pay rate $+$ department representatives' pay rate) $\times$ number of meetings during period
Postemployment acquisition and dissemination of information (R_5)	$=$ time required for acquiring and disseminating information $\times$ average personnel department employee's pay rate $\times$ number of turnovers replaced during period
In-house medical examinations (R_6) or Contracted medical examinations (R_7)	$=$ [(time required for examination $\times$ examiner's pay rate) $+$ cost of supplies used] $\times$ number of turnovers replaced during period $=$ rate per examination $\times$ number of turnovers replaced during period

Source: Adapted from Smith, H. C., and Watkins, L. E. "Managing Manpower Turnover Costs." *The Personnel Administrator,* April 1978, 23:48.

formulas for estimating them. As the exhibit indicates, there are six categories of replacement costs:

1. communication of job availability
2. preemployment administrative functions
3. entrance interviews
4. staff meetings
5. postemployment acquisition and dissemination of information
6. employment medical exams

The costs of communicating job availability will vary by type of job and targeted labor market. Depending on the methods used in recruitment, these costs may range from the cost of a classified advertisement in a local newspaper to employment agency fees borne by the employer (see Cascio, 1982, Chapter 9). Typically these costs can be obtained from existing accounting records. However, to the extent that this communication process requires considerable time from personnel department employees, the cost of their time should also be included in replacement costs.

Administratively, there are several tasks that are frequently undertaken in selecting and placing each new employee—for example, accepting applications, preemployment testing, and reference checking. These procedures can be expensive. In 1980, for example, firms using preemployment polygraph exams spent from $35 to $150 per candidate. Those requiring a background investigation spent an average of $300 per candidate ("Blood, Sweat, and Fears," 1980). Unfortunately, the time required to perform these activities is not routinely documented by organizational information systems. However, the methods described earlier for estimating exit interview time requirements may be applied in determining the time necessary for preemployment administrative functions.

Virtually all organizations use entrance interviews to describe jobs, to communicate employee responsibilities and benefits, and to make some general assessments of each candidate. The costs incurred when completing entrance interviews are a function of the length of the interview, pay rates of interviewers involved, and the number of interviews conducted. Clearly there are links between valid selection procedures and reduced turnover. If decision makers are to be able to make sound cost/benefit decisions regarding elements of the selection process, these costs (and benefits) must be documented. In this chapter we focus on costs; in Chapter 8 we will consider in more detail the benefits to be derived from valid selection procedures.

For some classes of employees, especially top level managers or other professionals, a meeting may be held between the personnel department and the department holding the vacant position. The estimated time required for this meeting multiplied by the sum of the pay rates for all employees involved provides a measure of this element of replacement costs.

Pertinent information for each new employee must be gathered, recorded, and entered into various subsystems of a human resource information system (for example, personnel records, payroll files, employee benefits records). If flexible, cafeteria-style benefits are offered by an organization, then considerable time may be spent in counseling each new employee. Managers must estimate the time required for this overall process for each replaced employee, and then multiply it by the wage rates of personnel department employees involved. Once this cost is multiplied by the number of turnovers, an estimate of the total cost of acquiring and disseminating information to new employees has been computed.

Preemployment medical examinations are the final element of replacement costs. The extent and thoroughness, and therefore the cost, of such examinations varies greatly. Some organizations do not require them at all, some contract with private physicians or clinics to provide this service, while others use in-house medical personnel. If medical examinations are contracted out, the cost can be determined from existing accounting data. If the exams are done in-house, their cost can be determined based upon the supplies used (for example, x-ray film, laboratory supplies) and the staff's time required to perform each examination. If the new employee is paid while receiving the medical examination, then his or her rate of pay should be added to the examiner's pay rate in determining total cost. Now let us estimate replacement costs for a one-year period based on Exhibit 2.3 for Wee Care Children's Hospital.

Job Availability (R_1)   Let us assume that fees and advertisements average $75 per turnover, that three more hours are required to communicate job availability, that the personnel specialist's pay rate is $7.80 per hour, and that 288 turnovers are replaced during the period. Therefore:

$$R_1 = [\$75 + (3 \times \$7.80)] \times 288 = \$28,339.20$$

Preemployment Administrative Functions (R₂)   Assume that the total time required by Wee Care's personnel department for preemployment administrative functions is three hours. Therefore:

$$R_2 = 3 \times \$7.80 \times 288 = \$6,739.20$$

Entrance Interview (R₃)   Assume that, on the average, three candidates are interviewed for every one hired. Thus, over the one-year period of this study, 864 (288 × 3) interviews were conducted. Therefore:

$$R_3 = 1 \text{ hour} \times \$7.80 \times 864 = \$6,739.20$$

In this example R_2 happens to be identical to R_3 because of the 3:1 interview-to-hire ratio, and because each interview was assumed to last one hour. However, this will not always be the case.

Staff Meeting (R₄)   Assume that each staff meeting lasts one hour, that the average pay rate of the new employee's department representative is $17.50, and that for administrative convenience such meetings are held, on average, only once for each three new hires (288 ÷ 3 = 96). Therefore:

$$R_4 = 1 \times (\$7.80 + \$17.50) \times 96 = \$2,428.80$$

Postemployment Acquisition and Dissemination of Information (R₅)   Assume that two hours are spent on these activities for each new employee. Therefore:

$$R_5 = 2 \times \$7.80 \times 288 = \$4,492.80$$

Preemployment Medical Examination (R₆ and R₇)   Assume that if the medical examinations are done at the hospital (in-house) each exam will take 30 minutes, the examiner is paid $22 per hour, supplies cost $14, and 288 exams are conducted. Therefore:

$$R_6 = [0.50 \times \$22) + \$14] \times 288 = \$7,200$$

If the exams are contracted out, let us assume that Wee Care will pay a flat rate of $30 per examination. Therefore:

$$R_7 = \$30 \times 288 = \$8,640$$

Wee Care therefore decides to provide in-house medical examinations for all new employees.

Total replacement costs (R_T) can now be computed (Σ R_1, R_2, R_3, R_4, R_5, R_6).

R_T = \$28,339.20 + \$6,739.20 + \$6,739.20 + \$2,428.80
    + \$4,492.80 + \$7,200
R_T = \$55,939.20

Training Costs

In virtually all instances, replacement personnel must be oriented and trained to a standard level of competence before assuming their regular duties. As we shall see in Chapter 10, this often involves considerable expense to an organization. For the present, however, let us assume that replacement employees are either placed in a formal training program or assigned to an experienced employee for some period of on-the-job training, or both. The cost elements and computational formulas for this category of turnover costs are shown in Exhibit 2.4. There are three major elements of training costs: (1) informational literature, (2) instruction in a formal training program, and (3) instruction by employee assignment.

The cost of any informational literature provided to replacement employees must be considered a part of orientation and training costs. Unit costs for those items may be obtained from existing accounting records. Multiplying the unit costs by the number of replacement employees hired during the period yields the first cost factor in determining training costs.

New employees may also be involved in a formal training program. The overall cost of the program can be determined by multiplying total hours of instruction during the period by the average pay rate for all trainers, but two other costs must also be considered. The first of these is the average pay rate for all trainees, and the second is the proportional cost of training that can be attributed to employee turnover. Since it cannot be assumed that the *total* cost of a training program is solely a result of turnover, managers must determine the extent to which formal training is considered to be a function of employee turnover. For the sake of simplicity, the costs of facilities, food, and other overhead expenses have not been included in these calculations.

Instead of, or in addition to, instruction in a formal training program, new employees may also be assigned to work with more experienced employees for a period of time or until they reach a standard level of

Exhibit 2.4 Measuring Training Costs

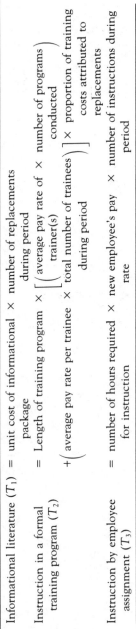

Informational literature (T_1) = unit cost of informational package × number of replacements during period

Instruction in a formal training program (T_2) = Length of training program × [(average pay rate of trainer(s) × number of programs conducted) + (average pay rate per trainee × total number of trainees during period)] × proportion of training costs attributed to replacements

Instruction by employee assignment (T_3) = number of hours required for instruction × new employee's pay rate × number of instructions during period competence. The overall cost of this on-the-job training must be determined for all replacement employees hired during the period, for it is an important element of training costs.

Notice that in Exhibit 2.4 the cost of reduced productivity of new employees while they are learning and of experienced employees while they are training is not included as an element of overall training costs. This is not because such a cost is unimportant. On the contrary, even if an organization staffs more employees to provide for a specified level of productivity while new employees are training, the cost of a decrease in the quantity and quality of goods or sevices produced is still very real. Less experienced employees may also cause an increase in operating expenses due to poor utilization of supplies and equipment. All of these costs are important, and when they can be measured reliably and accurately they should be included as an additional element of training costs. However, in many organizations, especially those providing services (for example, credit counseling, retail sales clerks, patient care in hospitals), the measurement of these costs is simply too complex for practical application.

Let us now estimate the total cost of training employee replacements at Wee Care. Using the formulas shown in Exhibit 2.4, Wee Care estimates the following costs over a one-year period.

Informational Literature (T_1) If the unit cost of informational literature is $4, and 288 employees are replaced,

$$T_1 = \$4 \times 288 = \$1,152$$

Instruction in a Formal Training Program (T_2) New employee training at Wee Care is conducted ten times per year, and each training program lasts 40 hours (one full week). The average pay rate for instructors is $13 per hour, the average pay rate for trainees is $7.80 per hour, and of the 576 employees trained, on the average, each year half are replacements for employees who left voluntarily or involuntarily. The total cost of formal training attributed to employee turnover is therefore:

$$T_2 = 40 \times [(\$13 \times 10) + (\$7.80 \times 576)] \times 0.50$$
$$= \$92,456$$

Instruction by Employee Assignment (T_3) To ensure positive transfer between training program content and job content, Wee Care requires each new employee to be assigned to a more experienced employee for an additional week (40 hours). Each experienced employee supervises two trainees. The total cost of such on-the-job training for replacement employees is therefore:

$$T_3 = 40 \times \$7.80 \times (288 \div 2)$$
$$= \$44,928$$

Total training costs can now be computed (ΣT_1, T_2, T_3)

$$T_T = \$1,152 + \$92,456 + \$44,928$$
$$= \$138,536$$

Having computed the costs of the three major components of employee turnover, the total cost of employee turnover can be represented by the following equation:

$$\text{total cost of employee turnover} = S_T + R_T + T_T$$

where S_T = total separation costs; R_T = total replacement costs; and T_T = total training costs. For Wee Care, the total cost of 288 employee turnovers during a one-year period was:

$$\$119,705.76 + \$55,939.20 + \$138,536 = \$314,180.96$$

This represents a cost of $1,090.91 for each employee who left the hospital.

It is important to stress that the purpose of measuring turnover costs is to improve management decision making. That is, once turnover figures are known, managers have a more realistic basis for choosing between current turnover costs and instituting some type of turnover reduction program such as increased compensation and nonwage benefits, job enrichment, realistic job previews, and expanded recruitment and selection programs. In our final section we examine this issue in greater detail.

Dealing with Employee Turnover

Now that we know how to cost turnover, and assuming management decides the costs are intolerable, how can we best deal with the problem? Although a complete treatment of solutions is beyond the scope of this chapter, let us focus on voluntary turnover, since much of this is controllable. Let us also distinguish voluntary turnover among newcomers from voluntary turnover among employees who have been with the organization for some time (at least a year).

One reason newcomers leave is that their inflated expectations about a job or organization are often not met after they begin working. Much of this turnover is unnecessary and therefore controllable. Over the last decade a number of studies have shown that when the expectations of job applicants are lowered to match organizational reality, job acceptance rates may be lower, but job satisfaction and job survival are higher for those who receive a realistic job preview (RJP). Wanous (1980) suggests three reasons why RJPs work so well. The first is a vaccination effect: job candidates are given a small dose of organizational reality during the recruitment stage to protect against the negative aspects of real organizational life. The second is a self-selection, matching effect: since people strive to be satisfied, they tend to choose organizations that they believe will lead to personal satisfaction. The better the information job candidates possess, the more effective their choices can be. A final reason for the success of RJPs is a personal commitment effect: when individuals believe that they made a decision without coercion or strong inducements from others, they tend to be much more committed to the decision.

Nevertheless, RJPs are not appropriate recruitment strategies for all types of jobs. They are most appropriate (1) when few applicants are actually hired; (2) when they are used with entry level positions (since those coming from outside to inside an organization are more likely to have inflated expectations than those who make changes internally); and (3) when unemployment is low (since job candidates are more likely to have other options).

As an example, consider a realistic recruitment program developed for telephone operators at Southern New England Telephone Company (SNET). The company-wide turnover rate at SNET was 30 to 40 percent per year, but for operators in the first six months it was 100 percent or higher. Even a modest reduction in the operator turnover rate would pay handsome dividends. Following the analysis of a telephone operator's job, an outline was prepared of the major positive and negative job characteristics, as reported by the operators and their supervisors. This outline served as the script for a fifteen-minute film to be used as an alternative to the traditional recruiting film that the organization was then using. Interviews with six experienced operators were videotaped for later editing. Exhibit 2.5 shows areas that were covered by both films, as well as those aspects unique to each one.

After an applicant saw the realistic film, he or she was given a pamphlet (see Exhibit 2.6) to reinforce the major points of the film. Applicants were

Exhibit 2.5 Job Characteristics Emphasized by Each Job Preview Film

---

Overlap Between Films

1. Customers can be quite unfriendly at times.
2. Work is fast paced.
3. Some operators receive satisfaction from helping out customers.
4. Action sequences of operators at work:
   a. emergency call
   b. "wise guy" calling operator
   c. credit card call
   d. overseas call
   e. directory assistance operators at work
   f. "nasty" customer calling operator
5. Dealing with others (customers, co-workers) is a large part of the job.

Nonoverlap Characteristics

Realistic film	*Traditional film*
1. Lack of variety.	1. Everyone seems happy at work.
2. Job is routine; may become boring.	2. Exciting work.
	3. Important work.
3. Close supervision; little freedom.	4. Challenging work.
4. Limited opportunity to make friends.	
5. Receive criticism for bad performance, but no praise when deserved.	
6. Challenging initially, but once learned is easy and not challenging.	

Source: J. P. Wanous. "Tell It Like It Is at Realistic Job Previews." *Personnel,* 1975, 52 (July-August):57. Copyright © 1975 by AMACOM, a division of American Management Associations. All rights reserved.

Exhibit 2.6   Pamphlet Used in Conjunction with Realistic Job Preview Films.

You have seen the film preview of the operator's job for two reasons:

1. We want you to know about the job before you decide if you want to be an operator.
2. If you become an operator, you will have a better idea of what to realistically expect on the job.

You are now given this folder which summarizes many important characteristics of the operator's job.

If you are a telephone operator, you can realistically expect:

varied schedules—work on weekends, holidays, and at odd hours

that regular attendance is required

to help people complete calls or look up numbers for them

that work will be closely supervised

steady employment; full pay during training; good benefits and retirement

routine work requiring strict attention to standard procedures

that wage increases will be determined by job performance

that accuracy and speed in work are required

Source: J. P. Wanous. *Organizational Entry.* Reading, Mass.: Addison-Wesley, 1980, p. 53.

shown the film after they had been offered a job but before they had accepted it.

The RJP program paid off. After the experiment 50 percent of the traditional-film group survived at least six months, while 62 percent of the realistic-film group survived, and with higher job satisfaction scores.

Job Performance Tests

Job performance or work sample tests have also been used to instill realistic attitudes in prospective employees. Performance tests usually refer to standardized measures of behavior whose primary objective is to assess the ability to do rather than the ability to know. Performance tests may be classified either as *motor*, involving physical manipulation of things (for example, tests for jobs like carpenter, mechanic, mason), or as *verbal*, involving problems that are primarily language-oriented or people-oriented (for example, tests for jobs like maintenance supervisor, programmer/ analyst, library assistant) (Asher and Sciarrino, 1974).

To demonstrate the impact of performance testing on turnover, Cascio and Phillips (1979) examined the results of a broad spectrum of performance tests (eleven motor and ten verbal) used by a city government over two years. The tests were matched as closely as possible (in tasks, tools, equipment, work setting, and proportion of time spent on various activities) to actual job requirements. For example, in the test for sewer pumping station operator (a promotional exam for laborers which requires no previous experience), all testing, proctoring, and rating was done underground at the sewer pumping station. During an initial one-hour instruction period a sewer mechanic explained and demonstrated, as if he were the applicants' supervisor, procedures for the general maintenance of sewer pipes and equipment—how to clean filters, grease fittings, read a pressure chart, and so on. Several applicants left immediately after the demonstration. During a second hour each applicant was required to repeat the demonstration (applicants were also free to ask questions) as if he or she were on the job. Applicants were then rated on the degree to which they: (1) understood instructions, (2) followed the prescribed procedures, (3) asked questions when they were unsure of something, and (4) followed safety practices (used protective masks and other equipment). Follow-up interviews revealed that those who qualified for and accepted the job had a good idea of what they were getting into and felt that for them the job represented a step up the career ladder.

To examine the impact of performance testing on turnover, data on turnover were gathered for one year prior to the introduction of performance testing and for a period (from nine to twenty-six months) after performance tests were introduced. Turnover rates for the twenty-one jobs during the year prior to performance testing varied from 0 to 300 percent, with an overall average of 40 percent. The turnover rate for these same jobs after performance tests was less than 3 percent. Using the formulas presented earlier for calculating actual turnover costs (separation, replacement, and training costs) the 37 percent reduction in turnover translated into savings of $336,199 for the city during the nine to twenty-six month period after the introduction of performance tests.

Changes in Compensation

Two other strategies for reducing turnover are increased salary and nonwage benefits, and job enrichment. In some circumstances noncompetitive compensation policies are a major cause of high turnover, especially if the attraction and expected utility of alternative jobs is high. Thus a large chain of convenience stores in the southeastern United States was experiencing a turnover rate among store clerks of over 100 percent a year before conducting an in-depth study of the causes of the turnover. Most of those who quit worked in hazardous areas during the evening or midnight shifts. Exit interviews and an attitude survey of present employees soon disclosed why. The parent company paid the legally required minimum wage to entry-level clerks at all stores regardless of work shift or store location. Further, security was lax and the stores were regularly robbed. To remedy this situation a security consultant was retained to implement tighter security measures at all outlets, and management instituted a shift differential of 150 percent (1978 minimum wage was $2.65 per hour × 1.50 = $3.98 per hour) for the midnight shift and 75 percent for the evening shift. On top of this a flat premium of $25 a week ($1,300 a year) was offered to those working in areas defined as hazardous. Within a year after these changes were instituted, turnover declined to 40 percent, still high but reduced by over 60 percent from the earlier situation. Unfortunately, since other changes (security procedures) were made along with the changes in compensation, we do not know the direct impact of the changes in compensation on turnover. However, we do know that the turnover problem was unlikely to improve by itself unless some changes were made.

Job Enrichment

As a final strategy for reducing turnover, let us briefly discuss job enrichment. While the theory and implementation of job enrichment are beyond the scope of this chapter (see Ford, 1969; Hackman and Oldham, 1980), let us describe an enrichment strategy applied by Hackman, Oldham, Janson, and Purdy (1975) to a key-punching job at the Travelers Insurance Company. The theory and technology underlying their approach is shown in Exhibit 2.7. According to the theory, positive personal and work outcomes (high internal work motivation, high work performance, high work satisfaction, and low absenteeism and turnover) result when three

Exhibit 2.7 A Theoretical Model of the Job Design Process.

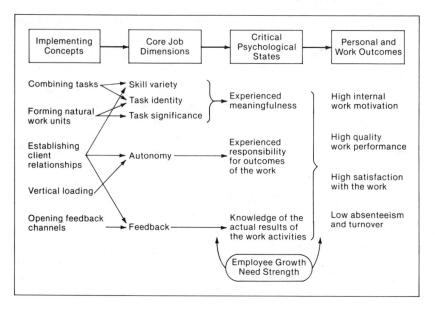

Source: J. R. Hackman, G. Oldham, R. Janson, and K. Purdy. A New Strategy for Job Enrichment. © 1975 by the Regents of the University of California. Reprinted from *California Management Review*, volume XVII, number 4, p. 62 by permission of the Regents.

critical psychological states (experienced meaningfulness of the work, experienced responsibility for work outcomes, and knowledge of results of work activities) are present for an employee. All three of the psychological states must be present for the positive outcomes to be realized.

The theory asserts that these critical psychological states are created by five core dimensions:

skill variety: the opportunity to perform a wide range of operations or use a wide variety of equipment and procedures

task identity: the opportunity to do an entire piece of work such that employees can clearly identify the result of their efforts *task significance:* the degree to which the job has a substantial impact on the lives or work of other people

autonomy: the extent to which employees have a major say in scheduling their work, selecting the equipment they will use, and deciding on procedures to be followed

feedback: the extent to which an employee receives useful, believable information regarding his or her job performance

This approach includes a set of *implementing concepts* that provide guides for action to be taken. The five implementing concepts are:

1. forming natural work units—identifying basic work items and grouping them into natural categories
2. combining tasks—if possible, combining existing and fractionalized tasks to form larger modules of work
3. establishing client relationships by identifying clients of the work, establishing the most direct contact possible, and setting up criteria by which the client can judge the quality of the product or service he receives
4. establishing vertical loading—closing the gap between planning, doing, and controlling the work, for example, by granting additional authority or discretion to the worker in setting schedules, quality control, and methods used
5. opening feedback channels by establishing client relationships, placing quality control close to the worker, providing summaries of performance to the worker

As shown in Exhibit 2.7, the implementing concepts are tied directly to the core job dimensions as follows:

1. Forming natural work units enhances task identity and task significance.
2. Combining tasks affects skill variety and task identity.
3. Establishing client relationships relates directly to skill variety, autonomy, and feedback.
4. Vertical loading fosters autonomy.
5. Opening feedback channels provides feedback to the worker.

This is the approach that Hackman et al. (1975) applied to the keypunching job at Travelers. After the existing operation was diagnosed on the five core dimensions (all five were deficient), an experiment was set up in which the jobs of one group of employees were enriched using all five of the implementing concepts, while a geographically separate control group, similar in size and demographic makeup, was monitored for comparison. After one year, the results were dramatic. In comparison to the control group, the experimental group showed significant improvements in work quantity (39.8%) and employee attitudes (job satisfaction scores increased 16.5%) and decreases in error rate (1.53% to 0.99%), and absenteeism (24.1%). The role of the supervisor also changed from closely supervising employees and dealing with crises to developing feedback systems and setting up work modules—that is, managing. Travelers estimated that the job-enrichment efforts would save the company $91,937 annually.

Clearly there are a number of alternative strategies for reducing turnover in organizations, but the first step, as we noted earlier, is to calculate the *cost* of turnover. Only then can managers make rational decisions based on the expected costs and benefits of each of the options available.

Exercises

1. Ups and Downs, Inc., a four-thousand-employee organization, has a serious turnover problem, and management has decided to estimate its annual cost to the company. Following the formulas presented in Exhibits 2.2, 2.3, and 2.4, a personnel specialist collected the following information. Exit interviews take about 45 minutes (plus 15 minutes preparation), the interviewer, a personnel specialist, is paid an average of $8.50 per hour, and over the last year Ups and Downs Inc. experienced a 27 percent turnover rate. Three groups of employees were primarily responsible for this: blue collar workers (40 percent), who make an average of $9.70 per hour; clerical employees (36 percent), who make an average of $7.60 per hour; and managers and professionals (24 percent), who make an average of $13.20 per hour. Administratively it takes about 90 minutes per terminating employee for the personnel department to perform the administrative functions related to terminations, and on top of that, each

terminating employee gets two weeks' severance pay. All of this turnover also contributes to increased unemployment tax (0.4 percent), and since the average taxable wage per employee is $8.90 this is likely to be a considerable (avoidable) penalty for having a high turnover problem.

It also costs money to replace those terminating. All preemployment physicals are done by Biometrics, Inc., an outside organization that charges $30 per physical. Advertising and employment agency fees run an additional $100, on the average, per termination, and personnel specialists spend an average of four more hours communicating job availability every time another employee quits. Preemployment administrative functions take another two and a half hours per terminating employee, and this excludes preemployment interview time (one hour, on average). Over the past year Ups and Downs Inc.'s records also show that for every candidate hired, three others had to be interviewed. For those management jobs being filled, a 90-minute staff meeting was also required, with a department representative (average pay of $12.75 per hour) present. In the last year seventeen of those were held. Finally, postemployment acquisition and dissemination of information took 75 minutes, on the average, for each new employee.

And of course all these replacements had to be trained. Informational literature alone cost $6.25 per package, the formal training program (run twelve times last year) takes four 8-hour days and trainers make an average of $11.35 per hour. New employees made an average of $9.45 per hour, and about 65 percent of all training costs can be attributed to replacements for those who left. Finally, on-the-job training lasted three 8-hour days per new employee, with two new employees assigned to each experienced employee. What did employee turnover cost Ups and Down, Inc. last year? How much per employee who left? (Use the worksheet provided for all computations.)

2. Management has decided that the cost of employee turnover at Ups and Downs, Inc., is intolerable. As an outside consultant, you have been retained to do two things. First, prepare a presentation to management that will help the managers better understand why employees leave. Second, recommend two *detailed* programs for reducing the turnover problem at Ups and Downs. (To do this, make whatever assumptions seem reasonable.)

Worksheet

Separation Costs

Exit interview cost of interviewer's time =

cost of terminating employees' time =

Administrative functions related to terminations =

Separation pay =

Unemployment tax =

Total separation costs =

Replacement costs

Communicating job availability =

Preemployment administrative functions =

Worksheet (continued)

Entrance interview =

Staff meeting =

Postemployment acquisition and dissemination of information =

Contracted medical examinations =

Total replacement costs =

Training Costs

Informational literature =

Instruction in a formal training program =

Instruction by employee assignment =

Total training costs =

Total turnover costs =

Total cost per terminating employee =

References

ASHER, J. J., and SCIARRINO, J. A. "Realistic Work Sample Tests: A Review." *Personnel Psychology,* 1974, 27:519–533.

"Blood, Sweat, and Fears." *Time,* September 8, 1980, p. 44.

CASCIO, W. F. *Applied Psychology in Personnel Mangement.* 2nd ed. Reston, Va.: Reston, 1982.

CASCIO, W. F., and PHILLIPS, N. F. "Performance Testing: A Rose Among Thorns?" *Personnel Psychology,* 1979, 32:751–766.

FLAMHOLTZ, E. G. "Toward a Theory of Human Resource Value in Formal Organizations." *The Accounting Review,* 1972, 47:666–678.

FORD, R. M. *Motivation Through the Work Itself.* New York: Amacom, 1969.

HACKMAN, J. R., and OLDHAM, G. R. *Work Redesign.* Reading, Mass.: Addison-Wesley, 1980.

HACKMAN, J. R., OLDHAM, G. R., JANSON, R., and PURDY, K. "A New Strategy for Job Enrichment." *California Management Review,* 1975, 17:57–71.

MACY, B. A., and MIRVIS, P. H. "Measuring the Quality of Work and Organizational Effectiveness in Behavioral-Economic Terms." *Administrative Science Quarterly,* 1976, 21:212–226.

SMITH, H. L., and WATKINS, L. E. "Managing Manpower Turnover Costs." *The Personnel Administrator,* 1978, 23 (April):46–50.

WANOUS, J. P. *Organizational Entry: Recruitment, Selection, and Socialization of Newcomers.* Reading, Mass.: Addison-Wesley, 1980.

3

The Hidden Costs of Absenteeism and Sick Leave

On a national level, employee absenteeism is estimated to cost workers (and the economy) $20 billion a year in lost pay alone, and cost employers $10 billion a year in sick pay and $5 billion in fringe benefits that continue whether or not the worker is at work (Robins, 1979). This is an enormous loss of productivity, a substantial debit in the national economic ledger. Unfortunately a national, or macro, perspective, while important, masks the costs borne by individual organizations in the economy. The costs of employee absenteeism can also be estimated at the level of the individual organization (at the micro level), although not quite as easily as regularly-computed expenditures such as rent, direct labor, building depreciation, or utilities. As one observer noted:

> Traditional accounting and personnel information systems simply don't generate data which reflect the estimated dollars-and-cents costs of absenteeism. While many organizations regularly compute *time* lost to absenteeism (hours, days, etc.) by employee and department, few organizations translate the collective act of staying away from work into *economic* terms. (Kuzmits, 1979, p. 29)

Despite these difficulties, it is important to emphasize that the costs of absenteeism are very real even if they are buried in an assortment of production, personnel, and accounting records. Until the magnitude of these costs is known, it will be difficult for management to determine the extent of the problem, to estimate its effect on overall productivity or profits, or to formulate strategies for dealing with it.

Before we begin to describe procedures for costing employee absenteeism let us first define absenteeism. The city of Baltimore's attendance monitoring and analysis program is quite specific on this issue: *absenteeism is any failure to report for or remain at work as scheduled, regardless of reason.* The use of the words "as scheduled" is significant, for this automatically excludes vacation, personal leave, jury duty leave, and the like. A great deal of confusion can be avoided simply by recognizing that if an employee is not on the job as scheduled he or she is absent, regardless of cause. The employee is not available to perform his or her job, and that job is probably being done less efficiently by another employee or is not being done at all.

Another point of primary importance is the fact that absenteeism is to be judged on the record, and the record only. While this may seem elementary, it is essential. There is a tendency to view some absences as "excusable" and others as "inexcusable." Judgments concerning the nature of illness causing the absence also tend to make some absences seem "better" or "worse" than others, and the length of service of the employee makes certain absences seem excusable. Actually, the only absence which is really inexcusable is the absence due to malingering, but, unfortunately, it is difficult or nearly impossible to provide evidence to substantiate malingering, and mere suspicions can be erroneous. Regardless, excused time is by no means a right. Absence is absence regardless of reason—even for medically verified illness. Failure to recognize this simple fact will result in an attempt to make judgments that simply cannot be made. (*City and County Government*, October 1980, 14:3.)

Estimating the Cost of Absenteeism

In the procedure to be described below,[1] we will estimate the cost of absenteeism for a one year period, although the procedure can be used just as easily to estimate these costs over shorter or longer periods as necessary.

---

[1]The method that follows is based upon that described by F. E. Kuzmits in "How much is absenteeism costing your organization?" *Personnel Administrator*, June 1979, 24:29–33.

Much of the information required should not be too time-consuming to gather if an organization regularly computes labor cost data and traditional absence statistics (for example, absenteeism rate = Σ (absence days ÷ average work force size) × working days or Σ (hours missed ÷ average work force size) × working hours). Although some estimates will involve discussions with both staff and management representatives, the time spent should be well worth the effort. The overall approach is shown in Exhibit 3.1.

To illustrate this approach, examples will be provided at each step. Using the hypothetical firm Presto Electric, a medium-sized manufacturer of electrical components employing two thousand people, we will make the examples as realistic as possible in order to illustrate the problems and costs related to employee absenteeism.

Step 1

Determine the organization's total employee-hours lost to absenteeism for the period for all employees—blue collar, clerical, management and professional. Include both whole-day and part-day absences, and time lost for all reasons except organizationally-sanctioned time off such as vacations, holidays, or official "bad weather" days. For example, absences for the following reasons should be included: illness, accidents, funerals, emergencies, or doctor's appointments (whether excused or unexcused).

As a basis for comparisons, Exhibit 3.2 illustrates monthly job absence rates as reported by the Bureau of National Affairs. While there is clearly a seasonal component to the time series data shown in Exhibit 3.2 (highest rates in January and February, lowest rates in June, July, and August), average monthly rates by year do not indicate a long-term trend, at least for the years shown.

In our example, let's assume that Presto Electric's personnel records show 124,776 total employee-hours lost to absenteeism for all reasons except vacations and holidays during the last year. This figure represents an absence rate of 3 percent of scheduled work time, about average for manufacturing firms (see Exhibit 3.2). It is derived as follows:

no. of employees × scheduled = total employee hours/month
             hours/month
(40 hours/week × 52 weeks/ = 2080 hours/year ÷ 12 months
             year

                    = 173.3 hours/month

Exhibit 3.1   Total Estimated Cost of Employee Absenteeism

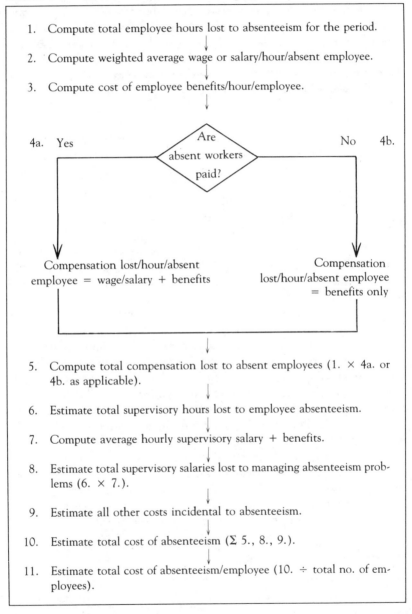

1. Compute total employee hours lost to absenteeism for the period.

2. Compute weighted average wage or salary/hour/absent employee.

3. Compute cost of employee benefits/hour/employee.

4a. Yes   Are absent workers paid?   No   4b.

Compensation lost/hour/absent employee = wage/salary + benefits

Compensation lost/hour/absent employee = benefits only

5. Compute total compensation lost to absent employees (1. × 4a. or 4b. as applicable).

6. Estimate total supervisory hours lost to employee absenteeism.

7. Compute average hourly supervisory salary + benefits.

8. Estimate total supervisory salaries lost to managing absenteeism problems (6. × 7.).

9. Estimate all other costs incidental to absenteeism.

10. Estimate total cost of absenteeism (Σ 5., 8., 9.).

11. Estimate total cost of absenteeism/employee (10. ÷ total no. of employees).

Exhibit 3.2 Typical Monthly Job Absence Rates

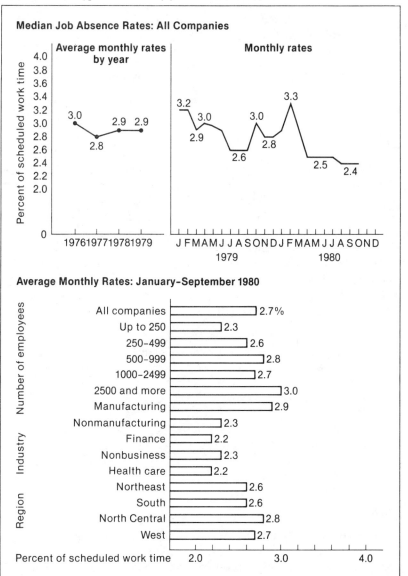

Source: "BNA's Job Absence and Turnover Report—3rd Quarter 1980." *Bulletin to Management,* Bureau of National Affairs, Washington, D.C., December 11, 1980, p. 1.

2,000 × 173.3 hours/month = 346,600

total employee hours/month × = hours/month lost
  monthly absenteeism rate
          346,600 × 0.03 = 10,398

hours/month lost × 12 months = total employee-hours/year lost
          10,398 × 12 = 124,776

Step 2

Compute the weighted average hourly wage/salary level for the various occupational groups that claimed absenteeism during the period. If absent workers are not paid, skip this step and go directly to step 3.

For Presto Electric, let us assume that about 75 percent of all absentees are blue collar, 20 percent clerical, and 5 percent management and professional. For purposes of illustration we will also assume that all employees are paid for sick days taken under the organization's employee benefits program. The average hourly wage rate per absentee is estimated by applying the appropriate percentages to the average hourly wage rate for each major occupational group. Thus:

Occupational group	Approximate percent of total absenteeism	Average hourly wage	Weighted average hourly wage
Blue collar	0.75	6.40	$4.80
Clerical	0.20	5.90	1.18
Management and professional	0.05	12.70	0.64
			$6.62 total

Step 3

Estimate the cost of employee benefits per hour per employee. Presently, the cost of employee benefits (profit-sharing, pensions, health and life insurance, paid vacations and holidays, and so on) is about 25 to 35 percent of total payroll costs nationally. By 1985 that figure is expected to increase to 50 percent (Henderson, 1979). One procedure for computing the cost of employee benefits per hour per employee is to divide the total cost of benefits per employee per week by the number of hours worked per week.

First, let us compute Presto's weekly cost of benefits per employee. Let's assume that the average annual salary per employee is $6.62/hour (which happens to correspond to the result we observed in step 2, though this need not be the case) × 2,080 (hours worked per year), or about $13,770. Let us further assume:

average annual salary × 33 percent = average cost of benefits per employee per year

$13,770 × 0.33 = $4,544

average cost of benefits per employee per year ÷ 52 weeks/year = average weekly cost of benefits per employee

$4,544 ÷ 52 = $87.38

average weekly cost of benefits per employee ÷ hours worked per week = cost of benefits per hour per employee

$87.38 ÷ 40 = $2.18

Step 4

Compute the total compensation lost per hour per absent employee. This figure is determined simply by adding the weighted average wage/salary per hour per employee (item 2) to the cost of employee benefits per hour per employee (item 3). Thus:

$6.62 + $2.18 = $8.80

Of course if absent workers are not paid, then item 4 is the same as item 3.

Step 5

Compute the total compensation lost to absent employees. Total compensation lost, aggregated over all employee hours lost, is determined simply by multiplying item 1 by item 4.a or 4.b, whichever is applicable. In our example:

124,776 × $8.80 = $1,098,028.80

Step 6

Estimate the total number of supervisory hours lost to employee absentee-ism for the period. Unfortunately, since existing records seldom provide the information necessary to compute this figure, it will be more difficult to estimate than wage and benefits estimates. As a first step, estimate the average number of supervisory hours spent per day dealing with all the problems stemming from employee absenteeism, problems such as:

1. production problems
2. instructing replacement employees
3. checking on the performance of replacements
4. counseling and disciplining absentees

Such an estimate can only be accurate if the staff member making it talks to the first-line supervisors and higher level managers who deal directly with employee absence problems. A representative sample of supervisors should be interviewed with a semi-structured interview format to help them refine their estimates. Areas to probe, in addition to those listed above, include the effects of typically high-absence days (Monday, Friday, days before and after holidays, days after payday). No published data, no industry-wide averages, are available to determine whether or not these estimates are reasonable. However, it is true of estimates in general that the more experience companies accumulate in making the estimates, the more accurate the estimates become (Wikstrom, 1971).

After you have estimated the average number of supervisory hours spent per day dealing with employee absenteeism problems, compute the total number of supervisory hours lost to the organization by multiplying three figures:

1. the estimated average number of hours lost per supervisor per day
2. the total number of supervisors who deal with problems of absenteeism
3. the number of working days for the period (including all shifts and weekend work)

In our example, let us assume that Presto Electric's data in these three areas are:

1. estimated number of supervisory hours lost per day: 0.5 hours
2. total number of supervisors who deal with absence problems: 53

Exhibit 3.4 (continued)

of a clearly defined standard and a misunderstanding as to the purpose of sick leave. The City sick leave benefit is designed to provide the continuation of income during times of legitimate illness. Sick leave is not to be considered as an alternate form of vacation time, comp time, holiday leave, or time off for personal business.

3. Action

   A. Effective immediately the following is established as the standard under which disciplinary action should be taken, and the progression of disciplinary action. It is important for supervisors to recognize that this standard has limited flexibility depending on each individual case. In addition, the standard is "occurrences," not "days."

   Oral Reprimand — at the 6th occurrence within a 12 month period
   Written Reprimand — at the 8th occurrence within a 12 month period
   Suspension of 3 days — at the 10th occurrence within a 12 month period
   Termination — at the 12th occurrence within a 12 month period

   B. Initiation of Disciplinary Process: Current Employees.

   Beginning immediately employees who have been absent on four (4) occasions since 1 January 1980, shall be counseled. Regardless of the current number of absences the employee will be given two (2) additional occurrences before progressive discipline begins (exception: If an employee is currently part of a progressive disciplinary process started before 1 July 1980, that process shall continue).

   C. Perpetuation of Disciplinary Process:

   It shall be the responsibility of the employee's immediate supervisor, beginning with the rank of Lieutenant, to administer this procedure. Authority to file charges, conduct hearings, and impose disciplinary action as outlined in paragraph A shall rest with the immediate supervisor up to and including termination.

Exhibit 3.4 (continued)

D. Time Period:

It is important to remember that the 12 month period begins with any employee absence and runs for the next 12 successive months. Anytime six (6) occurrences exist within any 12 month period, the standard shall apply.

E. Doctor's Notes:

Employees may be required to bring in a doctor's note for each additional absence up to a 90 day period, beginning with the written reprimand, set up within the progressive discipline process. Failure of an employee who has been previously warned in writing to furnish the required doctor's note may result in sick leave benefits being denied for the days in question.

A doctor's note does not in itself excuse an employee. Even with a doctor's note, supervisors may consider that absence as an occurrence. Supervisors should use good judgement, however, and evaluate each individual situation; employees with known medical problems may have the number of occurrences extended. Employees who bring doctor's notes indicating various common ailments or injuries, especially when the record indicates sick leave usage in conjunction with days off or during specific times of the year, should not be considered for any extension of occurrences.

Supervisors, at their discretion may choose to utilize two (2) progressively more severe suspensions before termination when the employee has a long and honorable work record and when the sick leave problem is a relatively new situation.

4. Self-cancellation

This order will remain in effect until revoked or superseded by competent authority.

J. D. Holt

J. D. HOLT, Deputy Director
Police Operations

each year to sick leave. This represents 96,000 hours or 3.8 percent of scheduled work hours in the 1,200-officer department. During the 1980 contract negotiations both the city's management and the police union's leaders agreed that abuse of sick leave had become a problem in the department. Once the contract was settled, department leaders developed new rules that defined sick leave abuse and established disciplinary procedures for those who break the rules.

Essentially the order gives an officer five sick leave occurrences before discipline begins. The more the officer calls in sick, the tougher the measures get (except for legitimate illnesses, no matter what the duration), from oral reprimands all the way to suspension and termination.

As part of the effort to curb sick leave abuse, the union agreed to counseling for every officer who was known to have a pattern of using sick leave, for example, during deer season or just before or just after regular days off. The general order was designed to deal with the pattern abuser, and it has been quite effective. A comparison of absenteeism rates in January, 1980 (before the new policy was issued) and August, 1980 (one month after it was issued) indicated a 65 percent drop. In January officers called in sick 457 times; in August only 159 calls were received ("Healthy Policemen," 1980). This pattern was sustained ten months after the order was issued, and the most serious disciplinary action taken up to that time was a written reprimand. Beyond that, the officers who originally had to cover for the sick leave abusers realized that it was in their best interest to support the general order, and their pressure on the sick leave abusers has also been an important factor in the overall success of the program (Real, 1981).

The Memphis approach is discipline-oriented, with peer pressure and counseling for pattern abusers as added incentives for sick leave reduction. A number of earlier discipline-oriented programs failed because they were based solely on punishment, and workers rapidly discovered how to beat the programs. For example, point systems used to be quite popular. Under such a system, the penalty for absence without notice might range from one point for an absence with a documented reason (a penalty which particularly infuriated conscientious workers) to seven points for an outright, no-excuse no-show. Forty points in twelve months meant dismissal. When June of one year began, the points accumulated the previous June no longer counted against a worker. Systems relying only on points often failed because workers soon learned how to beat them, for example, by keeping track of their own records and simply making sure that they didn't pass the dismissal level. As a supervisor at Ford Motor Company complained, "The group of chronic absentees just gets larger as more learn how to play the system" (Robins, 1979, p. 35). More recent "well pay" and attendance bonus programs have also had disappointing results. Three of the nation's largest farm equipment manufacturers have tried these programs and subsequently dropped them. Lateness and absenteeism were reduced somewhat temporarily, but chronic absentees remained chronic, and regular attendees earned the bonuses.

A different, and successful, approach to employee absenteeism control is based on the principle of job enrichment. Such programs, which attempt to give the worker more pride in his or her job and more appreciation of its importance to the company, have been used for over a decade, principally with white collar jobs. Now more enrichment programs are being tested on the factory floor and in blue collar jobs, where absenteeism is more of a problem.

At a General Electric lamp plant absences fell from 3.5 percent to 2.2 percent a year later after monthly plant-wide meetings were instituted to tell employees exactly what absenteeism costs the company. As the plant manager pointed out,

> Most of our efforts now go into awareness programs and enrichment. It's a matter of making workers feel they're important. There isn't anything that can beat that. We've tried to get our workers to realize just how important they are and how badly we need them here. (Robins, 1979, p. 35)

Worker teams meet with their supervisors weekly. They are congratulated when performance is good. When there is a poor production run on a certain type of light bulb, the supervisors don't point fingers; they ask for suggestions. The overall approach was summarized by the plant manager as follows:

> We don't feel that wages are the primary motivator. The real motivation is when the worker feels he's making a contribution. And a worker who feels he's contributing is the worker least likely to be an absentee problem. (Robins, 1979, p. 35)

Job enrichment programs clearly offer promise of alleviating absenteeism problems, but almost no one views any single approach as a permanent cure. This is part of the frustration—and challenge—inherent in preventing and controlling employee absenteeism. Like so many other areas of human resource management, absenteeism control requires meticulous attention combined with an enduring management commitment to deal successfully with the problem.

Exercises

1. Consolidated Industries, an 1,800-employee firm, is faced with a serious, and growing, absenteeism problem. Last year total employee-hours lost to absenteeism came to 119,808. Of the total employees absent, 65 percent were blue collar (average wage of $8.07 per hour), 25 percent were clerical (average wage of $7.16 per hour), and the remainder were management and professional (average salary $11.02 per hour). On the average, the firm spends 35 percent more of each employee's salary on benefits, and as company policy, workers are paid even if they are absent.

The 45 supervisors (average hourly salary of $9.86 per hour) involved in employee absenteeism problems estimate they lost 25 minutes per day just dealing with the extra problems imposed by those who fail to show up for work. Finally, the company estimates it loses $44,800 in additional overtime premiums, in extra help that must be hired, and in lost productivity from the more highly skilled absentees. As personnel director for Consolidated Industries your job is to estimate the cost of employee absenteeism so that management can better understand the dimensions of the problem. (Use the worksheet provided to record your answers.)

2. Inter-Capital Limited is a 500-employee firm faced with a 3.7 percent annual absenteeism rate. About 15 percent of absentees are blue collar (average wage $9.61 per hour), 55 percent are clerical employees (average wage $8.26 per hour), and the remainder are management and professional workers (average salary $12.14 per hour). About 38 percent more of each employee's salary is spent on benefits, but employees are not paid if they are absent from work. In the last six months, supervisors (average salary of $10.75 per hour) estimate that managing absenteeism problems costs them about an hour a day. It's a serious problem that must be dealt with, since about 20 supervisors are directly involved with absenteeism. On top of that, the firm spends approximately $28,000 more on costs incidental to absenteeism. Temporary help and lost productivity can really cut into profits. Just how much is absenteeism costing Inter-Capital Ltd. per year per employee? (Use the worksheet provided to record your answers.)

3. As a management consultant, you have been retained to develop two alternative programs for reducing employee absenteeism at Consolidated Industries (question 1). Write a proposal that addresses the issue in specific terms. Exactly what should the firm do? (To do this make whatever assumptions seem reasonable.)

Worksheet
Total Estimated Cost of Employee Absenteeism

Item	Consolidated Industries	Inter-Capital Limited
1. Total employee-hours lost to absenteeism for the period	_____	_____
2. Weighted average wage/salary per hour per absent employee	_____	_____
3. Cost of employee benefits per hour per employee	_____	_____
4. Total compensation lost per hour per absent employee		
a. If absent workers are paid (wage/salary plus benefits)	_____	_____
b. If absent workers are not paid (benefits only)	_____	_____
5. Total compensation lost to absent employees (total employee-hours lost × 4.a or 4.b, whichever applies)	_____	_____
6. Total supervisory hours lost on employee absenteeism	_____	_____
7. Average hourly supervisory wage, including benefits	_____	_____
8. Total supervisory salaries lost to managing problems of absenteeism (hours lost × average hourly supervisory wage—item 6 × item 7)	_____	_____
9. All other costs incidental to absenteeism not included in the above items	_____	_____

Worksheet (continued)

Item	Consolidated Industries	Inter-Capital Limited
10. Total estimated cost of absenteeism—summation of items 5, 8, and 9	————	————
11. Total estimated cost of absenteeism per employee (total estimated costs ÷ total number of employees)	————	————

References

"Healthy Policemen Draw Praise From Brass." *Memphis Press-Scimitar,* October 25, 1980, pp. 1, 6.

HENDERSON, R. I. *Compensation Management.* 2nd ed. Reston, Va.:Reston, 1979.

KUZMITS, F. E. "How Much Is Absenteeism Costing Your Organization?" *The Personnel Administrator,* June 1979, 24:29–33.

REAL, L., Director of Labor Relations, City of Memphis, Personal Communication, May 3, 1981.

ROBINS, J. "Costly Problem: Firms Try Newer Ways to Slash Absenteeism as Carrot and Stick Fail." *Wall Street Journal,* March 14, 1979, pp. 1, 35.

WIKSTROM, W. S. *Manpower Planning: Evolving Systems.* New York: The Conference Board, Report No. 521, 1971.

4

Costing the Effects of Smoking at the Work Place

Thousands of studies have been done on the health and behavioral consequences of smoking. When in 1964 the Surgeon General issued a report demonstrating the adverse effects of smoking on health, much of the general public was skeptical of its conclusions, and the tobacco industry challenged its validity. In 1979 the Surgeon General issued a second report on smoking, a report even more emphatic in its conclusions: "Thousands of additional studies remove any doubt as to the causal linkage between smoking and disease. . . . Smoking is far more dangerous than we ever imagined in 1964" (U.S. Department of Health and Human Services, 1979).

While the links between smoking and diseases such as cancer, heart disease, varicose veins, emphysema, and chronic bronchitis have been established firmly, the business implications of smoking are not very well understood. As with so many other areas of human resource costing, employers have not paid much attention to the costs of employee smoking. As of 1980 only about 2 percent of United States businesses imposed smoking bans at the work place, but these businesses reported uniformly high cost savings (Shannon, 1980). Research to be described in this

65

chapter indicates that the absenteeism rate among smokers can be as much as 85 percent higher than the rate for nonsmokers. Smokers' early disability rates and early mortality rates may be almost 300 percent higher than those for nonsmokers. The productivity loss can be substantial as well—as much as 25 percent of the work day may be lost to the smoking ritual. When these and other secondary consequences of smoking are translated into dollars, the incremental cost to business of hiring smokers is almost $5,000 per year per employee (Weiss 1981a). This chapter describes eight sources of these costs and develops dollar estimates based on current research. The eight areas we shall consider are:

absenteeism

medical care

morbidity and early mortality

insurance

on-the-job time lost

property damage and depreciation

maintenance

involuntary smoking

At the outset it is important to point out that the purpose of this chapter is not to advocate the imposition of no-smoking hiring and working policies. Rather, the purpose is to present current research on the effects of smoking at the work place, to discuss the cost implications for human resource management, and to let each reader decide whether smoking bans are warranted. Top managers of organizations may or may not choose to impose smoking bans, but whatever their decision, it should be based on a rational consideration of the costs and consequences of the issues involved. One final word of caution. The cost estimates described here are just that—estimates. Smoking behavior, employee mix, physical plant, type of production function, and other factors vary widely across business settings. In some circumstances our figures may be gross over- or under-estimates, but the factors involved and the methods for estimating their costs are likely to apply across settings. Many of the ideas in this chapter are drawn from the work of William Weiss (1980, 1981a, 1981b, 1981c), who has been responsible for much of the research done in this area. Let us begin with the easiest consequence of smoking to quantify—employee absenteeism.

Absenteeism

In the U.S. adult male population, 38 percent are smokers, and in the U.S. adult female population, 30 percent are smokers (U.S. Department of Health and Human Services, 1979). The impact of smoking on employee absenteeism can be illustrated by these incremental absenteeism rates (U.S. Departments of Health and Human Services, 1979; Commerce, 1974; and Public Health Service, 1967):

	Male smokers	Female smokers
Overall average	56.8%	45.1%
17–44 year olds	83.3%	23.3%
More than 40 cigarettes/day	65%	17.4%

Incremental absenteeism is the incidence of smokers' absenteeism over and above that of nonsmoking peers. The key figures in the illustration are the cross-sectional averages for all ages and all dosages, 56.8 percent (males) and 45.1 percent (females), or an absenteeism rate approximately 50 percent greater for smokers in general than for nonsmokers. This differential rate declines sharply after age forty-four, as many absence-prone smokers leave the work force altogether due to death or disability (U.S. Department of Health and Human Services, 1979).

Smoker and nonsmoker absenteeism rates may vary to some extent depending on each organization's mix of ages and education level (highly educated persons have much lower rates of smoking), but on the average each smoker on the payroll will be absent over three days per year more than nonsmokers. This figure is determined as follows:

Assume an overall company average absenteeism rate of approximately 2.5 percent of scheduled work time.

Incremental absenteeism for smokers is 50 percent; $0.025 \times 1.5 = .0375$, or 3.75 percent of scheduled work time.

Annual scheduled work time is 2,000 hours (40 hours/week $\times$ 50 weeks).

Hours absent for nonsmokers: $2,000 \times 0.025 = 50$ per year

Hours absent for smokers: $2,000 \times 0.0375 = 75$ per year

Days absent for nonsmokers: 6.25 per year

Days absent for smokers: 9.37 per year

Additional days absent for smokers: 3.12 per year

Since a detailed analysis of costing employee absenteeism was presented in Chapter 3, that analysis will not be repeated here. As an example though, let us adopt the all-company average estimated cost of absenteeism per year per employee ($620.38) we computed for Presto Electric. Let us assume that 30 percent of Presto's work force smokes; 1,200 × 0.30 = 360 employees. On the average, therefore, the annual cost of absenteeism for each nonsmoker is $620.38 − 25% = $465.28 and for each of the 360 smokers on the payroll $620.38 + 25% = $775.48.[1] The total additional cost per year per smoker is therefore $310.20.

Medical Care, Morbidity, and Premature Mortality

Differences between smokers and nonsmokers in the relative incidence of disease (morbidity), need for medical care, and premature mortality affect several factors that ultimately are paid for by the employer. Some of these factors are contributions to health, disability, and life insurance plans; taxes for state and federal unemployment compensation; and taxes for federal social security and medicare programs. The overall mortality rate for a cross section of adult age groups is 70 percent greater for smokers than nonsmokers, but this figure underestimates the differential for those in their prime working-age years. It also underestimates the differential for those who smoke a lot. Thus men between the ages of thirty-five and forty-four, for example, who smoke more than forty cigarettes per day suffer a mortality rate 272 percent higher than nonsmoking men in the same age bracket (U.S. Department of Health and Human Services, 1979). Heavy smokers also use the nation's health care system at least 50 percent more than nonsmokers do (Kristein, 1977).

Disability rates are also much higher among smokers. The Alexandria, Virginia, fire department observed that 73 percent of those taking early disability retirement between 1973 and 1978 were smokers. This is well

---

[1] Assuming absenteeism rates and costs are linearly related, a 50 percent differential in absenteeism rates for smokers and nonsmokers yields a savings, on the average, of 25 percent of the estimated all-company average absenteeism cost for nonsmokers, and an incremental cost, on the average, of 25 percent for smokers.

above the 33 percent smoking rate in the adult population. The department estimated that early retirements due to disability cost the fire district an additional $300,000 over normal retirements. Another way of stating the problem is that 33 percent of the employees were contributing 73 percent of the early retirements. This represents a disability rate for smokers that is five and a half times greater than that for nonsmokers. To illustrate: suppose 33 percent of a 4,000-person work force smokes (1,332 people). Suppose further that in any given year about 100 employees take early retirement. If, on the average, 73 of the early retirees are smokers, then:

1,332/73 or 1 of every 18.2 smokers takes early disability retirement, as compared with

2,668/27 or 1 of every 98.8 nonsmoking employees

98.8/18.2 = 5.43 as many smokers as nonsmokers who take early disability retirement

On the basis of these figures, Fire Chief Charles Rule decided to hire only nonsmokers—a decision that will ultimately save the taxpayers of Alexandria millions of dollars (*Wall Street Journal*, November 7, 1978).

For purposes of estimating the costs of increased medical care, morbidity, and premature mortality for smokers over nonsmokers, let us assume that all savings flow directly to the employer. This is a bit idealistic, but major insurance companies are starting to offer substantial discounts to nonsmokers. For example, on life insurance premiums the State Mutual Life Assurance Company of America is offering policies to nonsmokers at a cost 30 percent less than comparable coverage for smokers. The reduced rates are the result of an extensive study by the company that shows that death rates in all age categories were more than twice as high for smokers than for nonsmokers. For firms that have rigid no-smoking policies, fire insurance premium reductions of 25 percent and more can be negotiated (Weiss, 1981a).

Luce and Schweitzer (1978) reported in the *New England Journal of Medicine* that, on the average, smokers require an additional $230 per person per year for medical care alone, and an additional $765 per year for discounted lost earnings due to morbidity and premature mortality.[2] It may

---

[2]Estimates are in January 1981 dollars. Lost earnings are assumed to approximate the value lost to the employer from premature retirement or death, reflecting both the costs of investments in human resource development (amortized over a shorter time span than for nonsmokers) and the lost return for early termination of the employee's services.

be a while before the entire $995 per employee is realized by the organization, but the saving does represent a realistic objective in long-range policy projections.

Industries that invest substantial resources in training personnel should carefully consider the early disability and mortality differentials between smokers and nonsmokers at various age intervals. Consider an example presented by Weiss (1981c):

> . . . large public accounting firms defend their "youth only" hiring practices because of the 10 to 15 years needed to develop the skills and judgment required of partners. Wanting to enjoy at least 20 years of a partner's peak productivity makes it mandatory to begin the training process at an early age, preferably early twenties. If firms spent more time studying the disability and mortality rates during this period of peak productivity (ages 35–55), they might discover that age is not the only agent causing accountants to decay. The chance of living to take that mandatory retirement, for a 22-year-old smoker, is only one third of that for a 22-year-old nonsmoker. Is it worth the substantial investment to train young smokers to be good accountants (in the hereafter)? (p. 6)

Other Insurance Costs

There are other opportunity costs besides lost earnings that are associated with higher rates of mortality and disability among smokers. Economist Marvin Kristein of the American Health Foundation estimates that smokers cost an extra $90 per year in other insurance costs (Kristein, 1980). Accidental injury and related workers' compensation costs constitute $45 of this cost per year per smoker, and the remaining $45 is due to higher insurance premiums for fire, life, and wage continuation policies. These totals were based on studies showing that smokers have twice the accident rate of nonsmokers due to carelessness caused by attention loss, eye irritation, coughing, and hand interference.

On-the-Job Time Lost

Estimates of the amount of on-the-job time lost to the smoking ritual— lighting, puffing, informal breaks—vary among sources from a low of 8 minutes per day (Kristein, 1980) to a high of 15 to 30 minutes per hour (Weiss, 1980). The latter estimate was reported by a general contractor in

Seattle who stopped taking bids from smokers after firing a dry-wall crafts-man who lost 30 minutes of every hour to his smoking habit. As a basis for our cost estimate, let us use a conservative compromise of 30 minutes per day for cigarette smokers and 55 minutes per day for pipe smokers, as reported by the *Wall Street Journal* (Labor Letter, May 8, 1979).

If 30 minutes of every 8-hour work day is lost to the smoking ritual, then in a 250-day work year, 30 × 250 or 7,500 minutes are lost. Over a 120,000 minute work year this represents a 6.25 percent productivity loss. For pipe smokers approximately 11.25 percent of the work year is lost. Thus, assuming all other factors remain constant (that is, assuming all nonsmokers do not have a similar time-consuming habit, like drinking coffee), 8 nonsmokers can do the work of 9 pipe smokers. To carry this example further, if we assume that one of every five smokers puffs a pipe, then a weighted average of:

$$0.80 \times 30 = 24$$
$$0.20 \times 55 = \underline{11}$$

35 minutes per day is lost to smoking

In a 480-minute (8-hour) day, then 35/480 or 0.072916 of each day is lost to the smoking ritual. This represents 18.2 days per year in lost productivity:

120,000 minutes per work year × 0.072916 = 8,749 minutes per year loss

8,749 minutes per year ÷ 480 minutes per
work day = 18.2 days/year

Assuming an overall company average annual cost of absenteeism per employee of $620.38 (see Chapter 3) and an average of 6.25 days absent per year per employee, each day's absence costs the firm about $100. Therefore, 18.2 days costs employers an additional $1,820 per year per smoker. For jobs in construction and the trades where tools go down when smokers light up, the cost may be considerably higher.

Property Damage, Depreciation, and Maintenance

The estimates to be described in this category are based upon interviews reported by Weiss (1981a) with business owners and executives of orga-nizations that have implemented no-smoking policies. In some cases the estimates admittedly are rough, but as more firms begin to track costs in this category from before to after implementing smoking bans, the accuracy of the data will improve.

Property damage and depreciation[3] are roughly equivalent phenomena for estimating incremental costs for most businesses. Furniture, carpeting, and draperies are generally replaced when damaged, and the damage often results from cigarette burns. Estimates of the useful lives of commercial furnishings are primarily based on the employer's tolerance for burn spots and on the expected frequency of the appearance of burns. Since no-smoking policies eliminate a primary cause of depreciation, longer useful lives are to be expected.

The costs of removing tobacco odors should be considered. Tobacco odors are caused primarily by pyridine, a strong irritant that is produced when nicotine burns. Consider the effects on the operation of an air conditioner, for example. Controlled studies have shown that when someone lights a cigarette, cigar, or pipe in an air-conditioned environment, the air conditioning demands can jump as much as six times normal to control odor (American Lung Association, 1977).

At Radar Electric Company in Seattle, for example, intervals between furniture and fixture replacements are expected to at least triple as a result of the company's no-smoking policy. Firms that employ costly precision machinery have long recognized the damage that can be caused by smoke merely circulating in the surrounding air. Interview results indicate that employers expect to save at least $500 per smoker per year from the longer intervals between replacement of furnishings and equipment. This excludes occasional patch-up work on carpeting, which can run as high as $100 per repair.

Maintenance is another area of savings for smoke-free businesses. For example, Merle Norman Cosmetics trimmed general housekeeping maintenance costs by 10 percent per year since implementing its smoking ban in 1976 (Wall Street Journal, November 7, 1978). Routine cleaning may be reduced by as much as 60 percent, due in part (according to interviews with owners of smoke-free businesses) to a more cleanliness-conscious work force when smoking is banned (Weiss, 1981a). Some organizations are able to limit the washing of interior glass surfaces (windows, showcases) to an annual, instead of monthly, routine. Repainting of interior surfaces is also required less often.

---

[3]Depreciation, as used in estimating out-of-pocket costs, refers to *actual* deterioration of an asset's usefulness, as opposed to its usage in accounting terminology.

Estimates of savings resulting from reduced maintenance are again rough, but $500 per smoker was seen as reasonable by interviewees. One employer who had 40 smokers on his payroll before implementing a strict no-smoking policy was able to reduce his cleaning force by one person and reduce his average painting and window washing work by two-thirds, thereby saving $30,000 per year from maintenance alone—$750 per smoker. A $500 per smoker per year target seems to be a reasonably conservative estimate.

Involuntary Smoking and Employee Morale

Surprisingly, a number of employers are still oblivious to the health hazard imposed on nonsmokers who live and work around smokers, but the evidence is compelling. White and Froeb (1980) reported in the *New England Journal of Medicine* that they found a significant impairment of small airways function for nonsmokers who work around smokers. The damage from involuntary or "passive" smoking was equivalent to that suffered by light smokers (one to ten cigarettes per day), or approximately one-fifth the damage to normal smokers (Wynder and Stellman, 1977).

To gauge the impact of involuntary smoking on business costs, let us apply this one-fifth figure to our estimate of incremental costs from excess medical care, discounted lost earnings from morbidity and premature mortality, and incremental absenteeism.

medical care	$ 230
morbidity and early mortality (discounted lost earnings)	765
absenteeism:	310
total incremental cost	$1,305

total incremental cost ($1,305) × 1/5 = $261

Thus, on the average, each smoker is increasing the per worker expenses of nonsmokers by $261 per year. Furthermore, since two of every three workers are nonsmokers, the incremental cost due to the health impairment caused nonsmokers is $522 per smoker per year.

Although the incremental costs associated with smoking at the work place may appear substantial thus far, employers who have imposed no-smoking policies insist that the major savings, by far, stem from higher employee morale. They argue that smoke-free environments are clean, healthy, and conducive to good working relationships (Weiss, 1981b), but no cost data associated with higher morale are offered. This is understandable, since the benefits of higher morale are difficult to quantify (see Chapter 5). From a human resource management perspective, the important point is that the total cost that we are about to present in Exhibit 4.1 is probably a conservative estimate for it does not include what most employers regard as the most substantial savings of a no-smoking policy.

Aggregate Costs of Smoking at the Work Place

The additional yearly costs associated with each smoker on the payroll are summarized in Exhibit 4.1. Another way of viewing the entries in the exhibit is the cost savings that employers might expect from a policy that prohibits smoking on company premises and restricts all future hiring

Exhibit 4.1   Additional Annual Cost of Employing Smokers and Allowing Smoking at the Work Place

Absenteeism	$ 310[a]
Medical care	230[b]
Morbidity and early mortality (discounted lost earnings)	765[b]
Insurance (excluding health)	90[c]
On-the-job time lost	1,820[a]
Property damage and depreciation	500[d]
Maintenance	500[d]
Involuntary smoking	522[e]
Total cost per smoker per year	$4,737

Note: All costs are in January 1981 dollars.

[a]Assumes that overall company average cost of absenteeism is $620 per year and that smokers are absent 50 percent more often.

[b]Based on Luce and Schweitzer (1978) adjusted for 1981 dollars.

[c]Based on Kristein (1980) adjusted for 1981 dollars.

[d]Based on interviews by Weiss (1981a).

[e]Based on White and Froeb (1980), Wynder and Stellman (1977), and Luce and Schweitzer (1978).

Source: Adapted from W. L. Weiss. "Can You Afford to Hire Smokers?" The Personnel Administrator, May 1981, 26:71–78.

to nonsmokers. As we noted earlier, nonsmokers now constitute two-thirds of the adult population in the United States.

As the table indicates, the estimated total additional annual cost per smoker is $4,737. While some may quarrel with the accuracy of the numbers, they are based on the best estimates available. Indeed, future research may well show them to understate the actual costs significantly.

Is a Smoking Ban Legal?

As we noted earlier, some firms have banned altogether smoking by customers, clients, or employees on company premises. There are also firms that refuse to hire smokers—but are such bans legal? Given the power of the tobacco industry, a Supreme Court test is almost inevitable, although no such case has yet been decided. When the Johns-Manville Company announced in January, 1978, that smoking was prohibited in all of its asbestos mines and plants in the United States and Canada, legal questions arose. Concern was expressed about "smokers' rights" and the "undue restraint on the nervous system of the addicted smoker" imposed by the ban ". . . it is unjust for Johns-Manville to say [to current workers who smoke]: 'cold turkey or forfeit your job.' " (*Business Week*, May 29, 1978, p. 68).

On the other side, nonsmokers and employers raise two countervailing arguments: the rights of nonsmokers, whose health is impaired by side-stream and mainstream inhalation,[4] and the incremental costs to employers. Weiss (1980) argues persuasively:

> Recent studies showing adverse health effects on nonsmokers who are exposed to smoke at work should dispel any apprehensions as to the legality of a smoking ban. If anything, the legality of *not* imposing such a ban should be in doubt. You are not required to hire from a minority of applicants who, by choice, distinguish themselves with high rates of absenteeism, disability, early mortality, and substandard productivity, and whose habit is now known to be a major hazard for co-workers. (p.2)

There is no question today that smoking is permitted in the overwhelming majority of organizations in the United States and abroad. In

[4]Sidestream smoke goes directly into the air from the burning end of a cigarette, cigar, or pipe. Mainstream smoke is that which the smoker puffs through the mouthpiece when he or she inhales or puffs—and then exhales.

some of these firms smoking policies are the result of a rational weighing of the evidence. In others there has been no such conscious effort, for attempts to cost human resource management processes are of relatively recent origin. No one can guarantee that a smoking ban will immediately improve annual profits by $4,737 per reformed, or displaced, smoker. On the other hand, the accumulated evidence among firms that have imposed such bans indicates the following trends (Weiss, 1981a):

> Personnel costs decline. The same work load can be accomplished with 10 percent fewer employees.
>
> Maintenance costs decline.
>
> Actual physical depreciation on furniture and equipment slows substantially.
>
> Insurance rates can be decreased through renegotiation for new fire, health, accident, and disability coverage.
>
> Employee morale improves.
>
> Customers and clients adjust without adverse repercussions.

Smoking is a matter of individual choice in most organizations, and there are certainly other ways to increase productivity and profits without imposing a smoking ban. On the other hand, policy makers owe it to their organizations, to their employees, and to their stockholders to evaluate all of the available evidence bearing on this issue before adopting policies for or against smoking.

Exercises

1. You are the president and chief executive officer of a forty-person management consulting firm. Company headquarters consist of a six-room suite of offices in a downtown professional building. Most of your people are out in the field on business trips on any given day. Your work force is composed of the following:

Males	Females
10 aged 24–44	11 aged 24–44
14 aged 45–65	5 aged 45–65

Approximately one-third of each group (male-female) smokes. Write a one- to two-page memorandum to your employees explaining your reasoning for *not* imposing a smoking ban.

2. The Meyers Company employs 2,800 workers in the manufacture of precision components for medical and surgical equipment. About half the workers are male, most in their twenties and thirties. Two workers staff each work station, and work stations are spaced every six feet. Last month the company imposed a smoking ban, and the workers' union immediately filed a grievance on behalf of the 40 percent of the work force that smokes. As a personnel specialist assigned to the labor relations section, write a short paper summarizing management's arguments for the smoking ban.

3. As a staff member of the General Accounting Office of the federal government, your assignment is to review the evidence for and against smoking at the work place and prepare a report for use in upcoming congressional hearings on the subject. If a smoking ban is adopted it will affect over one million federal workers. You are a member of one four-to-six-person team working at a federal agency in Washington, D.C. Divide up the work any way you'd like, but be sure that your final report represents a balanced view of both sides of the issue.

References

American Lung Association. *Second-Hand Smoke.* New York: American Lung Association, 1977.

Companies Put Up the 'No-Smoking' Sign. Business Week, May 29, 1978, p. 68.

KRISTEIN, M. M. "Economic Issues in Prevention." *Preventive Medicine,* 1977, 6: 252–264.

KRISTEIN, M. M. *How Much Can Business Expect to Earn from Smoking Cessation?* Paper presented at the Connecticut Lung Association Conference, "Smoking in the Workplace," November 13, 1980, New Haven, Connecticut.

LUCE, B. R., and SCHWEITZER, S. O. "Smoking and Alcohol Abuse: A Comparison of Their Economic Consequences." *The New England Journal of Medicine,* March 9, 1978, pp. 569–571.

SHANNON, M. J. Business bulletin. *Wall Street Journal,* April 17, 1980, p. 1.

U. S. Department of Commerce, Bureau of the Census, *Statistical Abstract of the United States.* Washington, D. C.: Government Printing Office, 1974, p. 87.

U. S. Department of Health and Human Services. *Smoking and Health: A Report of the Surgeon General.* Washington, D. C.: Government Printing Office, 1979.

U. S. Public Health Service. *The Health Consequences of Smoking: A Public Health Service Review.* Washington, D. C.: Government Printing Office, 1967.

Wall Street Journal, November 7, 1978, p. 1.

Wall Street Journal, May 8, 1979, p. 1.

WEISS, W. L. "Improve Productivity Overnight." *The Collegiate Forum,* Fall 1980, p. 2.

WEISS, W. L. "Can You Afford to Hire Smokers?" *The Personnel Administrator,* May 1981, 26:71–78. (a)

WEISS, W. L. "Profits Up in Smoke." *Personnel Journal,* March 1981, 60. (b)

WEISS, W. L. "Warning: Smoking Is Hazardous to Your Business." Unpublished manuscript, Albers Graduate School of Business, Seattle University, Seattle, Washington, February 1981. (c)

WHITE, J. R., and FROEB, H. F. "Small Airways Dysfunction in Nonsmokers Chronically Exposed to Tobacco Smoke." *The New England Journal of Medicine,* March 27, 1980, pp. 270–273.

WYNDER, E. L., and STELLMAN, S. D. "Comparative Epidemiology of Tobacco-Related Cancers." *Cancer Research,* 1977, 37 (December):4608–4622.

II

Costing Employee Attitudes and Collectively Bargained Agreements

5

The Financial Impact
of Employee Attitudes

$\underbrace{}$A number of studies in behavioral science have examined the relationship between job attitudes and absenteeism, turnover, tardiness, job
performance, strikes, and grievances (see Mobley, Griffith, Hand, and
Meglino, 1979; and Porter and Steers, 1973 for reviews). Attitudes are
internal states that are focused on particular aspects of or objects in the
environment. They include three elements: *cognition*, the knowledge an
individual has about the focal object of the attitude; the *emotion* an
individual feels toward the focal object; and an *action* tendency, a readiness
to respond in a predetermined manner to the focal object.

Job satisfaction may be viewed as a multidimensional attitude; it is
made up of attitudes toward pay, promotions, co-workers, supervision, the
work itself, and so on. Management is interested in employees' job satisfaction principally because of the relationship between attitudes and behavior. Other things being equal, it is assumed that employees who are
dissatisfied with their jobs (hold negative attitudes about various aspects
of the work environment) will tend to be absent or late for work, or to quit
more often than those whose attitudes are positive. Work force productivity
therefore suffers. To explain the connection between attitudes and behav-

ior, we must look at the precursors of attitudes: each individual's beliefs (Ajzen and Fishbein, 1980). Attitudes are a function of beliefs.

Generally speaking, a person who believes that a particular behavior will lead mostly to positive outcomes will hold a favorable attitude toward that behavior. A person who believes that the behavior will lead mostly to negative outcomes will hold an unfavorable attitude. According to this approach, any behavior can be predicted from a person's attitude toward it, provided that the measure of attitude corresponds to that measure of behavior (that is, they are evaluated in similar terms). A review of the attitude-behavior literature supports this position (Ajzen and Fishbein, 1977). Experimental evidence in the organizational behavior literature also indicates that improved job satisfaction can reduce absenteeism, turnover, tardiness, and grievances (Marrow, Bowers, and Seashore, 1967).

From our perspective, the important questions are these: what is the financial impact of the behavioral outcomes associated with job attitudes, and can we measure the costs associated with different levels of job satisfaction and motivation? There is a strong need for behavioral scientists to be able to speak in dollars and cents terms when they argue the merits of human resource development programs designed to change attitudes or improve job satisfaction. As we saw in Chapters 2 and 3, methods for attaching costs to absenteeism and turnover are fairly well developed. Measures of employee attitudes are even more finely developed (Smith, Kendall, and Hulin, 1969; Taylor and Bowers, 1972). The purpose of this chapter is to show how the two types of measures, financial and attitudinal, can be synthesized to produce an estimate in dollars of the costs and benefits of human resource development programs designed to improve employee attitudes.

Let us begin by presenting a model of financial assessment (Exhibit 5.1) that was developed by Mirvis and Macy (1976). The exhibit depicts several different development programs (x_1 to x_5). There are three distinct accounting activities necessary for evaluating these programs. The first is a *cost model* needed for identifying the firm's direct costs and losses in productive time attributable to the development effort. The second is an *effectiveness model* used for measuring and validating the effects of a project on the work environment and employees' attitudes, behaviors, and performance, and expressing these effects in financial terms. The third is a *synthesizing model* to compare the costs and benefits of a program. Both social and financial goals can then be contrasted with project costs in order

Exhibit 5.1 Cost-Benefit Model for Human Resource Development Programs

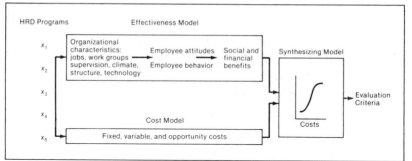

Source: P. H. Mirvis and B. A. Macy. "Accounting for the costs and benefits of human resource development programs: An interdisciplinary approach." *Accounting, Organizations, and Society,* 1976, *1*, 181.

to identify the most cost-beneficial development program (see Chapter 10). That is, programs are judged successful if expenditures are outweighed by the present value of future benefits.

Measuring the Costs of Development Programs

Although this issue is considered in much greater detail in Chapter 10, for the present let us distinguish three broad classes of costs: fixed, variable, and opportunity costs (see p. 7). Fixed costs include salaries, wages, and benefits associated with employees' lost time and the resulting unabsorbed overhead costs (see Chapters 2 and 3). Variable costs include, for example, consultants' fees and expenses associated with their activities. These costs vary depending on the type of program and the intensity and duration of the development activities. They should be reported in deflated dollar terms. The work site also incurs variable costs in the form of lost worker productivity and overtime. Finally, opportunity costs reflect the profit contribution of the employees' lost time. We can also conceive of an additional opportunity cost, the "opportunities foregone" (Rothenberg, 1975) that might have been realized had the resources allocated to the program been directed toward other organizational ends.

On the other side of the ledger we can distinguish fixed, variable, and opportunity savings resulting from successful development programs. Fixed savings might be realized if some of the service demands placed on the personnel, industrial relations, safety, and quality control departments were reduced. Variable savings might include improved marginal productivity through increased product quality and quantity, limited overtime, reduced consumption of supplies and materials, and less unscheduled maintenance. Wages and other expenses due to absenteeism, accidents, and grievances (including the expense of maintaining a replacement work force) might also decrease. Finally, opportunity savings might be realized if the work time of supervisors that was spent in replacing absent employees or turnovers could be put to more productive use (Mirvis and Macy, 1976). Behavioral-economic measurement provides the methods for documenting these cost savings. Conceptually the synthesis of costs and effectiveness measures seems straightforward. Indeed, two studies have proposed methods for undertaking such calculations. Let us examine the limitations of each method in order to illustrate the complexity of the problem. We will then present a third approach that circumvents many of the shortcomings of the first two methods.

Early Attempts to Estimate the Financial Impact of Attitudes

Human Asset Valuation

Myers and Flowers (1974) present a simple framework for measuring human assets. Job performance is viewed as the end product of a five-part flow process: knowledge, skills, health, availability, attitudes, job performance. The individual's knowledge enables him or her to direct his or her skills, and the individual's health enables him or her to apply them. The individual must be available when needed and must have the desire to apply his or her talents and energy toward productive effort. The five dimensions are not additive, so that if any one of them is lacking, the others are rendered ineffective. Before deciding to improve one dimension, therefore, consideration must be given to the level of the others. Thus it may not be cost-effective to improve the job knowledge of an employee if his or her attitude is poor. The first priority may well be to improve attitudes before attempting to improve job knowledge.

According to Myers and Flowers (1974) job attitudes are a symptom of the other four human assets as these are interpreted by each individual's personal value system. Therefore a quantitative, reliable measure of attitudes is probably the best single measure of how well all five assets are being utilized. However, attitude survey results should not be lumped together indiscriminately. Each attitude score should be weighted by the individual's job grade level and company tenure. The higher the job grade level and the longer the tenure with the firm, the higher the weight attached to that individual's score. Myers and Flowers (1974) attempt to quantify attitudes by multiplying salary dollars times weighted attitude scores to measure the potential dollar value increases that would be associated with improved employee attitudes (see Exhibit 5.2).

This approach is a traditional approach to human asset valuation; it assigns a value to individuals rather than to their behavior. Employees' salaries are equated with their value to the organization, and it is assumed that attitudinal improvements make employees more valuable to the or-

Exhibit 5.2 Human Asset Valuation Approach to Dollarizing Attitudes

Unit: Digital Assembly

Individual	Annual salary	Job grade	Tenure	Attitude Weight	Attitude score	Weighted attitude score
1. Tom Hill	$ 25,000	18	15	6	1.05	6.30
2. Cindy Fleming	15,000	12	6	3	1.12	3.36
3. Ben Williams	33,000	23	22	9	1.25	11.25
4. Judy Francis	15,000	12	6	3	1.26	3.78
5. Amy Fox	27,000	19	15	7	1.16	8.12
	$115,000			28		32.81

$$\text{attitude index} = \frac{(\Sigma \text{ weighted attitude score})}{(\Sigma \text{ attitude weights})} = \frac{32.81}{28} = 1.17$$

$$\begin{aligned}\text{dollarized} &= \text{attitude index} \times \text{annual} = 1.17 \times \$115,000 = \$134,550\\ \text{attitudes} &\qquad\qquad\qquad\qquad \text{payroll}\end{aligned}$$

gain = $134,550 - $115,000 = $19,550

gain per person = $3,910

ganization. As Mirvis and Lawler (1977) have noted, this approach suffers from three shortcomings. First, the effects of improved attitudes on job behavior are not stated. We don't know whether attitudinal improvement implies higher employee productivity, lower absenteeism, reduced turn-over, or some combination of these. Second, whether the actual savings associated with any behavioral changes will equal their estimated value improvement (that is, validation of predicted savings) is ignored by this approach. Finally, Myers and Flowers (1974) present no data on the relationship between the attitudes they measure and individuals' behaviors. At best, this framework provides a way for organizations to judge the impact of organizational investment on employee morale. It provides no clues to the direct financial impact of job satisfaction and motivation.

The Unit Cost Approach

The unit cost approach to assigning dollar values to attitudes was developed by Likert (1973) and Likert and Bowers (1973). Rather than trying to assign a value to the overall worth of an employee to an organization, this method attempts to determine the short-term costs of employee behavior. It does this by correlating standardized attitude scores with unit cost. It then predicts changes in unit cost from anticipated changes in attitudes and argues that the cost change represents the economic impact of the attitudes.

There are also problems with this approach, as Mirvis and Lawler (1977) have noted. This first problem stems from the choice of unit cost as a performance criterion. Cost per unit includes fixed costs (those incurred regardless of the number of units or level of service produced) and variable costs (those directly related to the level of activity). Only variable costs can be affected immediately by such employee behaviors as increased productivity and reduced absenteeism and turnover. Furthermore, both cost components are influenced by inflationary trends. The inclusion of fixed costs and inflationary trends in the criterion measure builds in a significant amount of variance that has nothing to do with changes in attitudes.

A second problem with this approach is that it ignores the processes that intervene between changes in attitude and changes in unit cost. That is, previous research suggests that improvements in job satisfaction should reduce levels of absenteeism and turnover, which in turn should result in lower unit cost. Simply relating attitudes to unit costs and bypassing the intervening processes ignores this sequential effect. The resulting relationship and financial consequences might well be over- or understated.

A third problem with the unit cost approach is its assumption of a constant attitude-behavior relationship over time. In fact, improvement in attitude scores could be accompanied by stronger or weaker predictive relationships to behavior. Predicted savings based on a constant relationship would understate the resulting benefits if the relationship was stronger than had been assumed, and it would overstate the benefits if the relationship was weaker than had been assumed. A final problem with this approach is that it relies on analysis at the work-group level, but much of the behavior change would occur at the individual level. Unless organizations are extremely large, relationships derived at the group level may be unreliable indicators of individual-level change.

In view of the shortcomings of the human asset valuation and unit cost approaches, we do not recommend that they be used. An awareness of their shortcomings is instructive, however, especially as a yardstick for measuring progress in methods proposed subsequently. The most recent of these approaches, behavior costing, was developed by Mirvis and Lawler (1977).

The Behavior Costing Approach

Behavior costing is based on the assumption that attitudinal measures are indicators of subsequent employee behaviors. These behaviors can be assessed using cost accounting procedures, and they have economic implications for organizations. Only short-term direct costs associated with the behaviors are used. This approach clearly builds on the unit cost approach of Likert and Bowers (1973).

The conceptual framework underlying behavior costing stems from expectancy theory, which emphasizes that employees' behavior at work is the result of choices about whether to appear at the work place ("participation-membership," March and Simon, 1958) and of choices about how to behave at work ("work strategies," Lawler, 1973). This framework assumes that employees will be more likely to come to work than be absent or quit if they obtain satisfaction from their jobs. And they are likely to give more effort and choose more effective job performance strategies if they expect to be rewarded either intrinsically or extrinsically for their efforts (Vroom, 1964).

These ideas suggest that attitudinal indexes of employee satisfaction and job involvement should be the best predictors of participation-membership since they reflect perceptions of the rewards associated with being at work (Lawler, 1973). Employee intrinsic motivation should be the best predictor of job performance, since it reflects some of the performance outcomes contingent on doing a good job: competence, achievement, and self-realization.

A Test of the Theory

These theoretical ideas were tested empirically on a sample of 160 tellers from 20 branches of a midwestern banking organization. The tellers (average age, thirty) were predominantly female (94 percent). They served as cashiers, handling customer deposits, withdrawals, and other transactions.

Attitude measures were taken from the Michigan Assessment of Organizations (Survey Research Center, 1975), and reflected intrinsic satisfaction (six items), organizational involvement (two items), and intrinsic motivation (three items). For example:

> *Intrinsic satisfaction:* please indicate how satisfied you are with the following aspects of your job: (1) the chances you have to do the things you do best; (2) the chances you have to learn new things; (3) the opportunity to develop your skills and abilities.

> *Organizational involvement:* is what happens in this branch really important to you?

> *Intrinsic motivation:* when you do your job well, do you feel you've done something worthwhile? Do you get a feeling of personal satisfaction from doing your job well?

Measures of participation-membership behavior and work performance were collected monthly after administration of the attitude questionnaire. Using standardized definitions and measures of behavioral outcomes (Macy and Mirvis, 1976), the following data were collected:

> *short-term absence or illness:* unauthorized absences of less than three consecutive days, including short-term illness and absence for personal reasons.

> *voluntary turnover:* voluntary employee departure from the bank, excluding terminations, maternity leaves or turnovers, and transfers.

teller balancing shortages: the number of shortages in tellers' balances (overpayments to customers).

Results of the Teller Study

Over a three-month period there was no statistical measure of relationship (correlation, r) between absenteeism and turnover, and there were few significant correlations between absenteeism and shortages (median $r = -0.06$) or turnover and shortages (median $r = 0.15$). The absenteeism measure reflected some stability across months 1, 2, and 3 ($r_{12} = 0.61$, $r_{23} = 0.71$, $r_{13} = 0.52$). However, no one who was absent the first month was absent the next two months. In contrast, the number of teller balancing shortages was more stable ($r_{12} = 0.82$, $r_{23} = 0.71$, $r_{13} = 0.59$).

Each behavior has a cost to the organization. We have already outlined the major cost elements associated with turnover and absenteeism in Chapters 2 and 3. With respect to teller shortages, the direct cost was estimated to be $8.23 per shortage. This figure includes the cash outlay minus recoveries, and is reported in constant dollar terms. Each incident of absenteeism was estimated to cost $66.45, of which $23.04 (salary) was a variable cost (since the supervisor must either find a suitable replacement or extend the existing staff). The total cost of each turnover incident was estimated at $2,522.03 of which $293.95 (direct hiring costs) was variable.

The distinction between variable and total costs is important, for a reduction in absenteeism and turnover will result in variable-cost savings only. A reduction in fixed costs or realization of opportunity costs depends on subsequent reallocation of fixed costs or staff workloads. Thus fixed and opportunity costs were not included in the financial estimates.

Exhibit 5.3 shows the relationship between teller attitudes and absenteeism, turnover, and balancing shortages three months later. Correlations between attitudes and turnover are low, negative, and significant (that is, statistical relationships of that magnitude would occur, on the average, fewer than five times out of a hundred by chance alone). This is consistent with results found in other research (Mobley et al., 1979). Notice also the significant negative correlation between tellers' intrinsic motivation and shortages three months later. Finally, the high negative correlation between satisfaction and absenteeism is probably an artifact. July is a primary vacation month for the tellers and some took additional, unauthorized days off. The findings suggest that the most dissatisfied employees took

Exhibit 5.3   Relationship Between Attitudes and Behavior (Lagged Three Months)

Attitudes (measured in April)	Behaviors (measured in July)		
	Absenteeism	Turnover	Shortages
Intrinsic satisfaction	−0.81[a]	−0.20[b]	0.10
Job involvement	0.08	−0.29[a]	−0.12
Intrinsic motivation	−0.26[a]	−0.16[b]	−0.23[a]

[a] $p < 0.01$
[b] $p < 0.05$

Source: P. H. Mirvis and E. E. Lawler, III. Measuring the financial impact of employee attitudes. *Journal of Applied Psychology*, 1977, 62:4.

this extra time off. Further, individual absences varied over time, and the correlations between attitude measures and absenteeism fluctuated over the three-month reporting period. Thus the cost savings attributable to reduced absenteeism may be particular to the measurement period.

We are now in a position to relate the attitudinal measures to financial results and to estimate the potential benefits resulting from improvements in employee attitudes. The statistical approach for doing this was developed by Likert (1973). As an example, let us relate tellers' intrinsic motivation scores ($M = 6.11$, $SD = 0.96$)[1] and the average balancing shortages ($M = 3.07$, $SD = 1.74$). To estimate the potential savings from a 0.5 standard deviation improvement in motivation, the steps are as follows:

1. present cost level = average balancing shortage × cost per incident
   = 3.07 × \$8.23
   = \$25.27 per employee per month

2. planned attitudinal improvement = 0.5 SD

3. estimated behavioral improvement = (planned attitudinal improvement in SD units) × (SD of balancing shortages) × ($r_{mot., shortages}$)
   = .5 × 1.74 × −0.23
   = −0.20

[1]M = mean, SD = standard deviation, a measure of the variability or dispersion of scores about their mean.

4. new behavioral rate = present mean shortage + estimated behavioral improvement

   = 3.07 + −0.20

   = 2.87 per employee per month

5. new cost level = new behavioral rate × cost per incident

   = 2.87 × $8.23

   = $23.62 per employee per month

A similar procedure was used to estimate the cost levels associated with the other attitudes that were measured (see Exhibit 5.4). For most measures, more positive attitudes are associated with lower costs. The cost figures are conservative for they reflect only the variable costs per teller for one month. For the bank tellers as a whole ($N = 160$) over a one-year period, an improvement in teller satisfaction of 0.5 standard deviations was estimated to result in direct savings of $17,664. Potential total savings were estimated to be $125,160.

Advantages of the Behavior Costing Approach

Behavior costing has three important advantages associated with it. First, it is a practical method for relating attitudes to costs that can be used in a wide variety of organizations. Moreover, it has the potential to increase significantly the impact and usefulness of attitudinal data. By focusing

Exhibit 5.4 Costs per Month per Teller

Attitude	Change	Absenteeism	Turnover	Shortage	Total
		Cost (in dollars)			
	+0.5SD	2.40	10.17	25.98	38.55
Intrinsic satisfaction	0	5.44	17.04	25.27	47.75
	−0.5SD	8.48	23.93	24.55	56.96
	+0.5SD	5.74	7.08	23.62	36.44
Job involvement	0	5.44	17.04	25.27	47.75
	−0.5SD	5.14	27.01	26.91	59.06
	+0.5SD	4.45	11.55	24.41	40.41
Intrinsic motivation	0	5.44	17.04	25.27	47.75
	−0.5SD	6.43	22.54	26.13	55.10

Source: P. H. Mirvis and E. E. Lawler, III. "Measuring the Financial Impact of Employee Attitudes." Journal of Applied Psychology, 1977, 62:6.

attention on employee satisfaction and motivation, results of the behavior costing approach could stimulate changes designed specifically to improve satisfaction and motivation.

A second advantage of this approach is that it relates attitudes to future costs. Thus organizations could use it as a way of diagnosing future costs, and as a basis for initiating programs designed to reduce those costs. This makes it possible for managers to estimate the cost savings and potential benefits associated with improved morale and group functioning.

Conceptually, behavioral cost measures should be most sensitive (in comparison to other indicators) to changes in employee satisfaction and motivation (Lawler and Rhode, 1976). A third advantage of the behavior costing approach (the attitude-costs model presented in this chapter), therefore, is that it provides a method for an empirical test of that hypothesis. It yields the financial measure most related to employee attitudes. Traditionally human resource accounting has valued employee service at gross book value (the original investment expense), net book value (the original investment minus depreciation), and economic value (the anticipated financial return of the investment). In contrast, behavior costing shifts the emphasis from assigning a value to employees to assessing the economic consequences of their behavior (Mirvis and Lawler, 1977).

Problems with the Behavior Costing Approach

Despite its advantages, behavior costing also has a number of difficulties associated with it. One important issue concerns validation of the predicted cost savings. This can only be done by observing what happens when attitude changes actually occur. To test the validity of the cost figures presented earlier, Mirvis and Lawler (1977) collected data one year later from the same tellers. At that time the tellers' personal motivation had increased to 6.25 or 0.145 standard deviations. Actual shortages had decreased to $21.71 per month, somewhat below the anticipated level, but in the predicted direction. This kind of evidence suggests that the changes in attitude caused the changes in behavior, but since behavior costing is based upon correlational analyses, other causal explanations are possible.

Two additional problems in predicting behavioral rate changes and costs from attitudinal data stem from the nature of the attitude-behavior relationship. The first problem has to do with the appropriateness of the time lag. Mirvis and Lawler (1977) used a three-month lag, but they also examined one- and two-month lags. Relationships between attitudes and behavior were found in all cases, but the relationships were stronger in the three-month lag. The superiority of the three-month lag is consistent with findings in the economic literature (Katona, 1975), but findings in the organizational literature suggest that a variety of time lags produce significant effects (Taylor and Bowers, 1972). At this time, therefore, the safest course is probably to collect time-series data on attitudes and behavior at multiple measurement points, and then choose the interval that yields the most stable and representative relationships.

A related problem concerning the stability of attitude-behavior relationships is that the size and form of the relationship between these variables can change over time. In the Mirvis and Lawler (1977) study, for example, secondary analyses revealed that monthly time-series relationships between a single item measure of intrinsic satisfaction and teller shortages ranged from -0.67 to -0.06 over a four-month period. Unless this relationship is stable, predicted financial changes will not be accurate. In addition, the behavior costing model assumes a linear attitude-behavior relationship, but the actual relationship may well be curvilinear. Correlational methods are available to deal with curvilinear relations (for example, eta, the correlation ratio), but the point is that both the size and form of attitude-behavior relationships must be monitored over time with periodic corrections in the predicted savings based on the new relationships.

Special care must be taken not to over- or understate potential cost savings. Motivation and job satisfaction are likely to be improved by a combination of factors, such as job enrichment programs, participative management styles, or better employee selection procedures. Since the components of job attitudes (satisfaction, job involvement, intrinsic motivation, and so on) are rarely independent, to estimate separately the cost savings associated with each would overstate the resulting benefits. This suggests that monthly behavior measures should be related to the *set* of relevant attitude measures. This would probably result in more accurate estimates of the attitude-behavior relationships and the eventual financial benefits.

Financial benefits might also be overstated if there is substantial covariation among the rates or costs of absenteeism, turnover, and performance. It would seem appropriate, then, to remove statistically the effects of absenteeism and turnover from performance in estimating behavioral change and financial benefits.

Finally, it is important to stress that the costs of absenteeism, turnover, tardiness, and mistakes in job performance vary widely from one organization to another. Hence, comparisons across organizations may be less useful than intra-organizational comparisons of outcomes relative to baseline data.

A Final Word

The time has clearly arrived for behavioral scientists to begin to speak the language of business. The methods described in this chapter provide a useful start in that direction, but we hasten to add that the nonfinancial impact of changes in employee attitudes and motivation (for example, individual growth and well-being, organizational adaptability, and goodwill) cannot, and perhaps should not, be assigned an economic value. Management decisions made solely to optimize financial gains will miss completely the effects of organizational development or attitude change programs on nonfinancial results.

Nonetheless, while there are a number of problems associated with relating attitudes to costs (see Exhibit 5.5), and refinements may be needed in the methods described here, the potential of cost-benefit comparisons of attitude-behavior relationships is enormous. The potential payoffs in improved personnel and financial planning provide ample justification for expending the necessary effort and resources to develop further methods for estimating the financial impact of employee attitudes.

Exercises

1. You are given the following data relative to the five-member troubleshooting team of the Behrens Corporation:

Individual	Annual salary	Job Grade	Tenure	Attitude weight	Attitude score
1. D. Hobbs	$24,000	32	10	8	1.15
2. P. Smith	18,000	24	6	5	1.04
3. T. Studley	30,000	37	14	10	1.28
4. B. Woo	22,000	30	10	7	1.20
5. W. Finkel	17,500	23	5	4	0.78

Exhibit 5.5 Assumptions, Advantages, and Disadvantages of Attitude-Cost Models

Model	Assumptions	Advantages	Disadvantages
Human Asset Valuation	Salary = value to organization; therefore attitudinal improvement enhances value to the organization	a. Simple framework for measuring human assets b. Attitude Index may serve as a standard metric	a. Effects of improved attitudes on job behavior are unknown b. No validation of predicted savings
Unit Cost	Changes in unit costs can be predicted from anticipated changes in attitudes. Therefore cost change = economic impact of attitudes	a. Reduces errors associated with equating to zero changes in the value of human organization from Time 1 to Time 2. b. Offers statistical method for relating attitudinal measures to financial results	a. Inclusion of fixed costs + inflationary trends in cost per unit yields irrelevant variance b. Ignores intervening processes between changes in attitudes and changes in unit cost c. Assumes constant attitude-behavior relationship over time d. Analysis is at work-group level, not individual level

Exhibit 5.5 (continued)

Behavior Costing	Attitudinal measures are indicators of subsequent employee behaviors—participation-membership and job performance	a. Relates attitudes to future costs b. Yields the financial measure most closely related to employee attitudes c. Analysis is at individual, not work-group, level	a. Difficult to validate cost savings since analyses are based on correlational data b. "Best" time lag for determining attitude-behavior relationships is unknown c. Instability in attitude-behavior relationships yields inaccurate financial changes

    a. Use a human asset valuation approach to dollarize these attitudes, to compute the overall gain (or loss), and to compute the gain (or loss) per person.

    b. What are two advantages and two drawbacks of this approach?

2. a. What is the purpose of each of the three components of the cost-benefit model of human resource development programs shown in Exhibit 5.1?

    b. What are the three broad classes of costs (and savings) involved in human resource development programs? Give an example of each.

3. As a special project, top management wants to use behavior costing methodology as one input to its human resource planning model. Over a three-month period, you have found the correlation between job satisfaction and absenteeism to be -0.34 for a sample of clerical employees. Chronic absenteeism is a serious problem in this firm, and clerical employees average 2.2 days per month absent from work ($SD = 1.43$). Each such incident costs $78.06, of which $38.25 is a variable cost. If management were to institute a job enrichment program that would improve attitudes among the clerical employees by 0.45 standard deviation, what might be the potential savings per employee per month?

References

AJZEN, I., and FISHBEIN, M. "Attitude-Behavior Relations: A Theoretical Analysis and Review of Empirical Research." *Psychological Bulletin*, 1977, 84:888–918.

AJZEN, I., and FISHBEIN, M. *Understanding Attitudes and Predicting Social Behavior.* Englewood Cliffs, N. J.: Prentice-Hall, 1980.

KATONA, G. *Psychological Economics.* New York: Elsevier, 1975.

LAWLER, E. E. *Motivation in Work Organizations.* Monterey, Cal.: Brooks/Cole, Organizations." *Personnel*, 1973, 50:8–24.

LAWLER, E. E., and RHODE, J. G. *Information and Control in Organizations.* Pacific Palisades, Cal.: Goodyear, 1976.

LIKERT, R. "Human Resource Accounting: Building and Assessing Productive Organizations. *Personnel*, 1973, 50:8–24.

LIKERT, R., and BOWERS, D. G. "Improving the Accuracy of P/L Reports by

Estimating the Change in Dollar Value of the Human Organization." *Michigan Business Review*, 1973, 25:15–24.

MACY, B. A., and MIRVIS, P. H. "A Methodology for Assessment of Quality of Work Life and Organizational Effectiveness in Behavioral-Economic Terms." *Administrative Science Quarterly*, 1976, 21:212–226.

MARCH, J. O., and SIMON, H. A. *Organizations*. New York: Wiley, 1958.

MARROW, A. J., BOWERS, D. G., and SEASHORE, S. E. *Management by Participation*. New York: Harper & Row, 1967.

MIRVIS, P. H., and LAWLER, E. E., III. "Measuring the Financial Impact of Employee Attitudes." *Journal of Applied Psychology*, 1977, 62:1–8.

MIRVIS, P. H., and MACY, B. A. "Accounting for the Costs and Benefits of Human Resource Development Programs: An Interdisciplinary Approach." *Accounting, Organizations, and Society*, 1976, 1:179–193.

MOBLEY, W. H., GRIFFITH, R. W., HAND, H. H., and MEGLINO, B. M. "Review and Conceptual Analysis of the Employee Turnover Process." *Psychological Bulletin*, 1979, 86:493–522.

MYERS, M. S., and FLOWERS, V. S. "A Framework for Measuring Human Assets." *California Management Review*, 1974, 16 (4):5–16.

PORTER, L. W., and STEERS, R. M. "Organization, Work, and Personal Factors in Employee Turnover and Absenteeism." *Psychological Bulletin*, 1973, 80:151–176.

ROTHENBERG, J. "Cost-Benefit Analysis: A Methodological Exposition." In M. Guttentag and E. Struening, ed., *Handbook of Evaluation Research* (Vol. 2). Beverly Hills, Cal.: Sage Publishing Co., 1975.

SMITH, P. C., KENDALL, L. M., and HULIN, C. C. *The Measurement of Satisfaction in Work and Retirement*. Chicago: Rand-McNally, 1969.

Survey Research Center. *Michigan Organizational Assessment Package*. Ann Arbor, Mich.: Institute for Social Research, 1975.

TAYLOR, J., and BOWERS, D. *Survey of Organizations*. Ann Arbor, Mich.: Institute for Social Research, 1972.

VROOM, V. H. *Work and Motivation*. New York: Wiley, 1964.

6

Labor Contract Costing

By far the largest costs incurred by United States corporations are labor costs. In capital-intensive organizations such as commercial airlines, labor costs account for about 42 percent of total expenses (Carley, 1979), but in labor-intensive organizations, such as the U.S. Postal Service, labor costs can account for over 80 percent of total expenses. Given the magnitude of labor costs, their impact on profits is critical, and relatively small changes either in the size or in the compensation of the labor force can result in relatively large effects on profits. Hence it makes a difference, an important, practical difference, how management selects the best labor contract package to contribute to the achievement of organizational goals. Without a thorough knowledge of the effect of proposed labor expenditures on profits, cost control is impossible. In a collective bargaining situation, management must be able to know—or at least to estimate—the effect on profits of proposed changes in its labor contract before accepting or rejecting the changes.

To be sure, management's ability to control labor costs is limited by its bargaining power relative to that of the unions. Nevertheless, management can still exert considerable influence on labor costs since the overall cost of labor depends not only on the size of the compensation package, but also on its component parts. For example, suppose a union is indifferent with respect to two alternative contract changes—the two have identical utility to union members. Yet the effect on profits of the two alternatives might be entirely different. To the extent that management is free to choose between the two alternatives, it has the opportunity to exercise important control over labor costs.

Evaluation of the costs of changes in labor contracts is particularly important when the potential costs of poor decisions are considered. Since many collective bargaining contracts are for three-year periods, mistakes made during negotiations are not easily rectified. Benefits granted for the duration of a contract may become permanent if a union can exact a high enough price when management wants to reduce or eliminate a benefit to which employees have become accustomed. If management overestimates the effect on profits of a wage package, it might take a costly (though unnecessary) strike rather than accede to union demands. Should management underestimate the effect on profits, the firm may find itself unable to compete successfully with other companies that did not sign a similar contract.

The task of evaluating the financial impact of contract proposals is formidable for three reasons, as Granof (1973) has pointed out. First, the financial burden of fringe benefits (compensation in addition to direct payments) is difficult to estimate. Virtually all labor contracts contain provisions relating to fringe benefits, and the number of workers receiving a variety of benefits is increasing rapidly. Second, contract clauses that do not involve compensation directly, such as those dealing with work schedules, job classifications, seniority rules, and training programs, are not easily quantified yet have a considerable financial impact. Third, the relationships between labor costs and other aspects of a firm's operations are often elusive. For example, changes in volume, product mix, and capital investment are likely to affect the amount of labor required. But changes in the amount of labor may in turn affect the firm's volume, product mix, and capital investment. Thus, Yamazaki, Japan's largest maker of machine tools, decided to invest $18 million in a new computer-controlled manufacturing plant that employs just 12 workers, instead of upgrading older plants (at far less cost) that would have required more than 200 skilled workers to produce the same number of precision components per month ("Look No Hands," 1981).

In summary, during the collective bargaining process, one of the most useful pieces of information management *and* the union can possess is the effect of present demands on future costs of operation. Such information not only aids each party during negotiations but also helps to prepare for future management of the work place. The process by which costs for a future contract may be computed is commonly referred to as "costing out." In the following sections we shall present a method by which either party may cost out demands. The method is adapted from a 1978 U.S. Department of Labor publication, *The Use of Economic Data in Collective Bargaining*, and from the June 1980 issue of *Midwest Monitor*. This method of costing out requires two basic pieces of information: the average compensation costs for the bargaining unit and the true value of increased demands made during negotiations.

Average Compensation for the Bargaining Unit

Average compensation, or weighted average compensation, represents the employer's average expense for each person on the payroll. When a settlement proposal is offered, this figure will help both parties in reaching a decision regarding the proposal. To compute average compensation costs, the following information is necessary:

salary scales and benefit programs

the distribution of employees in the unit according to pay steps, shifts, and length of service

each employee's coverage status for each benefit offered

These figures may be chosen from a fixed point in time, preferably as close to the beginning of collective bargaining as possible. If the three figures above are known, almost all costs of compensation and the increases in compensation can be computed, except for overtime costs, which may vary from week to week.

The first step in computing compensation costs is to develop the *base* or existing compensation figure. This figure is essential in determining the percentage value of a requested increase in compensation. Thus a $500 increase means different things to a unit whose base compensation is $20,000 (a 2.5 percent increase) and to a unit whose base compensation is $10,000 (a 5 percent increase).

To illustrate the process of computing a base compensation figure and of costing out a contract settlement, we will use as an example a bargaining unit of nurses in a city hospital. Although procedures for costing labor settlements differ slightly for public and for private sector organizations, the rapid proliferation of public sector unions makes such an example particularly appropriate. The unit has the characteristics shown in Exhibit 6.1. The information in Exhibit 6.1 allows a base compensation figure to be computed. Knowing the distribution of employees according to each classification and each of their salaries, we can compute the weighted salary for each classification. When this figure is divided by the total number of employees, the result is the weighted average annual base salary (see Exhibit 6.1). This method will also provide the average annual cost for longevity pay (additional pay given for length of service). The combined average salary cost and average annual cost of longevity pay for the nurses' bargaining unit is therefore $14,578 ($14,073 + $505) per year or $7.009 ($14,578 ÷ 2080) per hour. The hourly rate is needed to compute the cost of certain fringe benefits—for example, overtime, shift differential, vacations, paid holidays, insurance, and pensions. Note that *both* salary and longevity pay are included in the weighted average hourly rate of pay. This is an important factor to consider when determining the effect of a salary increase on these benefits. Exhibits 6.2 through 6.5 show how the present cost of each of the above fringe benefits is calculated.

The nine figures derived thus far may then be grouped together to provide a total figure for average annual compensation per employee:

base salary (Ex. 6.1)	$14,073.00
longevity pay (Ex. 6.1)	505.00
overtime (Ex. 6.2)	486.75
shift differential (Ex. 6.3)	1,033.68
vacations (Ex. 6.4)	636.76
holidays (Ex. 6.5)	560.72
hospitalization (Ex. 6.5)	515.72
clothing allowance (Ex. 6.5)	150.00
pension (Ex. 6.5)	965.89
total	$18,927.52

The additional $4,854.52 each nurse receives in benefits ($18,927.52 − $14,073.00) represents 34 percent of base pay, about average in 1980 across all organizations (Walker, 1980).

Exhibit 6.1 Nurses' Bargaining Unit

a. **Employment and Salaries**

Classification	Number of nurses	Salary
Probationary		
Step 1	20	$11,100
Step 2	40	12,100
L.P.N.	125	13,100
R.N.	105	16,100
Head nurse	12	18,000
	302	

b. **Longevity Payments**

Longevity Step	Number of nurses	Longevity pay
Step 1	35 L.P.N.s + 30 R.N.s	$ 500
Step 2	58 L.P.N.s	1,000
Step 2	50 R.N.s	1,000
Step 2	12 Head nurses	1,000

c. **Hours of Work**

The scheduled hours consist of five 8-hour shifts, or an average of 40 hours per week and a total of 2,080 hours per year.

d. **Overtime Premium**

All overtime hours are paid at the rate of time-and-one-half. The nurses' bargaining unit worked a total of 14,000 overtime hours during the preceding year.

e. **Shift Differential**

The shift differential is 10 percent for all hours between 4 P.M. and 8 A.M. However, 82 members of the unit work exclusively on the day shift, from 8 A.M. to 4 P.M. They are 4 head nurses, 35 R.N.s at longevity step 2, and 43 L.P.N.s at step 2.

f. **Vacations**

60 employees (probationers): 5 shifts
122 employees (longevity 0 or 1): 10 shifts
120 employees (all others): 15 shifts

g. **Holidays**

Each nurse is entitled to 10 paid holidays and receives 8 hours pay for each holiday.

h. **Clothing Allowance**

$150 per employee per year.

Exhibit 6.1 (continued)

i.

Hospitalization

Type of coverage	Number of nurses	Employer's monthly payment
Single coverage	45	$20.00
Family coverage	257	47.00

Average Annual Base Salary

(1)	(2)	(3)	(4)
	Number of		Weighted salaries
Classification	nurses	Salary	(2) × (3)
Probationary			
Step 1	20	$11,100	$ 222,000
Step 2	40	12,100	484,000
L.P.N.	125	13,100	1,637,500
R.N.	105	16,100	1,690,500
Head nurse	12	18,000	216,000
			$4,250,000

average annual base salary = $4,250,000 ÷ 302
or $14,073 per year

j.

Pensions

The employer contributes an amount equal to 6 percent of the payroll (including basic salaries, longevity, overtime, and shift differentials).

Longevity Pay

(1)	(2)	(3)	(4)
	Number of		Total Longevity pay
Longevity step	nurses	Longevity pay	(2) × (3)
Step 1	65	$ 500	$ 32,500
Step 2	120	1,000	120,000
			$152,500

average annual longevity pay = $152,500 ÷ 302*
or $505 per year

*Since the unit is trying to determine its average base compensation—that is, all the salary and fringe benefit items its members receive collectively—the total cost of longevity pay must be averaged over the entire unit of 302 nurses.

Exhibit 6.2 Overtime

Overtime work for the nurses' bargaining unit is paid for at the rate of time-and-one-half. This means that part of the total overtime costs is an amount paid for at straight-time rates and part is a premium payment.

	(1) Annual Cost	*(2)* Number of Nurses	*(3)* Average Annual Cost *(1) ÷ (2)*
Straight-time cost ($7.00 × 14,000 overtime hours)[a]	$ 98,000	302	$324.50
Half-time premium cost (1/2 × $98,000)	49,000	302	162.25
Total overtime cost	147,000		$486.75

[a]Based on preceding year's total overtime hours.

Computing the Costs of Increases

Once the base compensation costs have been determined, increases in those costs can be computed. Assume that the nurses' bargaining unit negotiates a settlement which contains the following changes:

a 7 percent increase in base salaries

two additional vacation days for all employees at the second step of longevity

an improvement in the benefits provided by the hospitalization program, which amounts to an additional $4.00 a month per family coverage and $2.50 for single coverage

The objective in costing out this increase is to obtain the average cost of the increase per nurse per year. It is important to aggregate the costs of individual items in the contract so that the implications of the total "package" can be evaluated by both parties.

To compute the average annual increase, the base salary ($14,073) is multiplied by the percent increase (7 percent). This results in an increase of $985.11. There is no increase in longevity pay for this example. Had

Exhibit 6.3   Shift Differential

The nurses' bargaining unit receives a shift differential of 10 percent for all hours worked between 4 P.M. and 8 A.M. But 82 members of the unit who work exclusively on the day shift do not receive the differential. This leaves 220 nurses who do receive the differential.

(1) *Classification*	*(2)* *No. on* *Shift Pay*	*(3)* *Salary*	*(4)* *10% of (3)*	*(5)* *Total Cost* *(2) × (4)*
Probationary				
Step 1	20	$11,100	$1,110	$ 22,200
Step 2	40	12,100	1,210	48,400
L.P.N.s				
Longevity 0	32	13,100	1,310	41,920
Longevity 1	35	13,600[a]	1,360	47,600
Longevity 2	15	14,100[a]	1,410	21,150
R.N.s				
Longevity 0	25	16,100	1,610	40,250
Longevity 1	30	16,600[a]	1,660	49,800
Longevity 2	15	17,100[a]	1,710	25,650
Head Nurses	8	19,000[a]	1,900	15,200
	220			$312,170

average annual cost of shift differential = $312,170 ÷ 302[b] or $1,033.68 per year

[a]Base salary plus longevity pay ($500 for step 1 and $1,000 for step 2).
[b]Since the unit is trying to determine its average base compensation, that is, all the salary and fringe benefit items its members receive collectively, the total cost of the shift differential must be averaged over the entire unit of 302.

the longevity pay been tied to the base salary on a percentage basis there then would have been an increase in that amount also. As a result, the increase in the unit's average annual salary (base salary and longevity payments) is not 7 percent but 6.76 percent. This is determined by dividing the increase ($985.11) by the base salary plus longevity payments ($14,073 + $505 = $14,578).

Computing the cost of an increase is important because of the impact on the cost of fringe benefits. This impact on benefits is often referred to as the *roll up*. As salary increases, so does the cost of fringe benefits such

Exhibit 6.4 Vacations

Vacation costs for the unit are influenced by the amount of vacations received by employees with different lengths of service and the pay scales of those employees.

(1) Classification	(2) Number of Nurses	(3) Hourly Rate[a]	(4) Hours of Vacation[b]	(5) Total Vacation Hours (2) × (4)	(6) Total Vacation Costs (3) × (5)
Probationary					
Step 1	20	$5.336	40	800	$ 4,268.80
Step 2	40	5.817	40	1,600	9,307.20
L.P.N.s					
Longevity 0	32	6.298	80	2,560	16,122.88
Longevity 1	35	6.538	80	2,800	18,306.40
Longevity 2	58	6.779	120	6,960	47,181.84
R.N.s					
Longevity 0	25	7.740	80	2,000	15,480.00
Longevity 1	30	7.981	80	2,400	19,154.40
Longevity 2	50	8.221	120	6,000	49,326.00
Head nurses	12	9.135	120	1,440	13,154.40
	302			26,560	$192,301.92

average annual vacation cost = $192,301.92 ÷ 302, or $636.76 per year

[a]Derived from annual salaries (including longevity pay), divided by 2,080 hours (40 hours × 52 weeks).
[b]Since each nurse works an 8-hour shift (excluding overtime), the hours of vacation are derived by multiplying the number of work shifts of vacation entitlement (see Exhibit 6.1) by 8 hours.

Exhibit 6.5   Paid Holidays, Hospitalization Insurance, and Other Benefits

Paid Holidays

Unlike vacations, the number of holidays received by an employee is not typically tied to length of service. Where the level of benefits is uniform, as it is with paid holidays, the calculation to determine its average cost is less complex.

In the nurses' bargaining unit, each nurse receives 8 hours of pay for each of his or her 10 paid holidays, or a total of 80 hours of holiday pay.

average annual cost of paid holidays = $560.72 (80 hours × $7.009 average straight-time hourly rate derived from average salary cost plus average longevity cost)

Hospitalization Insurance

(1)	(2)	(3)	(4)
		Yearly	
		Premium	*Total Cost to*
Type of	*Number of*	*Cost to*	*Employer*
Coverage	*Nurses*	*Employer*	*(2) × (3)*
Single	45	$240	$ 10,800
Family	257	564	144,948
	302		$155,748

average annual cost of hospitalization insurance = $155,748 ÷ 302, or $515.72

Other Fringe Benefits

1. Pensions cost the employer 6 percent of payroll. The payroll amounts to $4,861,670 (salary cost of $4,250,000, longevity cost of $152,500, overtime cost of $147,000, and shift differential cost of $312,170). Six percent of this total is $291,700 which, when divided by 302, yields $965.89 as the average cost of pensions per nurse per year.
2. The yearly cost of the clothing allowance is $150 per nurse.

as vacations, holidays, and overtime premiums. The cost of the benefits increases even if the level of benefits does not go up. In the example on longevity pay, the roll up did not come into play because the longevity pay was a fixed amount. Other types of benefits which are often exempt from the roll up are shift differentials, clothing allowances, and most group insurance plans. Any of these examples might be affected by the roll up if their cost is tied to the base salary amount.

In our example, it has already been determined that there will be no change in longevity pay because it is a fixed dollar amount. The hours of work are not affected, nor is the clothing allowance. The remaining items in the budget will be affected to some degree. The next task is to identify exactly how they will be changed. In our example, the items whose cost will be changed as a result of the roll-up effect include overtime premiums, shift differentials, holidays, and pensions. These benefits are tied to the original average annual salary (base salary plus longevity). The 6.76 percent increase in the average annual salary will increase the cost of these benefits. The increased costs are shown in Exhibit 6.6.

Once the effect of roll up has been determined, the next step is to identify which items are changed by an increase in benefits. Items may be changed either by the roll-up effect or by an increase in benefits, or both. In the nurses' settlement, the hospitalization benefit costs are changed because of an increase in benefits. The cost is a fixed dollar amount and thus is not subject to an increase in benefits because of the roll up. Costing out this benefit for the new contract entails multiplying the cost of the new program by the employees receiving the benefits (see Exhibit 6.7).

Finally, one item is affected by both the roll up and an increase in benefits—the vacation program. All vacation days will be increased by the cost increase in base salaries plus an increase of two shifts (48 hours)

Exhibit 6.6 Roll-up Costs of Fringe Benefits in Nurses' Bargaining Agreement

(1)	*(2)*	*(3)*	*(4)*
	Base Average		*Increased*
	Annual	*Roll-up*	*Cost*
Fringe Benefit	*Cost* [a]	*Factor*	*(2)×(3)*
Overtime	486.75	0.0676	$ 32.90
Shift differential	1,033.68	0.0676	69.88
Holidays	560.72	0.0676	37.90
Pensions	965.89	0.0676	65.29
			$205.97

[a]As derived in Exhibits 6.2, 6.3, and 6.5.

Exhibit 6.7   Increased Cost of Hospitalization Benefits in Nurses'
Bargaining Agreement

(1)	*(2)*	*(3)*	*(4)*
		Annual	*Total New*
Type of	*Number*	*Cost of*	*Cost*
Coverage	*Covered*	*Improvement*	*(2) × (3)*
Single	45	$30	$ 1,350
Family	257	48	12,336
			$13,686

The unit's average hospitalization cost will be increased by $45.32 per year
($13,686 ÷ 302 employees).

for all employees at the second step of longevity. The first step in calculating
the total additional cost of the new vacation program is to compute the
cost of the two additional shifts prior to the 6.76 percent salary increase.
These costs are shown in Exhibit 6.8. As the exhibit demonstrates, with
no increase in salaries, the increase in vacation days would cost $14,621.63.
The next step is to compute the total cost of the 6.76 percent increase.
These figures are shown in Exhibit 6.9.

Exhibit 6.9 indicates two added costs to the vacation benefit: the
$14,621.63 that represents the increase in benefits, and the $13,988.02
that is a result of the increase in wages. When the two are summed and
divided by the number of nurses in the unit, the *total average cost* of the

Exhibit 6.8   Incremental Cost of Vacations at Present Hourly Rates

(1)	*(2)*	*(3)*	*(4)*	*(5)*
	Hours of	*Total*	*Existing*	*Cost of*
	Increased	*Hours*	*Hourly*	*Improvement*
Number of Nurses	*Vacation*	*(1) × (2)*	*Rates*[a]	*(3) × (4)*
58 L.P.N.s	16	928	6.779	$ 6,290.91
50 R.N.s	16	800	8.221	6,576.80
12 Head nurses	16	192	9.135	1,753.92
				$14,621.63

[a]See Exhibit 6.4 for derivation of hourly rates.

Exhibit 6.9 Incremental Cost of Vacations at Increased Hourly Rates

(1) Classification	(2) Existing Vacation Costs[a]	(3) Increase in Cost[b]	(4) Adjusted Base Costs (2) + (3)	(5) Roll-up Factor	(6) Increased Cost from Roll-up (4) × (5)
Probationary					
Step 1	$ 4,268.80	—	$ 4,268.80	0.0676	$ 288.57
Step 2	9,307.20	—	9,307.20	0.0676	629.17
L.P.N.s					
Longevity 0	16,122.88	—	16,122.88	0.0676	1,089.91
Longevity 1	18,306.40	—	18,306.40	0.0676	1,237.51
Longevity 2	47,181.84	$ 6,290.61	53,472.45	0.0676	3,614.74
R.N.s					
Longevity 0	15,480.00	—	15,480.00	0.0676	1,046.45
Longevity 1	19,154.40	—	19,154.40	0.0676	1,294.84
Longevity 2	49,326.00	6,576.80	55,902.80	0.0676	3,779.03
Head nurses	13,154.40	1,753.92	14,908.32	0.0676	1,007.80
	$192,301.92	$14,621.63	$206,923.55	0.0676	$13,988.02

[a]The base or existing vacation costs are from Exhibit 6.4 and are derived from average annual salary (base salary plus longevity).
[b]From Exhibit 6.8.

new vacation benefit is $94.73 ($28,609.65 ÷ 302 nurses). This calculation would have been different (and considerably easier) if the vacation improvement had been granted across-the-board, to everyone in the unit. If the entire bargaining unit were to receive an additional 16 hours of vacation, the total additional hours would then be 4,832 (16 × 302). These hours would then be multiplied by the unit's old average straight-time rate (7.009), in order to arrive at the cost of the additional vacation improvement, which in this case would have come to $33,867.49. In that case, the total cost of vacations (the across-the-board improvement plus the impact of the 6.76 percent average annual salary increase) would have been computed as follows:

roll up of old vacation costs ($192,301.92 × 0.0676)	$12,999.61
cost of vacation improvement	33,867.49
roll-up cost of improvement ($33,867.49 × 0.0676)	2,289.44
total incremental cost of vacations	$49,156.54

When spread over the entire bargaining unit, the increase in the average cost of vacations would have been $162.77 per nurse per year ($49,156.54 ÷ 302 nurses).

The method we have described above does not apply only to vacations. It applies to any situation where a salary-related fringe benefit is to be improved equally for every member of the bargaining unit (such as an additional paid holiday).

The Total Increase in the Average Cost of Compensation

Summing the increases in each of the items that will change in the nurses' contract settlement yields the total increase in the bargaining unit's *average cost of compensation*. The items that we have considered include:

base salary (p. 105)	$ 985.11
longevity pay	0
overtime (Exhibit 6.6)	32.90
shift differential (Exhibit 6.6)	69.88

vacations (p. 112)	$ 94.73
holidays (Exhibit 6.6)	37.90
hospitalization (Exhibit 6.7)	45.32
clothing allowance	0
pensions (Exhibit 6.6)	65.29
total increase	$1,331.13

Remember that the nurses' average annual compensation (base pay plus benefits) was $18,927.52. The total dollar increase amounts to $1,331.13, or 7.03 percent. This is the amount by which the nurses' settlement increased the employer's average yearly cost per nurse.

Despite the apparent comprehensiveness of coverage of the items in the nurses' settlement, all of the possible items affected by roll up were not considered. In addition to overtime premiums, shift differentials, and pensions, other possible items include:

Social security and unemployment insurance contributions: The employer's contribution to both of these programs is computed as a percentage of each employee's wage up to a fixed amount annually. To the extent that the annual earnings of some employees are less than the fixed amounts, an increase in wages will require an increase in social security and unemployment insurance contributions.

Life insurance: Often the amount of insurance coverage for which the employer pays is a percentage of wages or a varying amount corresponding to graduated wages in a table. As employee earnings increase, so too will the amount and cost of coverage.

Disability insurance premiums: To the extent that this benefit is a percentage of base pay, the employer's cost of providing it will also increase.

In costing out contract settlements, some analysts include the costs of holidays, vacations, rest periods, wash-up time, and paid absences in calculating roll up. Steckel (1980) has shown that including these items overstates the cost of roll up per se because a wage increase applies to the total 2,080 straight-time hours in a year (40 hours × 52 weeks). So, for example, if a company grants a 50¢ per hour wage increase, it is not going to cost any more than the 50¢ per hour whether the employee works and is paid or does not work, but is paid for the time. In other words, there is a 50¢ per hour increase, and no more than that, whether the employee works 1,880 hours a year and has 10 holidays and three weeks of vacation totalling 200 hours, or whether he or she works the full 2,080 hours in the year and has no established holidays and vacation. However, it will cost the company more than the 50¢ per hour for the overtime premium, shift premium, and the other roll-up benefits we noted above, because they are based on a percentage of wages and when the wages go up, there is a secondary impact of these benefits. To provide a more accurate picture of the cost of a labor settlement, a distinction should be made between gross hours per year and hours worked (Hazelton, 1979). Let us continue on with the nurses' bargaining unit example to show how this is done.

Computing the Hourly Cost of Compensation

In the case of the hourly computation, the goal is to obtain the cost per hour of *work*. Hence we must separate hours worked from hours paid for. The difference between the two is leave time.

In the nurses' bargaining unit, for example, each nurse receives an annual salary that covers 2,080 regularly scheduled hours. In addition, each works an average of 46 hours of overtime per year. The sum of these two—regularly scheduled hours and overtime, or 2,126—equals the total hours paid for.

However, hours paid for is not the same as hours worked, because some of those hours are paid leave time. Nurses in the bargaining unit receive paid leave time in the form of vacations and holidays. The number of hours actually worked by each employee is 1,958 (2,126 hours paid for, minus 168 hours of paid leave).

Each nurse receives 80 hours in paid holidays per year. The number of hours of vacation per year was derived as follows:

60 nurses (probationary) × 40 hours	2,400 hours
67 L.P.N.s × 80 hours	5,360 hours
58 L.P.N.s × 120 hours	6,960 hours
55 R.N.s × 80 hours	4,400 hours
50 R.N.s × 120 hours	6,000 hours
12 head nurses × 120 hours	1,440 hours
	26,560 hours

This averages out to 88 hours of vacation per nurse (26,560 ÷ 302) which, together with 80 holiday hours, totals 168 paid leave hours.

The paid leave hours are hours paid for above and beyond hours worked. Thus, in order to obtain the hourly cost that they represent, the annual dollar cost of these benefits is divided by the annual hours *worked.*

So it is with all fringe benefits, not only paid leave. In exchange for those benefits the employer receives hours of work (the straight-time hours and the overtime hours). Consequently, the hourly cost of any fringe benefit will be obtained by dividing the annual cost of the benefit by the annual number of hours *worked.* In some instances that cost is converted into money that ends up in the employee's pocket, as is the case with fringe benefits like shift differentials, overtime premiums, and clothing allowances. In other instances—such as hospitalization and pensions—the employee is provided with benefits in the form of insurance programs. And in the case of paid leave time, the return to the employee is in terms of fewer hours of work. Now let us return to the problem of computing the hourly cost of compensation.

The average annual costs of the fringe benefits of the nurses' bargaining unit were developed earlier in connection with the computations of the unit's average annual base compensation. In order to convert the costs of these fringe benefits into an average hourly amount, they are divided by 1,958, the average hours worked during the year by each employee in the unit. As can be seen in Exhibit 6.10, the hourly cost of all fringe benefits amounts to $2.055.

In addition to the fringe benefit costs, compensation includes the base pay. For the nurses in our example, this is $14,578 per year (average salary plus average longevity payments). On a straight-time hourly basis, this comes to $7.009 ($14,578 ÷ 2.080 hours). Even with the straight-time portion for the year's overtime included ($324.50), the average straight-time hourly rate of pay will remain at $7.009 ($14,902.50 ÷ 2,126 hours).

Let us now recapitulate these salary and fringe benefit cost data on an average annual compensation basis and on an average hourly compensation basis:

	Annually	*Hourly*
Straight-time earnings	$14,902.50 ÷ 2,126	$7.009
Fringe benefits	4,025.02 ÷ 1,958	2.055
Total compensation	$18,927.52	$9.064

Exhibit 6.10   Hourly Cost of Fringe Benefits

(1) Cost of Benefit	*(2)* Average Annual Cost	*(3)* Average Hours Worked	*(4)* Average Hourly Cost (2) ÷ (3)
Overtime premium[a]	$ 162.25	1,958	0.083
Shift differential	1,033.68	1,958	0.528
Vacations	636.76	1,958	0.325
Holidays	560.72	1,958	0.286
Hospitalization	515.72	1,958	0.263
Clothing allowance	150.00	1,958	0.077
Pensions	965.89	1,958	0.493
	$4,025.02		$2.055

[a]Includes only the premium portion of the pay for overtime work.

The $18,927.52 figure is identical to the figure developed earlier in the chapter to represent average annual compensation per employee, even though the method used to arrive at it is different. Essentially the same process is followed if the *increase* in compensation is to be measured on an hourly (instead of annual) basis.

The 7 percent pay increase received by the nurses would be worth 47¢ per hour ($14,073 × .07 = $985.11 ÷ 2,080 = $0.47). The annual increase in the unit's fringe benefits costs per nurse—$324.09 for all items combined (overtime premium only, shift differential, vacations, holidays, hospitalization, and pensions)—works out to 16.55 cents per hour ($324.09 ÷ 1,958 hours).

Together these represent a gain in average compensation of 63.55 cents per hour, or 7.01 percent ($0.6355 ÷ $9.064). This is 0.02 percent off the amount of increase (7.03 percent) reflected by the annual data— a difference due to the rounding of decimals during computation.

Conclusion

If the data that were used for the nurses' bargaining unit in our discussion are available for an actual unit, almost all demands can be evaluated in terms of future costs. Costing out demands requires careful documentation and thorough record keeping. But in return, both of the parties will have the ability to see what effect the increases will have on the budget. Costing out prepares the parties for realistic negotiations; offers and demands are supported by the facts obtained through costing out. Finally, because costing out is a clearly defined method, it reduces the discrepancies and disagreements over budget items. Although costing out will not provide answers to every question that arises, it will provide important information for the parties' use during collective bargaining.

Role of the Computer in Collective Bargaining

Studies of the use of computers in preparation for collective bargaining indicate that the most common use of the computer is to produce routine reports similar to those prepared by conventional methods (Caples, 1969; Granof, 1973). It appears that few companies use, on an ongoing basis during negotiations, mathematical models or simulations to test the effects of alternative demand packages. However, software packages have been developed to allow the simulation of a negotiation session or to negotiate a series of contracts (Cascio and Awad, 1981; Fraser and Hipel, 1981).

New approaches to the determination of the financial impact of proposed labor contracts are clearly needed, and computers can help enormously in this effort. For example, cost-of-living adjustments (COLAs) present special analytical problems since the amount of increase to be granted over the life of a contract not only is variable, but also is beyond the control of managements. Computer simulation would permit evaluation of financial impact on a "what if?" basis. That is, what if the maximum increase required by the proposed contract is the actual increase that must be granted? What if the price index reaches this level, or that one; what will it cost us?

The computer would also permit the application to labor contracts of techniques used to evaluate long-term capital projects (for example, buildings, equipment) such as the discounted cash flow model, since the algorithms (step-by-step procedures) necessary to do the computations can be stored easily in computer memory. The discounted cash flow model requires a user to estimate the incremental (i.e., differences in) cash flows that would result from accepting each capital project under consideration.

Using an appropriate discount rate[1] (usually a "cost of capital" or "internal rate of return") expressed as a percentage, the expected cash flows over the life of the project are discounted back to the present. That is, the present value of the sums of the cash flows are computed. Projects are then ranked according to the magnitude of their net cash flows.

If such a model were used to evaluate alternative labor contract proposals, managers would similarly have to take into account both direct and indirect changes in cash flows attributable to the new contract. They would have to recognize explicitly changes in price, volume, product mix, and labor-capital mix, as well as any other changes the firm might make in its attempt to adjust to the new contract, changes that would not specifically be recognized if traditional cost-oriented methods were used. Perhaps the major advantage of the model is that it permits the firm to take into account increases in revenues, as well as expenses, and thereby to determine the impact of contract changes on profits instead of only on costs. Furthermore, the model enables the firm to add another dimension, the time value of money, to the review of contract proposals (Granof, 1973). Exhibit 6.11 is an example of a computer printout from such a program. The printout shows the present value of alternative proposals that might either be spread evenly over the life of the contract or "front-loaded"—that is, granted at the beginning of the contract.

Models such as these will probably be more widely used in the future as both labor and management continue to demand more information as a basis for decision making, and as personal computers, and their prepackaged specialty programs, become more popular among those who do not have the time or inclination for computer programming. At the same time, however, it is important to put the role of computers in collective bargaining in proper perspective, for content (actual contract elements) as well as process (interpersonal dynamics) issues are both important determinants of bargaining outcomes. To the extent that computer models could track accurately union and management preference curves for particular settlements, then ultimately collective bargaining would cease to exist as we know it. The issues would become mere pawns in a computerized chess game, and the political aspects of the process would be scuttled. Since that prospect seems rather remote at this time, the most likely role of computers in collective bargaining for the foreseeable future will probably be to help the parties make decisions regarding content issues.

---

[1]Discounting is the reverse of compounding.

Exhibit 6.11 Printout from a Computer Program Designed to Identify Equally Acceptable Wage Proposals

---

Information entered into terminal by executive is indicated in italics

$RUN
#EXECUTION BEGINS

WHAT IS THE INTERNAL RATE OF RETURN OF YOUR COMPANY?
WRITE IN DECIMAL FORM, I.E. .05
.16

BY WHAT PERCENT DO YOU EXPECT WAGES TO INCREASE EACH CONTRACT AFTER THE FIRST? WRITE IN DECIMAL FORM, I.E. .20
.18

WHAT IS THE LENGTH, IN YEARS, OF YOUR CONTRACT?
3

WHAT IS YOUR TIME PERSPECTIVE, IN NUMBER OF CONTRACTS?
3

WHAT IS THE PRESENT WAGE?
5.00

INDICATE, IN DOLLARS, THE PROPOSED INCREASES DURING THE FIRST CONTRACT. TYPE THE INCREASE FOR EACH YEAR ON A NEW LINE.
.50
.35
.15

RATE = .16
GROWTH RATE = .18
CONTRACT LENGTH = 3
PERSPECTIVE = 3
CURRENT WAGE = 5.00

PROPOSED INCREASES = 0.50   0.35   0.15

IS ABOVE DATA CORRECT? ANSWER YES OR NO
YES

YOU PROPOSED A TOTAL INCREASE OF 20.0 PERCENT
ALTERNATIVELY YOU WOULD BE AS WELL OFF BY GIVING THE FOLLOWING INCREASE SPREAD OVER THE LIFE OF THE CONTRACT:
PERCENT INCREASE: 21.48

Exhibit 6.11 (continued)

TOTAL DOLLAR INCREASE: 1.074
ANNUAL DOLLAR INCREASE: 0.358
NEW WAGE AT END OF CONTRACT: 6.074

OR YOU COULD ALSO HAVE PROPOSED A FRONT-LOADED
CONTRACT AS FOLLOWS:
PERCENT INCREASE: 17.64
TOTAL DOLLAR INCREASE: 0.882
NEW WAGE AT END OF CONTRACT: 5.882

PRESENT VALUES OF PROPOSALS

CONTRACT NO.	YOUR PROPOSAL	EVEN SPREAD	FRONT LOADED
1	12.9328	12.7582	13.2108
2	23.0939	23.0257	23.2025
3	30.7589	30.7589	30.7589
4	36.5428	36.5865	36.4732
5	40.9085	40.9801	40.7944

DO YOU WANT TO TRY AGAIN? WRITE YES OR NO
NO
STOP
#EXECUTION TERMINATED
#$SIGNOFF

Source: M. H. Granof. *How to Cost Your Labor Contract.* Washington, D.C.:
Bureau of National Affairs, 1973, pp. 120, 121.

Exercises

1. a. Break the class into two, with three or four students withdrawing
to act as judges for the debate to follow. Half the class will
prepare a debate, resolved that computer-based mathematical
models that test the effects of alternative sets of demands should
be widely used in preparation for collective bargaining. The
other half prepares to argue that such computer-based models
should not be widely used in preparation for collective
bargaining.

   b. Each team should appoint a discussion leader and spokesperson.
Prepare arguments for about twenty minutes. During this time

the judges should decide on the criteria they will use to evaluate the presentations.

c. The class should reassemble, and the arguments should be presented. Post arguments short-hand style on the board. Each group is allowed five minutes to make its presentation. After the presentations each group is given one minute for rebuttal. Judges act as timekeepers.

d. Judges then meet in front of the participants and decide on the winner. In announcing their decision, they should state clearly why they decided as they did.

2. a. Exhibit 6.12 gives you information about a firefighters' bargaining unit. Based on this information, compute the average annual compensation of each firefighter. Include the cost of the following items: base salary, longevity pay, overtime, shift differential, vacations, holidays, hospitalization, clothing allowance, and pensions.

b. Assume the bargaining unit negotiates a settlement that contains the following changes:

an 8 percent increase in base salaries and longevity pay

an additional vacation day for all employees in the bargaining unit

improvements in hospitalization insurance that amount to $6 a month for family coverage and $3 a month for single coverage.

Cost out the average annual increases in the nine items noted in Exhibit 6.12.

c. Cost out the increases computed in part b on an average *hourly* basis.

Exhibit 6.12 Firefighters' Bargaining Unit

a. Employment and Salaries

Classification	Number of firefighters	Salary
Probationary		
Step 1	5	$10,100
Step 2	10	11,100
Private	65	12,100
Lieutenant	15	13,500
Captain	5	14,500
	100	

b. Longevity Payments

Longevity step	Number of firefighters	Longevity pay
Step 1	20 Privates	$ 500
Step 2	10 Privates	1,000
Step 2	15 Lieutenants	1,000
Step 2	5 Captains	1,000

c. Hours of Work

The scheduled hours consist of one 24-hour shift every three days (one on, two off) or an average of 56 hours per week and a total of 2,912 hours per year.

e. Shift Differential

The shift differential is 10 percent for all hours between 4 P.M. and 8 A.M. However, 10 members of the unit work exclusively on the day shift, from 8 A.M. to 4 P.M. They are 1 captain, 3 lieutenants, 3 privates at longevity step 1, and 3 privates at step 2.

f. Vacations

15 employees (probationers): 5 shifts
35 employees (privates): 10 shifts
50 employees (all others): 15 shifts

g. Holidays

Each firefighter is entitled to 10 paid holidays and receives 8 hours pay for each holiday.

h. Clothing Allowance

$150 per employee per year.

i. Hospitalization

Type of Coverage	Number of firefighters	Employer's monthly payment
Single coverage	15	$20.00
Family coverage	85	47.00

d. Overtime Premium

All overtime hours are paid at the rate of time-and-one-half. The members of the bargaining unit worked a total of 5,000 overtime hours during the preceding year.

j. Pensions

The employer contributes an amount equal to six percent of the payroll (including basic salaries, longevity, overtime, and shift differentials).

References

CAPLES, W. G. "The Computer's Uses and Potential in Bargaining: A Management View." In A. J. Siegel, ed., *The Impact of Computers on Collective Bargaining*. Cambridge, Mass.: MIT Press, 1969.

CARLEY, W. M. "Squaring Off: United Airlines Strike Reflects Industry Drive to Curb Labor Costs." *Wall Street Journal*, May 11, 1979, p. 1.

CASCIO, W. F., and AWAD, E. A. *Human Resources Management: An Information Systems Approach*. Reston, Va.: Reston, 1981.

"Costing Out in the Public Sector." *Midwest Monitor*, May/June, 1980, pp. 1–7.

FRASER, N., and HIPEL, K. "Computer Assistance in Labor-Management Negotiations." *Interfaces*, April 1981, 11:22–30.

GRANOF, M. H. *How to Cost Your Labor Contract*. Washington, D. C.: Bureau of National Affairs, Inc., 1973.

HAZELTON, W. A. "How to Cost Labor Settlements." *Management Accounting*, 1979 (May) 57:19–23.

"Look, No Hands." *Time*, November 16, 1981, p. 127.

STECKEL, R. G. "The Misuse of Roll-up in Costing Contract Settlements." *The Personnel Administrator*, 1980 (March), 25: pp.33–34.

WALKER, J. W. *Human Resource Planning*. New York: McGraw-Hill, 1980.

III

Personnel Programs:
A Return on Investment
Perspective

7

Utility: The Concept and Its Measurement

In the past, personnel programs have often been selected and implemented because they were fashionable (especially human relations programs) or commercially appealing, or because of the entertainment value they offered the target audience. But personnel costs continue to consume larger and larger portions of the total cost of doing business; for example, in 1980 U.S. Postal Service labor costs accounted for 86 percent of total expenses ("Postal Service," 1980). As this trend continues we may expect to see increased pressure on personnel executives to justify new or continuing personnel programs. Such justification requires a consideration of the relative utilities to the organization of alternative strategies for reaching targeted objectives.

Utility analysis is the determination of institutional gain or loss (outcomes) anticipated from various courses of action. When faced with a choice among strategies, management must choose the strategy that maximizes the expected utility for the organization across all possible outcomes (Wiggins, 1973). To make the choice, management must be able to estimate the utilities associated with various outcomes. Estimating utilities has traditionally been the Achilles heel of decision theory (Cronbach and

Gleser, 1965), but the problem is less acute in business settings. Although extremely difficult to calculate, institutional gains and losses may be estimated by relatively objective cost-accounting procedures, that is, in dollars.

Our objective in this chapter is to introduce the concept of utility analysis, to describe three different models of utility analysis, and to describe situations in which each is most appropriate. We will then build on these ideas in Chapters 8, 9, and 10 to show how personnel programs can be evaluated from a return-on-investment perspective.

Overview

Utility analysis (or decision theory) is a tool that is particularly well suited to applications in business settings because it insists that costs and expected consequences of decisions always be taken into account. It stimulates the decision maker to formulate clearly what he or she is after, as well as to anticipate the consequences of alternative courses of action. Decision makers must clearly state their overall objectives and attempt to anticipate the consequences of each alternative before they make the decision.

It should serve as some comfort to know that all personnel decisions can be characterized identically. In the first place there is an individual about whom a decision is required. Based on certain information about the individual (for example, performance appraisals, assessment center ratings, a disciplinary report), decision makers may elect to pursue various alternative courses of action. Let us consider a simple example.

After an extensive screening process, an organization has narrowed its list of candidates for vice president of finance to three candidates. Each candidate has particular strengths especially attractive to the company. Candidate A works for a large eastern conglomerate, candidate B is employed by an elite firm in the midwest, and candidate C works for a small, innovative company on the west coast. The candidates' financial requirements are all within $1,000 of each other, so the personnel cost to the company is an inconsequential measure of the comparative value of each candidate. The task for the organization, then, is to construct a payoff model and to determine payoff measures for each candidate. The organization must process the list of choices (candidates) according to well-defined criteria, and then select the alternative that best satisfies its objectives. The payoffs assigned to each possible outcome must therefore be assessed in value units consistent with these objectives. These value units may not be measurable in dollars. Let us assume that the organization selects technical knowledge, human relations skills, and administrative skills as valid measures of value payoff to associate with each candidate. On the basis of assessment results, the organization assigns a rating of zero to ten to measure the contribution for each component of payoff for each candidate. These ratings are shown in Exhibit 7.1.

To combine the components of payoff, the organization must decide what the relative importance of these three components to payoff is. Suppose the organization views technical knowledge as the most important, twice as important as either human relations or administrative skills for this position. Thus a weight of 2 is assigned to the scaled values for technical skills, and weights of 1 to human relations skills and administrative skills. The following payoff measures may then be obtained:

$$\text{payoff, candidate } A = 6(2) + 6(1) + 7(1) = 25$$

$$\text{payoff, candidate } B = 4(2) + 9(1) + 6(1) = 23$$

$$\text{payoff, candidate } C = 10(2) + 5(1) + 4(1) = 29$$

On the basis of these results, candidate C should be selected.

Let us summarize our presentation thus far. In any given situation some strategies are better than others. Strategies are better or worse when evaluated against possible outcomes or consequences of decisions (payoffs). The first and most difficult step is to assign values to possible outcomes. Once this is accomplished, particular decisions or general strategies can then be compared, as Cronbach and Gleser (1965) noted:

> The unique feature of decision theory or utility theory is that it specifies evaluations by means of a payoff matrix or by conversion of the criterion to utility units. The values are thus plainly revealed and open to criticism. This is an asset rather than a defect of this system, as compared with sys-

Exhibit 7.1   Payoff Table for Selection Problem

	Candidate A	*Candidate B*	*Candidate C*
Technical knowledge	6	4	10
Human relations skills	6	9	5
Administrative skills	7	6	4

tems where value judgments are imbedded and often pass unrecognized. (p. 121)

Utility theory provides a framework for making decisions by forcing the decision maker to define goals clearly, to enumerate the expected consequences or possible outcomes of his or her decision, and to attach differing utilities or values to each. Such an approach has merit since resulting decisions are likely to rest on a foundation of sound reasoning and conscious forethought.

Utility Models

In the context of personnel selection, three of the best known utility models are those of Taylor and Russell (1939); Naylor and Shine (1965); and Brogden (1946, 1949) and Cronbach and Gleser (1965). *The utility of a selection device is the degree to which its use improves the quality of the individuals selected beyond what would have occurred had that device not been used* (Blum and Naylor, 1968). Quality, in turn, may be defined in terms of (1) the proportion of individuals in the selected group who are considered successful, (2) the average standard score on some job performance criterion for the selected group, or (3) the dollar payoff to the organization resulting from the use of a particular selection procedure. The remainder of this chapter considers each of these utility models and its associated measure of quality in greater detail.

The Taylor-Russell Model

Taylor and Russell (1939) developed perhaps the most well-known utility model and pointed out that the overall utility of a selection device is a function of three parameters: the validity coefficient (the correlation between a predictor of job performance and a criterion measure of actual job performance), the selection ratio (the proportion of applicants selected), and the base rate (the proportion of applicants who would be successful without the selection procedure). This model demonstrates convincingly that even selection procedures with relatively low validities can increase substantially the percentage successful among those selected when the selection ratio is low. Let us consider the concepts of selection ratio (SR) and base rate (BR) in greater detail.

Whenever a quota exists on the total number of applicants that may be accepted, the selection ratio is a major concern. As the *SR* approaches 1.0 (all applicants must be selected), it becomes high or unfavorable from the organization's perspective. Conversely, as the *SR* approaches zero, it becomes low or favorable; the organization can afford to be selective. The wide-ranging effect that the *SR* may exert on a predictor with a given validity is illustrated in Exhibit 7.2. In each case, X_c represents a cutoff score on the predictor. As can be seen in Exhibit 7.2, even predictors with very low validities can be useful if the *SR* is low and if an organization needs to choose only the cream of the crop. Conversely, given high selection ratios, a predictor must possess very high validity in order to increase the percentage successful among those selected.

It might thus appear that given a particular validity, decreasing the *SR* (becoming more selective) should always be advocated. Unfortunately, the optimal strategy is not this simple (Sands, 1973). When the personnel manager must achieve a certain quota of satisfactory individuals, lowering the *SR* forces the recruiting and selection effort to be expanded. This strategy may not be cost-effective.

Utility, according to Taylor and Russell (1939), is also affected by the base rate (the proportion of applicants who would be successful without the selection measure). In order to be of any use in selection, the measure must demonstrate incremental validity by improving on the *BR*. That is, the selection measure must result in more correct decisions than could be

Exhibit 7.2 Effect of Varying Selection Ratios on a Predictor with a Given Validity

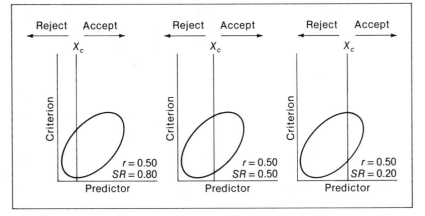

made without using it. As Exhibit 7.3 demonstrates, the higher the BR, the more difficult it is for a selection measure to improve upon it.

In each case X_c represents the minimum criterion standard (criterion cutoff score) necessary for success. Obviously, the BR can be changed by raising or lowering this minimum standard on the criterion. Exhibit 7.3 illustrates that with a BR of 0.80, it would be difficult for any selection measure to improve on the base rate. In fact, when the BR is 0.80 and half of the applicants are selected, a validity of 0.45 is required in order to produce an improvement of even 10 percent over base rate prediction. This is also true at very low BRs (as would be the case, for example, in the psychiatric screening of job applicants). Given a BR of 0.20 and SR of 0.50 and a validity of 0.45, the percentage successful among those selected is 0.30—once again representing only a 10 percent improvement in correct decisions. Selection measures are most useful, however, when BRs are about 0.50 (Taylor and Russell, 1939). As the BR departs radically in either direction from this value, the benefit of an additional predictor becomes questionable, especially in view of the costs involved in gathering the additional information. The lesson is obvious: applications of selection measures to situations with markedly different SRs or BRs can result in quite different predictive outcomes and cost-benefit ratios. When significant incremental validity cannot be demonstrated by adding a predictor, then the predictor should not be used, since it cannot improve on classification of persons by the base rate.

Exhibit 7.3   Effect of Varying Base Rates on a Predictor with a Given Validity

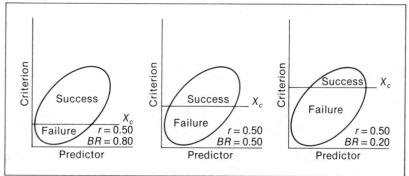

Taylor and Russell (1939) published a series of tables illustrating the interaction of the validity coefficient, the selection ratio, and the base rate on the success ratio (the proportion of selected applicants who are subsequently judged successful). The success ratio, then, serves as an operational measure of the value or utility of a selection device, when used in conjunction with methods presently used to select applicants.

The Taylor-Russell approach is presented graphically in Exhibit 7.4. In this figure, the criterion cutoff (arbitrarily set by managerial consensus concerning minimally acceptable performance) separates the present employee group into satisfactory and unsatisfactory workers. The predictor cutoff (set by the selection ratio) defines the relative proportion of workers who would be hired at a given level of selectivity. Areas A and C represent correct decisions. That is, if the selection measure were used to select applicants, those in area A would be hired and become satisfactory employees. Those in area C would be correctly rejected because they scored below the predictor cutoff and would have performed unsatisfactorily on

Exhibit 7.4   Effect of Predictor and Criterion Cutoffs on a Bivariate Distribution of Scores

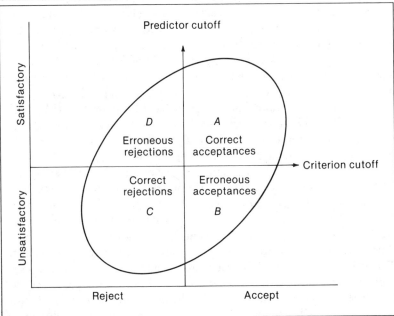

the job. Areas B and D represent erroneous decisions. Those in area B would be hired because they scored above the predictor cutoff, but they would perform unsatisfactorily on the job. Those in area D would be rejected because they scored below the predictor cutoff, but they would have been successful if hired.

The ratios used by Taylor and Russell (1939) in developing their tables were as follows:

$$\text{base rate} = \frac{A + D}{A + B + C + D} \tag{1}$$

$$\text{selection ratio} = \frac{A + B}{A + B + C + D} \tag{2}$$

$$\text{success ratio} = \frac{A}{A + B} \tag{3}$$

By specifying the validity coefficient, the base rate, and the selection ratio, and making use of Pearson's "Tables for Finding the Volumes of the Normal Bivariate Surface" (1931), Taylor and Russell developed their tables (see Appendix A). The usefulness of a selection measure can thus be assessed in terms of the success ratio which will be obtained if the selection measure is used. The gain in utility to be expected from using the instrument (the expected increase in the percentage of successful workers) can then be derived by subtracting the base rate from the success ratio (equation 3 minus equation 1). For example, given an *SR* of 0.10, a validity of 0.30, and a *BR* of 0.50, the success ratio jumps to 0.71—a 21 percent gain in utility over the base rate (to verify this figure, see Appendix A).

It is important to note that the validity coefficient referred to by Taylor and Russell (1939) is based on present employees who have already been screened using methods other than the new selection procedure. The selection ratio is then applied to this population.

The Taylor-Russell approach also makes three other assumptions. First, it assumes fixed treatment selection (that is, individuals are chosen for one specified treatment or course of action that cannot be modified). For example, if a person is selected for Treatment A, a training program for slow learners, transfer to Treatment B, fast-track instruction, is impossible regardless of how well the person does in Treatment A. Second, the Taylor-Russell model does not take into account the percentage of rejected individuals who would have been successful if hired (erroneous rejections). Finally the model classifies accepted individuals into successful and unsuccessful groups. All individuals within a group are regarded as making equal contributions. Because of these assumptions Taylor and Russell (1939) find different shapes for the validity-utility relation at different selection ratios and nonlinear relationships given high validities and high base rates. However, it should be pointed out that the Taylor-Russell model is not used to choose optimal selection ratios (or cutoff scores), but rather only to evaluate those already selected.

Perhaps the major shortcoming of this utility model is that it is cast so that the usefulness of a predictor is reflected only in the success ratio and nothing else. Criterion performance is described as a dichotomous classification—successful and unsuccessful—and as the tables in Appendix A demonstrate, when validity is fixed the success ratio increases as the selection ratio decreases. (Turn to Appendix A, choose any particular validity value, and note what happens to the success ratio as the selection ratio changes from 0.95 to 0.05.) Under these circumstances the success ratio tells us that more people are successful, but not *how much more* successful. While in practice there may be situations where the average level of job performance would not be expected to change as a function of higher selection standards, for many, if not most, jobs increased criterion mean performance would be expected to result from increased selectivity as long as the relationship between performance on the predictor and performance on the job can best be described by a straight line (is linear). If the predictor-criterion relationship is not linear, then the Taylor-Russell tables are inappropriate anyway, since they are based on the assumptions of bivariate normal,[1] linear, homoscedastic[2] relationships between predictor and criterion. In short, when it is reasonable to assume that the use of higher cutoff scores will lead to higher average job performance by those selected, the Taylor-Russell (1939) tables will underestimate the actual amount of gain to be expected.

The Naylor-Shine Model

In contrast to the Taylor-Russell utility model, the Naylor-Shine (1965) approach assumes a linear relationship between validity and utility. This relationship holds at all selection ratios. That is, given any arbitrarily defined cutoff on a selection measure, the higher the validity, the greater

---

[1] *Bivariate normal* means that the two variables in question (in this case, predictor and criterion scores) are each normally distributed, that is, scores are dispersed in a bell-shaped fashion.

[2] *Homoscedastic* means that the variability in criterion scores is the same at high predictor scores as it is at low predictor scores.

the increase in average criterion score for the selected group over that observed for the total group (mean criterion score of selectees minus mean criterion score of total group). Thus the Naylor-Shine index of utility (originally derived by Kelley, 1923) is defined in terms of the increase in average criterion score to be expected from the use of a selection measure with a given validity and selection ratio. Like Taylor and Russell, Naylor and Shine assume that the relationship between predictor and criterion is bivariate normal, linear, and homoscedastic, and that the validity coefficient used is based on the concurrent validity model.[3] Unlike Taylor and Russell, however, use of the Naylor-Shine model does not require that employees be dichotomized into satisfactory and unsatisfactory groups by specifying an arbitrary cutoff on the criterion (job performance) dimension that represents minimally acceptable performance. Thus less information is required in order to use the Naylor-Shine utility model than the Taylor-Russell model. The basic equation underlying the Naylor-Shine (1965) model is:

$$\overline{Z}_{yi} = r_{xy}\frac{\lambda_i}{\phi_i} \tag{4}$$

where $\overline{Z}_{yi}$ is the mean criterion score (in standard score units[4]) of all cases above the predictor cutoff; r_{xy} is the validity coefficient; λ_i is the ordinate of the normal distribution at the predictor cutoff, Z_{xi} (expressed in standard score units); ϕ_i is the selection ratio. Equation 4 applies whether r_{xy} is a zero order correlation coefficient or a multiple regression coefficient.[5]

Using equation 4 as a basic building block, Naylor and Shine (1965) present a series of tables (see Appendix B) which specify, for each selection ratio, the standard (predictor) score corresponding to that selection ratio, the ordinate of the normal curve at that point, and the quotient λ_i/ϕ_i. The table can be used to answer several important personnel questions. (1)

[3]That is, the new selection procedure is administered to present employees who have already been screened using other methods. The correlation (validity coefficient) between scores on the new procedure and the employees' job performance scores is then computed.

[4]To transform raw scores into standard scores, the following formula is used: x − x̄, where x is the raw score, x̄ is the mean of the distribution of scores, and /SD is the standard deviation of the distribution. Assuming the raw scores are normally distributed, about 99 percent of the standard scores will lie within the range − 3 to + 3. Standard scores (Z-scores) are expressed in standard deviation units.

[5]A zero order correlation coefficient is based on two variables. A multiple regression coefficient represents the correlation between a criterion and two or more predictors.

Given a specified selection ratio, what will be the average performance level of those selected? (2) Given a desired selection ratio, what will $\bar{Z}_{yi}$ be? (3) Given a desired improvement in the average criterion score of those selected, what selection ratio and/or predictor cutoff value (in standard score units) should be used? Let us work through some examples, using the tables in Appendix B.

In each of the following examples assume that r_{xy}, the validity of our predictor, is positive and equal to 0.40.

1. Given the selection ratio $\phi_i = 0.50$, what will be the average performance level of those selected?
Solution: Enter the table at $\phi_i = 0.50$ and read $\lambda_i/\phi_i = 0.80$.
$\bar{Z}_{yi} = r_{xy} \lambda_i/\phi_i = (0.40) (0.80) = 0.32$
Thus, the mean criterion score of those selected, using a selection ratio of 0.50, is 0.32 Z-units better than the unselected sample.

2. Given the desired cutoff score $Z_{xi} = -0.96$, what will $\bar{Z}_{yi}$ be?
Solution: Enter the table at $Z_{xi} = -0.96$ and read $\lambda_i/\phi_i = 0.30$.
$Z_{yi} = r_{xy} \lambda_i/\phi_i = (0.40) (0.30) = 0.12$
Thus, using this cutoff score on our predictor results in an improvement of 0.12 Z-units in the average criterion score of selected personnel.

3. Given the desired improvement in the average criterion score of those selected $\bar{Z}_{yi} = 0.50$, what selection ratio and/or predictor cutoff value should be used?
Solution: Since $\bar{Z}_{yi} = r_{xy} \lambda_i/\phi_i$, then
$\lambda_i/\phi_i = \bar{Z}_{yi}/r_{xy} = 0.50/0.40 = 1.25$
Enter the table at $\lambda_i/\phi_i = 1.25$ and read $\phi_i = 0.2578$ and $Z_{xi} = 0.65$. Thus, to achieve an average improvement of 0.50 (one half) standard deviation in job performance a selection ratio of 0.26 is necessary, and to achieve that particular ratio, one should employ a cutoff score on the predictor of 0.65 in Z-score units.

In each of the following examples assume that r_{xy}, the validity of our predictor, is negative and equal to -0.40. The general rule for this case is to reverse the sign of r_{xy} and Z_{xi} everywhere in the calculations.

1. Given the selection ratio $\phi_i = 0.50$, what will be the average performance level of those selected?
Solution: Enter the table at $\phi_i = 0.50$ and read $\lambda_i/\phi_i = 0.80$.
Taking the sign reversal on r_{xy} into account,
$\bar{Z}_{yi} = (-r_{xy}) \lambda_i/\phi_i = -(-0.40) (0.80) = 0.32$

Thus, the mean criterion score of those selected, using a selection ratio of 0.50, is 0.32 Z-units better than the unselected sample.

2. Given the desired cutoff score $Z_{xi} = -0.96$, what will Z_{yi} be?
Solution: When r_{xy} is negative, ϕ_i is in the *left* tail of the score distribution instead of the right tail as it is when r_{xy} is positive. Thus, a cutoff score of -0.96 for the negative case is equivalent to a cutoff score of 0.96 with r_{xy} positive. We therefore reverse the sign of Z_{xi}, enter the table at $Z_{xi} = 0.96$, and read $\lambda_i/\phi_i = 1.49$. Taking the sign reversal on r_{xy} into account, we have

$$\overline{Z}_{yi} = (-r_{xy}) \lambda_i/\phi_i = -(-0.40)(1.49) = 0.596$$

Thus, using a cutoff score of $Z_{xi} = -0.96$ on our predictor results in an improvement of about 0.60 Z-units in the average criterion score of selected personnel.

3. Given the desired improvement in the average criterion score of those selected $\overline{Z}_{yi} = 0.50$, what selection ratio and/or predictor cutoff value should be used?
Solution: Reversing the sign on r_{xy} gives

$$\overline{Z}_{yi} = (-r_{xy})\frac{\lambda_i}{\phi_i}$$

or

$$\frac{\lambda_i}{\phi_i} = \frac{\overline{Z}_{yi}}{(-r_{xy})}$$

Therefore,

$$\frac{\lambda_i}{\phi_i} = \frac{0.50}{-(-0.40)} = 1.25$$

Enter the table at $\lambda_i/\phi_i = 1.25$ and read $\phi_i = 0.2578$ and $Z_{xi} = -0.65$ (note that the sign on Z_{xi} has been reversed). Thus, to achieve the desired improvement in average criterion performance, a selection ratio of 0.26 is necessary, and to achieve that particular ratio, one should employ a cutoff score on the predictor of -0.65 in Z-score units.

The Naylor-Shine utility index appears more generally applicable than the Taylor-Russell index because in many if not most cases, given valid selection procedures, an increase in average criterion performance would be expected as the organization becomes more selective in deciding whom to accept. However, neither of these models formally integrates the concept of cost of selection, or dollars gained or lost, into the utility index. Both simply imply that larger differences in the percentage of successful employees (Taylor-Russell) or larger increases in average criterion score (Naylor-Shine) will yield larger benefits to the employer in dollars saved.

The Brogden-Cronbach-Gleser Model

Brogden (1946) showed that when the predictor and criterion are continuous (i.e., they can assume an infinite number of values theoretically) and identical (not necessarily normal, but identical) in distribution form, the regression of the criterion on the predictor is linear, and the selection ratio is held constant, then the validity coefficient itself is a direct index of selective efficiency. If criterion performance is expressed in standard score units, then over all individuals r_{xy} represents the ratio of the average criterion score made by persons selected on the basis of their predictor scores ($\Sigma \bar{Z}_y$) to the average score made by selecting the same number of persons on the basis of their criterion scores ($\Sigma Z_{y'}$). That is:

$$r_{xy} = \frac{\Sigma \bar{Z}_y}{\Sigma Z_{y'}} \qquad (5)$$

As an illustration, suppose a firm wants to hire 20 persons for a certain job and must choose the best 20 from 85 applicants. Ideally, the firm would hire all 85 for a period of time, collect criterion data, and retain the best 20, those obtaining the highest criterion scores. The average criterion score of the 20 so selected would obviously be the highest obtainable by any possible combination of 20 of the 85 original workers. Since such a procedure is usually out of the question, we administer a selection measure and select the 20 highest scorers. Equation 5 indicates that the validity coefficient may be interpreted as the ratio of the average criterion performance of the 20 persons selected on the basis of their predictor scores to the average performance of the 20 who would have been selected had the criterion itself been used as the basis for selection. Thus if persons could be selected on the basis of actual criterion behavior (or by means of a perfect selection device), and this would save an organization $100,000 per year over random selection, then a selection device with a validity of 0.50 could be expected to save $50,000 per year. Utility is therefore a direct linear function of validity, given the assumptions noted above.

Although equation 5 does not formally include the cost of selection and was not advanced as an estimate of utility, in a later paper (1949),

Brogden used the principles of linear regression to demonstrate the relationships of cost of selection, validity, and selection ratio to utility. The derivation is straightforward.

Let r_{xy} equal the correlation between a predictor (x) and job performance measured in dollars (y). The basic linear model is:

$$y = \beta Z_x + \mu_y + e$$

where:

y = job performance measured in dollars

β = the linear regression weight on the predictor for forecasting job performance

Z_x = performance on the predictor in standard score form in the applicant group

μ_y = mean job performance in dollars of randomly selected employees

e = error of prediction

For those selected (s), the equation that gives the average job performance in this group is:

$$E(y_s) = E(\beta Z_{x_s}) + E(\mu_y) + E(e)$$

Since the expected value of e is zero, and β and μ are constants, the equation reduces to:

$$\overline{Y}_s = \beta \overline{Z}_{x_s} + \mu_y$$

Remember that $\beta = r_{xy}(SD_y/SD_x)$, where SD_y is the standard deviation of dollar-valued job performance among randomly selected employees. Since $SD_x = 1.00$, $\beta = r_{xy}SD_y$. We therefore obtain:

$$\overline{Y}_s = r_{xy}SD_y\overline{Z}_{x_s} + \mu_y$$

This equation tells us the *absolute* dollar value of average job performance in the selected groups. What we really want, however, is an equation that gives the *increase* in dollar value of average performance that results from using the predictor. To get that equation, let us suppose that the new predictor was not used. Then $\overline{Y}_s = \mu_y$, for mean job performance in the selected group would be the same as mean performance in a group selected randomly from the applicant pool. Thus the increase due to use of a valid predictor is $r_{xy}SD_y\overline{Z}_{x_s}$. The equation we want is produced by transposing μ_y to give

$$\overline{Y}_s - \mu_y = r_{xy}SD_y\overline{Z}_{x_s}$$

The right side of the above equation represents the difference between mean productivity in the group selected using the new predictor and mean productivity in a group selected without using the new predictor, that is, a group selected randomly. The equation thus gives mean gain in productivity per selectee (marginal utility) resulting from the use of the new predictor, that is,

$$\Delta\overline{U}/\text{selectee} = r_{xy}SD_y\overline{Z}_{x_s} \qquad (6)$$

where $\overline{U}$ is utility and $\Delta\overline{U}$ is marginal utility.

Equation 6 states that the average productivity gain in dollars per person hired is the product of the validity coefficient, the standard deviation of job performance in dollars, and the average standard score on the predictor of those hired. The value $r_{xy}\overline{Z}_{x_s}$ is the mean standard score on the dollar criterion of those selected, $\overline{Z}_y$.

Assuming predictor scores are distributed normally and the predictor-criterion relationship is linear, then $\overline{Z}_{x_s}$ for the selected group may be computed by the formula λ/ϕ, where λ is the height of the normal curve at the point of cut, and ϕ is the percentage in the selected group (the selection ratio). $\overline{Z}_{y_s}$ (the average standard criterion score for the selected group) is then obtained as the product $r\,\lambda/\phi$. This is the same formula (equation 4) used by Naylor and Shine (1965) to derive the values in their tables.

The total utility of the new predictor depends on the number of persons hired. The total utility (total productivity) gain is simply the mean gain per selectee times the number of people selected, N_s. That is, the total productivity gain is:

$$\Delta U = N_s r_{xy}SD_y\lambda/\phi \qquad (7)$$

Suppose the average marginal utility is $5,000. If 10 people were hired, the actual utility would be $50,000. If 100 people were hired, then the utility would be $500,000. Obviously, the total dollar value of the new predictor is greater for large employers than for small employers. However, this fact can be misleading. On a percentage basis it is average gain in utility that counts, and that is what counts to each individual employer. The cost of selection is a further factor which must be considered in estimating the savings expected from a selection program. Since the expected saving per individual selected is $r_{xy}SD_y\lambda/\phi$, the saving with allowance for the cost of testing can be determined by subtracting c/ϕ from the above value, where c is the cost of testing a single individual. Cost of testing is divided by ϕ, so that c/ϕ represents the total cost of the testing required to fill one vacancy. The expected saving per selectee corrected for the cost of testing is therefore:

$$\Delta U = r_{xy}SD_y\lambda/\phi - c/\phi$$

The effect of the cost of testing can be evaluated, as Brogden (1949) has shown, by computing the ratio, per applicant cost of testing/(validity $\times$ SD_y). This value represents the ratio of the cost of testing to the expected gain in dollar value of production with an increase in applicant test score of one standard deviation unit. Thus, if the cost of evaluating an applicant for an executive position is $300, the validity of the selection procedure is 0.35, and the criterion standard deviation is $15,000, then the ratio is about 0.06. If this ratio can be held below 0.05, then Taylor and Russell's (1939) conclusions are substantially correct. That is, a low selection ratio can be just as important or more important than high validity in achieving savings; even selection procedures with low validities can produce considerable savings if the selection ratio is also low; and finally, if nearly all applicants must be hired, even highly valid selection procedures are of little value.

Cronbach and Gleser (1965) elaborated and refined Brogden's (1949) derivations with respect to utility in fixed treatment selection and, in addition, thoroughly explored the application of utility theory to selection with adaptive treatment, two-stage and multistage selection, placement decisions, and classification decisions. With respect to utility in fixed treatment selection, Cronbach and Gleser (1965) adopt Taylor and Russell's (1939) interpretation of the validity coefficient for utility calculations, that is, concurrent validity. The validity coefficient based on present employees presupposes a population that has been screened using information other than the new selection measure. It is to this population that the selection ratio will be applied.

Cronbach and Gleser (1965) argue, as did Taylor and Russell (1939) and Naylor and Shine (1965), that selection procedures should be judged on the basis of their contribution over and above the best strategy available that makes use of prior information. Thus, any new procedure must demonstrate incremental utility before it is put to use. With respect to fixed treatment selection Cronbach and Gleser (1965) make the following assumptions:

1. Decisions are made regarding an indefinitely large population. This "a priori population" consists of all applicants after screening by any procedure which is presently in use and will continue to be used.

2. Regarding any person, i, there are two possible alternative decisions: accept (t_a) and reject (t_b).

3. Each person has a test score, y_i, which has zero mean and unit standard deviation. [Test scores are assumed to be distributed normally.]

4. For every person there is a payoff e_{it_a} which results when a person is accepted. This payoff has a linear regression on test score. The test will be scored so that r_{ye} is positive.

5. When a person is rejected, the payoff e_{it_b} results. This payoff is unrelated to test score, and may be set equal to zero.

6. The average cost of testing a person on test y is c_y, where $c_y > 0$.

7. The strategy will be to accept high scorers in preference to others. A cutoff y' will be located on the y continuum so that any desired proportion $\phi(y')$ of the group falls above y'. Above that point the probability of acceptance is 1.00; below it, 0.00. Cochran (1951) shows that such a strategy is optimal for selection with fixed quota.[6]

The assumption of a normal distribution of test scores (assumption 3 above) implies that the expected payoffs from randomly selected persons are also normally distributed. As both Brogden (1949) and Cronbach and Gleser (1965) have noted, this assumption may not always be met, nor would it be desirable that it always be met. Standards set by management often place a lower limit on production (which produces a positively skewed payoff distribution), while voluntary restrictions on output by a work group skew the curve negatively. In the extreme, complete task standardization eliminates variability entirely among those who remain on

---

[6]L. J. Cronbach, and G. C. Gleser. *Psychological Tests and Personnel Decisions.* 2nd ed. Urbana, Ill.: University of Illinois Press, 1965, p. 307.

the job. However, with highly skewed distributions, as long as linear regression is present, payoffs resulting from cutoff points on the tail of the distribution skew could be relatively greater than those obtained at the same percentile point of cut with a normally distributed variable. This implies a comparison of relative payoffs at different selection ratios.

When the assumptions noted earlier are met, however, Cronbach and Gleser (1965) demonstrate that the net gain in utility from testing N persons in fixed treatment selection is

$$\Delta U = NSD_e r_{ye} \lambda(y') - Nc_y \qquad (9)$$

where c_y is the cost of testing one person; r_{ye} is the correlation of the selection procedure with the dollar-scale-evaluated criterion in the a priori population; SD_e is the standard deviation of this criterion; y' is the cutoff score on the selection procedure; and $\lambda(y')$ is the ordinate of the normal curve at that point. In this expression, $SD_e r_{ye}$ is the slope of the payoff function relating expected payoff to score. An increase in validity leads to an increase in slope, but as equation 9 demonstrates, slope also depends on the dispersion of criterion scores. For any one treatment SD_e is constant and indicates both the magnitude and practical significance of individual differences in payoff. Thus a selection procedure with $r_{xy} = 0.25$ and $SD_e = \$10,000$ for one selection decision is just as useful as a procedure with $r_{xy} = 0.50$ and $SD_e = \$5,000$ for some other decision (holding other parameters constant). Even procedures with low validity can still be useful when SD_e is large.

If equation 9 is expressed as the net gain in utility per person accepted in fixed treatment selection, it is identical to Brogden's (1949) formula (equation 8). Therefore,

$$\Delta U = SD_e r_{ye} \frac{\lambda(y')}{\phi(y')} - \frac{c_y}{\phi(y')} \qquad (10)$$

where all terms are as defined above. In short, both Brogden (1946, 1949) and Cronbach and Gleser (1965) arrived at the same conclusions regarding the effects of r, SD_e, the cost of selection, and the selection ratio on utility in fixed treatment selection. Utility is properly regarded as a linear function of validity and, if cost is zero, is proportional to validity. Contrary to the Taylor-Russell results, the linear relation holds at all selection ratios. A summary of the three approaches discussed so far is presented in Exhibit 7.5.

Exhibit 7.5 Summary of the Utility Indexes, Data Requirements, and Assumptions of the Taylor-Russell, Naylor-Shine, and Brogden-Cronbach-Gleser Utility Models

Models	Utility Index	Data Requirements	Distinctive Assumptions
Taylor-Russell (1939)	Increase in percentage successful in selected group	Validity, base rate, selection ratio	All selectees classified as either successful or unsuccessful. Equal criterion performance by all members of each group; cost of selection = $0.
Naylor-Shine (1965)	Increase in mean criterion score of selected group	Validity, selection ratio	Validity linearly related to utility; cost of selection = $0.
Brogden-Cronbach-Gleser (1965)	Increase in dollar payoff of selected group	Validity, selection ratio, criterion standard deviation in dollars	Validity linearly related to utility; cost of selection ≠ $0; criterion performance evaluated in dollars.

Note: All three models assume a validity coefficient based on present employees (concurrent validity).

Source: W. F. Cascio. "Responding to the Demand for Accountability: A Critical Analysis of Three Utility Models." *Organizational Behavior and Human Performance*, 1980, 25:42.

Appropriate Application of Each Model

Only by understanding thoroughly the theory, assumptions, and data requirements of the various utility models can the models be used properly. Yet their proper (and more widespread) use is essential in order to satisfy the demand for accountability in personnel programs. Let us consider the Taylor-Russell model first.

Taylor-Russell

The Taylor-Russell (1939) model is most appropriate under the following circumstances: (1) differences in ability beyond the minimum necessary to perform the job do not yield differences in benefit (for example, in various types of clerical or technician's jobs). (2) Individuals are placed into two (or more) groups based on their scores on a test battery, interest inventory, or other procedure. All individuals remain within the organization, but they are treated differently. By assigning particular values to "hits" and "misses" for each possible assignment, cutoff scores can be adjusted to maximize expected utility. (3) Differences in output are believed to occur, but are presently unmeasurable (for example, in nursing care, teaching performance, or credit counseling). In these instances estimating utility according to the magnitude of the increase in the success ratio makes good sense. It makes even better sense, however, to attach cost estimates to expected payoffs. Thus Sands (1973) developed the cost of attaining personnel requirements (CAPER) model on the basis of the Taylor-Russell (1939) approach. CAPER is a decision-oriented system whose objective is to determine an optimal recruiting-selection strategy for minimizing the total cost of recruiting, inducting, selecting, and training a sufficient number of persons to meet a quota of satisfactory employees. There are two major advantages to such an approach: (1) results can easily be communicated and understood by operating managers (that is, they are given in numbers of persons and dollar costs), and (2) by broadening the perspective of personnel selection from selection per se to all phases of the personnel system (from initial recruiting through the completion of training), the likelihood of over- or under-optimization of one component of the system at the expense of all others is minimized. Nevertheless, CAPER, like the Taylor-Russell model, can only be justified under the conditions noted above. Its lack of general applicability is its major drawback.

Naylor-Shine

The Naylor-Shine model is most appropriate when differences in criterion performance cannot be expressed in dollar terms, but when it can be assumed that the function relating payoff (performance under some treatment) to predictor score is linear. Consider the following examples:

1. In classification and placement decisions (for example, in the military or in large organizations) all selected individuals are assigned to available treatments (jobs, training programs) so that individual and institutional outcomes are maximized. In classification, for example, the decision maker has a number of available jobs on the one hand and a number of people on the other. The objective is to make the most effective matching of people and jobs (Ghiselli, 1956). Thus criterion performance must be forecast for each individual for each job, for example, by using least-squares estimates.[7] If the predicted criterion scores for each job (units produced, dollar value of sales, and so on) are expressed in standard score units, then the expected increase in mean criterion performance as a function of variation in the selection ratio can be assessed by means of the Naylor-Shine model.

2. In the prediction of labor turnover, expressed as a percentage, based on scores from a predictor which demonstrates some validity, if percentages are expressed as standard scores, then the expected decrease in the percentage of turnover can be assessed as a function of variation in the selection ratio (the predictor cutoff score). If appropriate costing procedures are used to calculate actual turnover costs (see Chapter 2), expected savings resulting from reduced turnover can then be estimated.

3. In the selection of students based on predicted academic performance in college or graduate school, or in training programs where the cost per trainee is high (for example, academy training), if academic performance is expressed in standard score units, institutions might profitably examine variations in expected criterion performance as a function of variations in predictor scores by means of the Naylor-Shine utility model.

[7]In attempting to forecast job performance on the basis of a composite of predictor scores, a mathematical formula (regression equation) must be developed. Although many such equations are possible, statisticians generally agree that the best (most accurate) equation is that for which the sum of the squared deviations between actual and predicted job performance scores is a minimum. Thus the term, least-squares.

Brogden-Cronbach-Gleser

The Brogden-Cronbach-Gleser continuous variable utility model is potentially the most versatile utility model available, but to date it has not received widespread attention. It is most appropriate in situations where criterion performance can be expressed in dollars and where linear regression of the criterion on the predictor can be assumed. In short, this model provides a direct estimate of the monetary value of a selection program by making use of the "dollar criterion" (Brogden and Taylor, 1950). Consider the following examples:

1. Roche (1965) used cost accounting procedures to estimate the payoff from a program designed to select radial drill operators in a manufacturing operation. Although the cost accounting methods were relatively straightforward, many subjective estimates and arbitrary allocations entered into the estimated profit accruing to the firm as a result of the radial drill operator's work. Such elements as the cost of materials used in producing the company's products, the cost of direct labor hours consumed in the manufacture of a product, and the cost of capital investment, jigs, fixtures, power, perishable tools, and floor space all had to be expressed in dollars. The determination of the standard deviation of criterion outcomes expressed in dollars is clearly a complex undertaking, but through the joint efforts of personnel psychologists and cost accountants it can be done. Chapter 8 is devoted exclusively to this problem.

2. In a service organization, Schmidt and Hoffman (1973) applied the Brogden-Cronbach-Gleser model to a weighted application blank developed to predict turnover among nurse's aides. Using cost accounting methods, the dollar cost of turnover was estimated. When actual dollar savings over a two-year period were compared to estimated dollar savings at two selection ratios using the Brogden-Cronbach-Gleser model, the differences were no greater than 7 percent.

3. In a sales organization Cascio and Silbey (1979) estimated the utility of an assessment center in selection by means of the Brogden-Cronbach-Gleser utility model. Like the CAPER (Sands, 1973) model, the costs of recruiting, selecting, inducting, and training a sufficient number of persons to meet a quota of satisfactory employees were explicitly included in the cost of selection (c_y). Like CAPER, this decision-oriented system broadens the perspective of personnel selection from selection per

se to all phases of the personnel system. Thus, the likelihood of over- or underoptimization of one component of the system at the expense of all others is minimized. Unlike CAPER, however, this model requires fewer restrictive assumptions and is potentially applicable to a much wider variety of selection situations.

In summary, as personnel costs and the costs of personnel programs continue to escalate, demands for accountability are also likely to escalate. Utility-based decision systems can meet this challenge, but their proper application requires careful attention to the assumptions and data requirements of each model. "Garbage in—garbage out" is as true in this context as it is in the context of an information system.

Exercises

1. Use the Taylor-Russell tables (Appendix A) to solve these problems:

Validity	SR	BR	Success Ratio
0.25	0.20	0.30	_____
0.55	0.70	0.80	_____
0.20	0.70	0.80	_____
0.10	0.50	0.50	_____
0.55	0.50	0.50	_____

2. Use the Naylor-Shine tables (Appendix B) to solve these problems:

r_{xy}	ϕ_i	Z_{xi}	$\overline{Z}_{yi}$
0.35	0.7019		____
0.22		−0.30	____
0.47	____	____	0.65
−0.47	____	____	0.65

3. Using the Brogden-Cronbach-Gleser continuous variable utility model, what is the net gain over random selection (ΔU) overall, and per selectee, given the following information?

quota for selection: 20

SR: 0.20

SD_e (standard deviation of job performance expressed in dollars): $10,000

r_{ye}: 0.25

$\lambda(y')$: 0.28

c_y: $25

Hint: To find N, the number recruited, divide the quota for selection by the SR.

4. As in question 3, find the net gain in utility (ΔU) over random selection overall and per selectee, given the following information:

quota: 125

SR: 0.50

SD_e: $7,500

r_{ye}: 0.35

$\lambda(y')$: 0.3988

c_y: $400

5. Given the following information on two selection procedures, and using the Brogden-Cronbach-Gleser model, what is the relative *difference* in payoff (overall and per selectee) between the two procedures? For both procedures, quota = 50, SR = 0.50, $\lambda(y')$ = 0.3989, and SD_e = $15,000.

r_{y_1} : 0.20 c_1: $100

r_{y_2} : 0.40 c_2: $500

6. You are a management consultant whose task is to do a utility analysis using the following information regarding secretaries at Inko, Inc. The validity of the Secretarial Aptitude Test (SAT) is 0.40, applicants must score 70 or better (Z of 0.5) to be hired, and only about half of those who apply are actually hired. Of those hired, about half are considered satisfactory by their bosses. How selective should Inko be if it desires to upgrade the average criterion score of

those selected by $Z = 0.5$? What utility model did you use to solve the problem? Why?

References

BLUM, M. L., and NAYLOR, J. C. *Industrial Psychology: Its Theoretical and Social Foundations.* Rev. ed. New York: Harper & Row, 1968.

BROGDEN, H. E. "On the Interpretation of the Correlation Coefficient as a Measure of Predictive Efficiency." *Journal of Educational Psychology,* 1946, 37:64–76.

BROGDEN, H. E. "When Testing Pays Off." *Personnel Psychology,* 1949, 2:171–185.

BROGDEN, H. E., and TAYLOR, E. K. "The Dollar Criterion—Applying the Cost Accounting Concept to Criterion Construction." *Personnel Psychology,* 1950, 3:133–154.

CASCIO, W. F., and SILBEY, V. "Utility of the Assessment Center as a Selection Device." *Journal of Applied Psychology,* 1979, 64:107–118.

COCHRAN, W. G. "Improvement by Means of Selection." In J. Neyman, ed., *Second Berkeley Symposium on Mathematical Statistics and Probability.* Berkeley: University of California Press, 1951.

CRONBACH, L. J., and GLESER, G. C. *Psychological Tests and Personnel Decisions.* 2nd ed. Urbana, Ill.: University of Illinois Press, 1965.

GHISELLI, E. E. "The Placement of Workers: Concepts and Problems." *Personnel Psychology,* 1956, 9:1–16.

KELLEY, T. L. *Statistical Method.* New York: Macmillan, 1923.

NAYLOR, J. C., and SHINE L. C. "A Table for Determining the Increase in Mean Criterion Score Obtained by Using a Selection Device." *Journal of Industrial Psychology,* 1965, 3:33–42.

PEARSON, K. *Tables for Statisticians and Biometricians,* Part 2. London: Biometric Laboratory, University College, 1931, pp. 78–109.

"Postal Service Plans to Hike Mail Rates." *The Miami Herald,* March 30, 1980, p. 8A.

ROCHE, W. J., JR. "The Cronbach-Gleser Utility Function in Fixed Treatment Employee Selection." (Doctoral dissertation, Southern Illinois University, 1961.) *Dissertation Abstracts International,* 1961-1962, 22:4413. (University Microfilms No. 62-1570.) Portions reproduced in C. J. Cronbach and G. C. Gleser, eds., *Psychological Tests and Personnel Decisions.* Urbana: University of Illinois Press, 1965.

SANDS, W. A. "A Method for Evaluating Alternative Recruiting-Selection Strategies: The CAPER Model." *Journal of Applied Psychology,* 1973, 57:222–227.

SCHMIDT, S. L., and HOFFMAN, B. "An Empirical Comparison of Three Methods of Assessing the Utility of a Selection Device." *Journal of Industrial and Organizational Psychology*, 1973, 1:1–11.

TAYLOR, H. C., and RUSSELL, J. T. "The Relationship of Validity Coefficients to the Practical Effectiveness of Tests in Selection." *Journal of Applied Psychology*, 1939, 23:565–578.

WIGGINS, J. S. *Personality and Prediction: Principles of Personality Assessment*. Reading, Mass.: Addison-Wesley, 1973.

8

Estimating the Economic Value of Job Performance

Despite the fact that the powerful Brogden-Cronbach-Gleser continuous variable utility model has been available for years, it has not received widespread attention. Perhaps the major reason for this is the extreme difficulty, in most cases, of obtaining all of the information called for in the equations. Certainly the numbers of people tested, the cost of testing, and the selection ratio can be determined reasonably accurately, since much of this information is a matter of record. The element most difficult to obtain has been the estimate of the standard deviation of dollar-valued job performance, SD_y (Cronbach and Gleser, 1965, p. 121). In the past it has been assumed that SD_y could be estimated only by using complicated cost-accounting methods that are both costly and time consuming. In general, these procedures involve first costing out the dollar value of the job behaviors of each employee (Brogden and Taylor, 1950) and then computing the standard deviation of these values. Two newer approaches require only estimates from knowledgeable persons. In this chapter we shall examine briefly the cost-accounting approach to estimating SD_y, and then we shall examine the two newer estimation procedures in greater detail.

Cost-Accounting Approach

Let us begin by considering the objectives of a business enterprise. In the simplest terms, the objective of a business is to make money. Consequently, monetary gain is the appropriate measure of the degree to which on-the-job activity of the individual contributes to or detracts from this overall objective. Brogden and Taylor (1950) summarize this idea as follows:

> Only after we have succeeded in evaluating on-the-job performance in these terms can we be sure that our criterion measures conform to the objectives of the organization. . . . Unless criterion elements are of such a nature that they can be expressed in dollar units, their use as criterion measures cannot be justified and do [sic] not satisfy the requirement of logical face validity. (p. 139–40).

In using cost accounting to develop a dollar criterion a number of elements must be considered. Brogden and Taylor list the following as examples:

1. Average value of production or service units.
2. Quality of objects produced or services accomplished.
3. Overhead—including rent, light, heat, cost depreciation, or rental of machines and equipment.
4. Errors, accidents, spoilage, wastage, damage to machines or equipment due to unusual wear and tear, etc.
5. Such factors as appearance, friendliness, poise, and general social effectiveness where public relations are heavily involved. (Here, some approximate or arbitrary value would have to be assigned by an individual or individuals having the required responsibility and background.)
6. The cost of time of other personnel consumed. This would include not only the time of the supervisory personnel but also that of other workers (p. 146).

Roche (1961) attempted to apply these ideas to 291 beginning level radial drill operators (RDO-1s) working in a large midwestern industrial plant that employs about 25,000 persons. The company's job description for an RDO-1 is:

> Sets up and operates a radial drill, performing drill, ream, line ream, tap (stud, pipe, and standard), countersink, chamfer, bore, counterbore, spotface, backface, and hollow mill operations. Involves various types of parts

such as castings, forgings, bar stock, structural steel and welded fabrications. Grinds drills when necessary.

Work assignments to the RDO-1s are made by the planning department according to machine number, not according to specific operators. Consequently, the RDO-1s have no control over the type of parts on which they perform machining operations. Typically, any single worker will work on a variety of parts, and the mix differs from worker to worker.

It was assumed that the dollar profit that accrues to the company as a result of an individual's work provides the best estimate of his or her worth to the company. The following cost-accounting procedures were used to develop this dollar criterion. As described by Roche (1961), the method is one of "standard costing," which is an effective tool for volume production accounting. It also permits the application of the "principle of exception," whereby attention is directed chiefly to variations from standard cost that indicate trends in volume output. Standard cost for the company's products is determined by procuring costs on three basic factors: material used to produce products; direct labor hours used to alter the size, shape, quality, or consistency of material; and facility usage required to perform direct labor. Standard cost must remain stable or fixed for a specific period in order to attain its objective. Usually all standards remain frozen for a period of five years, or until a general cost revision is officially authorized.

The company uses "lifo" (last in–first out) inventory accounting,[1] so that latest costs are used first to allocate costs in a manner closely related to price levels prevailing at the time of sale. The seven major cost elements in the accounting are:

material, unformed steel

material, grey iron castings

material, forgings, stampings, and so on

material, purchased finished

direct labor

general burden

machine burden

---

[1]Using lifo, the earliest-acquired stock is assumed to be still on hand; the last-acquired stock is assumed to have been used immediately. Lifo releases the most recent (or last) inventory costs as cost of goods used or sold. It attempts to match the most current cost of obtaining inventory against sales for a period (Horngren, 1972).

Prime product costs are built up from costs of piece-parts or units into costs for assemblies, then costs for groups, arrangements, and finally for the general arrangements or complete model. The total cost figure has four basic components: variable, fixed, office, and parts warehousing. Variable or out-of-pocket cost includes only those costs that fluctuate with production output; it includes actual cost of material, plus material-handling burden; direct labor cost plus an allocation to cover indirect labor, supplies, and so on; and facility usage, which generally reflects normal maintenance, power consumption, perishable tool usage, and facility supplies. These variable costs are most useful in determining costs where facility usage is not affected; however, fixed costs are used where facility usage is affected. Fixed costs are based on a given percentage of the production capacity of the plant. In determining them allocations are made to cover portions of material-handling burden, plant labor and burden (such as overtime premium, special indirect labor, and management salaries), and plant facility usage (such as building and machinery depreciation, repairs and maintenance, tool design). Office and parts warehousing costs are figured as a percentage allocation.

The income from the RDO-1's work is readily determined, since the parts manufactured are sold to dealers, and a price for each part has been established. Subtracting the cost at standard production from the price yields a profit figure.

Measuring Each Individual's Productivity

A productivity measure called the *performance ratio* was developed to express the payoff for each individual. Since the length of time it takes a competent operator to complete a machining operation on a particular piece-part was established by standard time study procedures, the number of piece-parts per hour that an operator should be able to process was known. A performance ratio for any period of work could then be computed by dividing actual production per hour by the standard hourly production for the piece-part on which an RDO-1 was then working. For example, if the standard production for a piece-part is ten pieces per hour and an operator produces seven pieces in an hour, his or her performance ratio for that one hour's work is 0.70. This index makes it possible to determine the operator's performance ratio over a month or more during which he or she has worked on a number of different piece-parts, each of which has a different production standard. Only rarely does an operator turn out more than standard production over an extended period of time. At the time of the study operators had varying lengths of time of company service, ranging from a few months to over ten years. A rigid attempt to control the experience factor would have seriously reduced the size of the group. Management personnel stated that most individuals with no previous machine operator experience could reach their typical level of RDO-1 performance within a few weeks. In Roche's (1961) study, therefore, performance ratios for each operator were obtained monthly for a six-month period, and the mean was taken as the operator's typical performance. These results are shown in Exhibit 8.1. An analysis of variance indicated that the mean performance ratios over the six-month period were not significantly different from each other. Thus, it was concluded that the group's performance was stable over the period of study, and the mean performance for each of the operators was used as his or her typical performance.

The Burden Adjustment

If an operator produces at less than standard, the actual burden per hour for this inefficiency is greater than the standard burden per hour determined for his or her operation. An operator producing at 80 percent of standard actually takes one and one-quarter hours to produce an hour's work. In order to take into account this additional burden, each below-standard performance ratio was corrected. It was assumed that the amount of burden in excess of the standard burden reduced in a proportional amount an

Exhibit 8.1   Monthly Performance Ratios for RDO-1s as a Group

Month	Mean	SD
First	79.92	17.84
Second	81.21	17.88
Third	79.70	16.71
Fourth	83.16	16.87
Fifth	79.23	20.25
Sixth	80.69	17.72

Source: W. J. Roche, Jr. "A Dollar Criterion in Fixed Treatment Employee Selections," In L. J. Cronbach and G. C. Gleser, eds., *Psychological Tests and Personnel Decisions.* Urbana: University of Illinois Press, 1965, p. 262.

operator's contribution. The formula used for such corrections was $2 - 1/PR$, where PR = performance ratio. Thus, where a person is working at 80 percent of standard, the burden is 1.25 hours instead of 1.00 hours, and the corrected performance ratio is 0.75.

Determination of Payoff

The procedures for determining each operator's payoff (y) were as follows:

1. Computation of each operator's typical performance ratio. This figure was his or her mean performance ratio for the six-month period of the study.

2. Adjustment of the typical performance ratio for below-standard production (the burden adjustment).

3. Computation of the average profit at standard production, attributable to the radial drill operation.

a. Tabulation of the standard production rate for each type of piece-part machined by radial drill operators. These data were provided by the time study division.

b. Profit for each type of piece-part attributable to the radial drill operation.

c. Profit per hour for each piece-part attributable to the radial drill operation at standard production. These figures were determined by multiplying the profit per piece by the standard production rate for the piece.

d. Average hourly profit attributable to the radial drill operation at standard production. This was determined by weighting the profit per hour for each piece-part (step 3c) by the number of such parts in the work flow.

4. Determination of y, the profit for each radial drill operator at his or her corrected performance ratio and the standard hourly profit.

5. Computation of SD_y. This is merely the standard deviation of the y values computed in step 4.

In actually computing the payoff values, Roche (1961) reported that the 291 radial drill operators worked on approximately 2,500 different piece-parts. Because an enormous amount of clerical work would be involved in determining the profit attributable to the radial drill operation for every piece-part, a random sample of 275 parts (about 10 percent of the total) was drawn and the necessary computations were performed for these. Averaged over the sample of parts, the profit per hour attributable to the radial drill operation was $5.512; the standard deviation was $3.947.[2] This is not directly a part of company earnings. Out of this line in the balance sheet must come various costs of doing business, such as interest on loans and bonds and taxes.

The y value for each operator was the hourly profit at standard production attributable to RDO-1 multiplied by his or her corrected performance ratio. The standard deviation of this distribution (SD_y) was $0.585.[3]

Despite the complexity and apparent objectivity of the cost-accounting approach, Roche (1961) admitted that "many estimates and arbitrary allocations entered into the cost accounting" (Cronbach and Gleser, 1965, p. 263). The development of an estimate of SD_y clearly required a prodigious effort in the Roche study. (The actual utility estimates will be described in the next chapter.) This is probably a major reason why more such studies were not undertaken for over fifteen years following its publication. However, in the late 1970s two new approaches for estimating the economic value of job performance were developed. Since both require considerably less effort than the cost-accounting approach, they may encourage wider use of the Brogden-Cronbach-Gleser utility model. In the following two sections we shall consider these approaches in more detail.

Global Estimation of the Dollar Value of Job Performance

Fortunately it is not critical that estimates of utility be accurate down to the last dollar. Utility estimates are typically used to make decisions about selection procedures, and for this purpose only errors large enough to lead to incorrect decisions are of any consequence. Further, errors may be as frequent or more frequent when cost-accounting procedures are used. As we noted earlier, Roche (1961) found that even in the case of the simple

---

[2]These figures are in 1961 dollars. Assuming an 8 percent inflation rate over 20 years, the comparable figures in 1981 dollars are $25.69 and $18.40, respectively.

[3]$2.73 in 1981 dollars.

and structured job he studied, the cost accountants were frequently forced to rely on subjective estimates and arbitrary allocations. This is generally true in cost accounting and may become a more severe problem as one moves up the corporate ladder. What objective cost-accounting techniques, for example, can be used to assess the dollar value of an executive's impact on the morale of his or her subordinates? It is precisely the jobs with the largest SD_y values, that is, the jobs for which ΔU/selectee is potentially greatest, that are handled least well by cost-accounting methods. Rational estimates, to one degree or another, are virtually unavoidable at the higher job levels.

One procedure for obtaining rational estimates of SD_y has been developed by Schmidt, Hunter, McKenzie, and Muldrow (1979). This method was used in a pilot study by 62 experienced supervisors of budget analysts to estimate SD_y for that occupation. Supervisors were used as judges because they have the best opportunities to observe actual performance and output differences among employees on a day-to-day basis. The method is based on the following reasoning: if job performance in dollar terms is normally distributed, then the difference between the value to the organization of the products and services produced by an employee at the eighty-fifth percentile in performance and that of an employee at the fiftieth percentile in performance is equal to SD_y. Budget analyst supervisors were asked to estimate both these values; the final estimate was the average difference across the sixty-two supervisors. The estimation task presented to the supervisors may appear difficult at first glance, but only one out of sixty-two supervisors objected and stated that he did not think he could make meaningful estimates. Use of a carefully developed questionnaire to obtain the estimates apparently aided significantly. Such a global estimation procedure (in which a total figure is derived directly instead of summing individual cost elements) has at least two advantages. First, the mental standard to be used by the supervisor-judges is the estimated cost to the organization of having an outside consulting firm provide the same products or services. In many occupations, this is a relatively concrete standard. Second, the idiosyncratic tendencies, biases, and random errors of individual experts can be controlled by averaging across a large number of judges. Unless there is an upward or downward bias in the group as a whole, such an average should be fairly accurate. In the budget analyst example, the standard error of the mean was $1,120. This means that the interval $9,480 to $13,175 should contain 90 percent of such estimates.

Thus to be extremely conservative one could employ the lower bound of this interval in calculations.

Methods similar to this global estimation procedure have been used successfully by the Decision Analysis Group of the Stanford Research Institute to scale otherwise unmeasurable but critical variables. Resulting measures have been used in the application of the principles of decision theory to high-level policy decision making in such areas as nuclear power plant construction, corporate risk policies, investment and expansion programs, and hurricane seeding (Howard, 1966; Howard, Matheson and North, 1972; Matheson, 1969). All indications are that the response to the work of this group has been positive; these methods have been judged by high-level decision makers to contribute valuably to improvement of socially and economically important decisions.

Let us now describe in detail how the global estimation procedure has been used to estimate SD_y. The application to be described was reported by Schmidt et al. (1979) using supervisors of computer programmers in ten federal agencies. To test the hypothesis that dollar outcomes are normally distributed, the supervisors were asked to estimate values for the fifteenth percentile (low-performing programmers), the fiftieth percentile (average programmers), and the eighty-fifth percentile (superior programmers). The resulting data thus provide two estimates of SD_y. If the distribution is approximately normal, these two estimates will not differ substantially in value.

The instructions to the supervisors were as follows: The dollar utility estimates we are asking you to make are critical in estimating the relative dollar value to the government of different selection methods. In answering these questions, you will have to make some very *difficult judgments*. We realize they are difficult and that they are judgments or estimates. You will have to ponder for some time before giving each estimate, and there is probably no way you can be absolutely certain your estimate is accurate when you do reach a decision. But keep in mind three things:

(1) The alternative to estimates of this kind is application of cost accounting procedures to the evaluation of job performance. Such applications are usually prohibitively expensive. And in the end, they produce only imperfect estimates, like this estimation procedure.

(2) Your estimates will be averaged in with those of other supervisors of computer programmers. Thus errors produced by too high and too low estimates will tend to be averaged out, providing more accurate final estimates.

(3) The decisions that must be made about selection methods do not require that all estimates be accurate down to the last dollar. Substantially accurate estimates will lead to the same decisions as perfectly accurate estimates.

Based on your experience with agency programmers, we would like for you to estimate the yearly value to your agency of the products and services produced by the average GS 9–11 computer programmer. Consider the quality and quantity of output typical of the *average programmer* and the value of this output. In placing an overall dollar value on this output, it may help to consider what the cost would be of having an outside firm provide these products and services.

Based on my experience, I estimate the value to my agency of the average GS 9–11 computer programmer at _____ dollars per year.

We would now like for you to consider the *"superior" programmer.* Let us define a superior performer as a programmer who is at the 85th percentile. That is, his or her performance is better than that of 85% of his or her fellow GS 9–11 programmers, and only 15% turn in better performances. Consider the quality and quantity of the output typical of the superior programmer. Then estimate the value of these products and services. In placing an overall dollar value on this output, it may again help to consider what the cost would be of having an outside firm provide these products and services.

Based on my experience, I estimate the value to my agency of a superior GS 9–11 computer programmer to be _____ dollars per year.

Finally, we would like for you to consider the *"low-performing" computer programmer.* Let us define a low-performing programmer as one who is at the 15th percentile. That is, 85% of all GS 9–11 computer programmers turn in performances better than the low-performing programmer, and only 15% turn in worse performances. Consider the quality and quantity of the output typical of the low-performing programmer. Then estimate the value of these products and services. In placing an overall dollar value on this output, it may again help to consider what the cost would be of having an outside firm provide these products and services.

Based on my experience, I estimate the value to my agency of the low-performing GS 9–11 computer programmer at _____ dollars per year. (Schmidt et al., 1979, p. 621)

The wording of this questionnaire was carefully developed and pretested on a small sample of programmer supervisors and personnel psychologists. None of the programmer supervisors who returned questionnaires in the study reported any difficulty in understanding the questionnaire or in making the estimates. Participation in the study was completely voluntary. Of 147 questionnaires distributed 105 were returned (all in usable form), for a return rate of 71.4 percent.

Results

The two estimates of SD_y were similar. The mean estimated difference in dollar value of yearly job performance between programmers at the eighty-fifth and fiftieth percentiles in job performance was $10,871 ($SE$ = $1,673). The difference between the fiftieth and fifteenth percentiles was $9,955 ($SE$ = $1,035). The difference of $916 was roughly 8 percent of each of the estimates and was not statistically significant. Thus the hypothesis that computer programmer productivity in dollars is normally distributed could not be rejected. The distribution was at least approximately normal. The average of these two estimates, $10,413, was the SD_y figure used in the utility calculations to be described in Chapter 9. This figure must be considered an underestimate, since it applies to incumbents rather than to the applicant pool. As can be seen from the two standard errors, supervisors showed better agreement on the productivity difference between low-performing and average programmers than on the difference between the average and superior programmers. Although this global estimation procedure is easy to use and provides fairly reliable estimates across supervisors, it has two drawbacks: (1) as we noted in Chapter 7, both Brogden and Cronbach and Gleser pointed out that dollar outcomes are often not normally distributed, and (2) the procedure lacks face validity (that is, it does not look like it measures what it purports to measure) since the components of each supervisor's estimate are unknown and unverifiable. An alternative procedure that avoids some of these difficulties is described next.

The Cascio-Ramos Estimate of Performance in Dollars (CREPID)

The Cascio-Ramos estimate of performance in dollars (CREPID), the third approach that we shall discuss for estimating SD_y, was developed under the auspices of the American Telephone and Telegraph Company, and tested in the Comptroller's Division of a Bell operating company. The rationale underlying CREPID is as follows. Assuming an organization's compensation program reflects current market rates for jobs, then the economic value of each employee's labor is best reflected in his or her annual wage or salary. CREPID breaks down each employee's job into its principal activities, assigns a proportional amount of the annual salary to each principal activity, and then requires supervisors to rate each employee's job performance on each principal activity. The resulting ratings are then translated into estimates of dollar value for each principal activity. The sum of the dollar values assigned to each principal activity equals the economic value of each employee's job performance to the company. Let us explain each of these steps in greater detail.

1. *Identify principal activities.* In many job analysis systems, principal activities (or critical work behaviors) are expressly identified. In others they can be derived. As an illustration, consider Exhibit 8.2, a portion of a hypothetical job description for an accounting supervisor. As Exhibit 8.2 indicates, this job involves eight principal activities.

2. *Rate each principal activity in terms of time/frequency, importance, consequence of error, and level of difficulty.* It has long been recognized that rating job activities simply in terms of the time or frequency with which each is performed is an incomplete indication of the overall weight to be assigned to each activity. For example, a nurse may spend most of the work week doing the routine tasks of patient care. However, suppose the nurse must respond to one medical emergency per week that requires, on an average, one hour of his or her time. To be sure, the time/frequency of this activity is short, but its importance is critical, its level of difficulty is high, and the consequence of an error may be the loss of a life. In fact, to derive a more accurate indication of the overall weight to be assigned each principal activity, four ratings are needed: time/frequency, importance, consequence of error, and level of difficulty. Each of these should be expressed on a scale that has a zero point so that in theory it is possible to indicate complete absence of a property. Sample rating scales for principal activities are shown in Exhibits 8.3, 8.4, and 8.5. The definitions of various levels of difficulty in Exhibit 8.4 are used to rate managerial jobs. They can easily be modified (especially levels 0 and 1) for lower level jobs to reflect more accurately a 0 or 1 level of difficulty.

3. *Multiply the numerical rating for time/frequency, importance, consequence of error, and level of difficulty for each principal activity.* The purpose of this step is to develop an overall relative weight to assign each principal

Exhibit 8.2   Portion of a Job Description for an Accounting Supervisor

Function: Under general supervision of the Manager-Accounting (Accounts analysis and Bills and Vouchers) Supervises the Accounts Payable System of the Central Region.

Know How: This position is responsible, through subordinates, for the processing, payment, and journalization of suppliers' bills (all bills except those handled by inter-company settlement) and employees' expense vouchers through input to the accounts payable system. Bills and vouchers are received along with authorization forms from company employees initiating the expense. The following steps then take place:

> Receive summaries and log into accounts payable system by office, summary, and total dollars for control purposes.
>
> Edit for correctness, for example proper authorization or coding.
>
> Enter bill and voucher information into accounts payable system for check issuance and subsequently into mechanized system for journalization.
>
> Return erroneous bills and vouchers to employee originating for correction and then correct the initial cumulative total in accounts payable system.
>
> Update the master file of suppliers contained in system.

Incumbent is directly responsible for the manual processing, payment, and journalization of special bills that cannot be processed via computer (for example, relocation expenses, tuition aid, employee refunds and commissions) and various special reports. Also responsible for the issuance of Forms 1099—U.S. Information Return-to-suppliers and the Internal Revenue Service.

Incumbent must have a thorough knowledge of accounting principles, of the accounts payable data entry system, and of the bill payment process. Also needed is a familiarity with disbursement accounting practices and other guides and reference manuals. Incumbent must have analytical and investigative ability, communicative skills, mathematical aptitude, and supervisory skills.

Subordinates consist of eleven Senior Clerks.

Principal Activities

1. Performs normal supervisory functions.
2. Receives questions on billing problems from suppliers. Investigates and furnishes answers, expedites late checks.

Exhibit 8.2 (continued)

3. Adjudicates bills and vouchers for legitimacy of purpose or amount when clerks cannot make determination. Contacts originators at all levels of management when necessary.

4. Verifies and signs reports sent to Corporate Books and other departments.

5. Performs immediate action in the event of computer problems, notifies programmer if necessary.

6. Interprets procedural changes, trains subordinates or arranges for formal training.

7. Coordinates the review of bills and vouchers by internal and external auditors or state authorities.

8. Ensures implementation of proper security precautions.

Problem Solving: The incumbent's major problems involve questions from subordinates and other departments regarding correct chargeable account, if expenditure is reimbursable, etc.; investigating and answering suppliers' inquiries regarding late or improper payment of bills; maintaining work production with a consistently changing force; contending with computer breakdowns.

Accountability: Incumbent in this position is accountable for receiving, logging, totaling, editing, payment, and journalization of all company vouchers and bills (except those handled through inter-company settlements) for the Central Region. Incumbent is also accountable for acting as the information center where suppliers and other departments can call to have their questions answered regarding bill payments and voucher processing information. Subordinates' salaries approximately $XXX,000 annually.

$$\text{Bills processed} = \$\text{XX},000 \text{ per month}$$
$$\text{Totaling} = \$\text{XX}.\text{X million}$$

activity. The ratings are multiplied together so that if a zero rating is assigned to any category, the relative weight of that principal activity is zero. Thus, if an activity is never done, or it is totally unimportant, or there is absolutely no consequence of an error, or there is zero difficulty associated with its performance, then the relative weight for that activity should be zero. As an illustration, let us present hypothetical ratings of the

Exhibit 8.3   CREPID Rating Scales for Principal Activities

1. *Time/frequency*: Please rate each principal activity on a 0–100 scale. Stepping back and looking at the whole job, say, over a one-year period, how would you allocate the principal activities in terms of the time/ frequency with which each is done so that the percentages total 100 percent?

2. *Importance*: Please rate each principal activity on a 0–7 scale that reflects, in your opinion, how important that principal activity is to overall job performance. Use the scale below as a guide to help you rate.

0	1	2	3	4	5	6	7
of no importance		moderately important		very important		of greatest importance	

3. *Consequence of error*: Again rate each principal activity on a 0–7 scale that reflects, in your opinion, the consequences of an error in that principal activity. In other words, as far as ongoing operations are concerned, how serious are an employee's mistakes in doing that principal activity?

0	1	2	3	4	5	6	7
error is of no consequence	slightly serious consequences		moderately serious consequences		extremely serious consequences		

4. *Level of difficulty*: See attached "Level of Difficulty" rating form (Exhibit 8.4).

eight principal activities identified for the accounting supervisor's job shown in Exhibit 8.2

Principal activity	Time/ frequency	× Importance	× Consequence of error	× Level of difficulty	=	Total	Relative weight (%)
1	25	4	5	4	=	2,000	15.7
2	35	7	6	5	=	7,350	57.6
3	10	5	5	6	=	1,500	11.8
4	5	3	4	2	=	120	0.9
5	5	7	6	2	=	420	3.3
6	10	4	5	1	=	200	1.6
7	5	3	7	3	=	315	2.5
8	5	6	7	4	=	840	6.6
						12,745	100.0%

Exhibit 8.4 CREPID Rating Scale for Level of Difficulty
(Management Jobs)

Level	Definition
0	Inputs, outputs, tools, equipment, and procedures are all specified. Almost everything the worker needs to know is contained in his or her assignment. The worker is supposed to turn out a specified amount of work or a standard number of units per hour or day.
1	Inputs, outputs, tools, and equipment are all specified, but the worker has some leeway in the procedures and methods used to get the job done. Almost all the information needed is in his or her assignment. Production is measured on a daily or weekly basis.
2	Inputs and outputs are specified, but the worker has considerable freedom as to procedures and timing, including the use of tools and equipment. He or she has to refer to several standard sources for information (handbooks, catalogs, wall charts). Time to complete a particular product or service is specified, but this varies up to several hours.
3	Output (product or service) is specified in the assignment, which may be in the form of a memorandum or of a schematic (sketch or blueprint). The worker must work out ways of getting the job done, including selection of tools and equipment, sequence of operations (tasks), and obtaining important information (handbooks, etc.). The worker may either carry out work him- or herself or set up standards and procedures for others.
4	Same as 3 above, but in addition the worker is expected to know and employ theory to understand the whys and wherefores of the various options that are available for dealing with a problem and can independently select among them. The worker may have to do some reading in the professional and/or trade literature in order to gain this understanding.
	Various possible outputs are described that can meet stated technical or administrative needs. The worker

5	must investigate the various possible outputs and evaluate them in regard to performance characteristics and input demands. This usually requires creative use of theory well beyond referring to standard sources. There is no specification of inputs, methods, sequences, sources, or the like.
6	There is some question as to what the need or problem really is or what directions should be pursued in solving it. In order to define it, control and explore the behavior of the variables, and formulate possible outputs and their performance characteristics, the worker must consult largely unspecified sources of information, and devise investigations, surveys, or data analysis studies.
7	Information and/or direction comes to the worker in terms of needs (tactical, organizational, strategic, financial). The worker must call for staff reports and recommendations concerning methods of dealing with them. He or she coordinates both organizational and technical data in order to make decisions and determinations regarding courses of action (outputs) for major sections (divisions, groups) of the organization.

After all the multiplication is done, the overall ratings assigned each principal activity are totaled (12,745 in the example above). The overall rating for each principal activity is then divided by the grand total to derive the relative weight for that activity (for example, 2000 ÷ 12,745 = 0.157 or 15.7 percent). Knowing each principal activity's relative weight allows us to allocate proportional shares of the employee's overall salary to each principal activity. This is done in step 4.

4. *Assign dollar values to each principal activity.* Take an average (or weighted average) annual rate of pay for all participants in the study (employees in a particular job class), and allocate it across principal

Exhibit 8.5   CREPID Summary Rating Form For Principal Activities

Principal Activity	Time/ Frequency	Importance	Consequence of Error	Level of Difficulty
1				
2				
3				
4				
5				
6				
7				
8				
•				
•				
•				
N				
	100%			

activities according to the relative weights obtained in step 3.

To illustrate, suppose the annual salary of each accounting supervisor is $35,000.

Principal activity	Relative weight (%)	Dollar value
1	15.7	5,495
2	57.6	20,160
3	11.8	4,130
4	0.9	315
5	3.3	1,155
6	1.6	560
7	2.5	875
8	6.6	2,310
		$35,000

5. *Rate performance on each principal activity on a zero to two hundred scale.* Now that we know what each employee does, the relative weight of each principal activity, and the dollar value of each principal activity, the next task is to determine *how well* the employee does each principal activity. The higher the rating on each principal activity, the greater the economic value of that activity to the organization. CREPID uses magnitude estimation (Stevens, 1971) to obtain information on performance.

In order to use this procedure, a value (say 100) is assigned to a referent concept (for example, the average employee, one at the fiftieth percentile in job performance), and then all comparisons are made relative to this value. Discussions with operating managers indicated that, given current selection procedures, it is highly unlikely that even the very best employee is more than twice as effective as the worst employee. Thus a continuous 0–200 scale was used to rate each employee on each principal activity. The actual form used is shown in Exhibit 8.6. Managers reported that they found this format helpful and easy to use.

Exhibit 8.6   Performance Appraisal Form Used with CREPID

In this last part of the exercise we would like you to rate the job performance of your subordinate, _____, relative to the principal activities identified in Part I. Use the rating scale below for each of the principal activities listed in the job analysis to rate your subordinate.

0	50	100	150	200
	better than 25% of employees I've seen do this activity	better than 50%	better than 75%	better than 99%

In your opinion, based on the principal activities described in the job analysis and relative to others you have seen do these activities, how does the job performance of _____ compare? (Use any number of the 0–200 scale shown above.)

Principal Activity   *Points Assigned*

1   _____

2   _____

3   _____

4   _____

5   _____

6   _____

7   _____

8   _____

6. *Multiply the point rating (expressed as a decimal number) assigned to each principal activity by the activity's dollar value.* To illustrate, suppose the following point totals are assigned to accounting supervisor C. P. Ayh:

Principal activity	*Points assigned*	×	*Dollar value of activity*	=	*Net dollar value*
1	1.35		5,495	=	7,418.25
2	1.00		20,160	=	20,160.00
3	1.25		4,130	=	5,162.50
4	2.00		315	=	630.00
5	1.00		1,155	=	1,155.00
6	0.50		560	=	280.00
7	0.75		875	=	656.25
8	1.50		2,310	=	3,465.00

7. *Compute the overall economic value of each employee's job performance by adding the results of step 6.* In our example, the overall economic value of Mr. Ayh's job performance is $38,927 or $3,927 more than he is being paid.

8. *Over all employees in the study, compute the mean and standard deviation of dollar-valued job performance.* When CREPID was tested at a Bell operating company, the mean of dollar-valued job performance was only $177 more than the average salary of all employees in the study, but the standard deviation (SD_y) was over $17,000. Thus supervisors reported very high variability in the job performance of their subordinates. This was not due to the tendency of some supervisors to rate their subordinates high and others to rate low. In fact, the lowest range of difference (highest minus lowest rating assigned to subordinates' job performance) for any individual supervisor was about $15,000. As we shall see in Chapter 9, this is precisely the type of situation where valid selection procedures have the greatest payoff—when individual differences in job performance are high, and therefore the cost of error is substantial.

It is important to point out that CREPID requires only two sets of ratings from a supervisor: (1) a rating of each principal activity in terms of time/frequency, importance, consequence of error, and level of difficulty (this is the job analysis phase); and (2) a rating of a specific subordinate's performance on each principal activity (this is the performance appraisal phase). The actual identification of principal activities (step 1), multiplication of the numerical ratings assigned during the job analysis phase (step 3), the assignment of dollar values to each principal activity (step 4), and the determination of the overall economic value of job performance (steps 6, 7, and 8) is done by personnel specialists. A summary of the entire CREPID procedure is presented in Exhibit 8.7.

This completes our review of the three procedures for estimating the economic value of job performance. Each provides an estimate of SD_y, the major stumbling block to wider use of the powerful Brogden-Cronbach-Gleser utility model. While the three procedures differ in terms of time, cost, and ease of use, particular circumstances might well dictate a preference for a specific method. Given the range of options now available for estimating SD_y, there should be no excuse for failure to make utility analysis an integral part of the justification for personnel programs. In our next chapter we will show how such justification can and has been done.

Exhibit 8.7   Summary of the Cascio-Ramos Procedure for Determining the Economic Value of Management Performance

---

1. Identify principal activities.

2. Rate each principal activity in terms of time/frequency, importance, consequence of error, and level of difficulty.

3. Multiply the numerical rating for time/frequency, importance, consequence of error, and level of difficulty for each principal activity.

4. Assign dollar values to each principal activity. Take an average rate of pay of participants in the study and allocate it across principal activities according to the results obtained in step 3.

5. Rate each principal activity on a 0–200 point scale.

6. Multiply (for each principal activity) its dollar value by point rating assigned (expressed as a decimal number).

7. Compute overall economic value of job performance by adding together results of step 6.

8. Over all employees in the study, compute the mean and standard deviation of dollar-valued job performance.

Exercises

1. Divide into four-to-six-person teams and do either a or b depending on feasibility.

   a. Choose a production job at a fast food restaurant and, using the standard costing approach described by Roche (1961), estimate the mean and standard deviation of dollar-valued job performance.

   b. The Tiny Company manufactures components for word processors. Most of the work is done at the 2000-employee Tiny plant in the midwest. Your task is to estimate the mean and standard deviation of dollar-valued job performance for Assembler-1s (about 200 employees). You are free to make any assumptions you like about the Tiny Assembler-1s, but be prepared to defend your assumptions. List and describe all of the factors (along with how you would measure each one) your team would consider in using standard costing to estimate SD_y.

2. Using the instructions provided for the Schmidt et al. (1979) global estimation procedure, each class member should attempt to estimate the mean, standard deviation, standard error of the mean $SD/\sqrt{N}$, and 90 percent confidence interval[4] for the mean value of a stockbroker working for a major brokerage firm in New York. Each class member should make three estimates of the dollar value to the firm: (a) the value of a stockbroker at the fiftieth percentile in merit, (b) at the eighty-fifth percentile in merit, and (c) at the fifteenth percentile in merit. For purposes of this exercise, accuracy of your estimates is less important than your understanding of the process and mechanics fo the estimation procedure.

3. Jim Hill is manager of subscriber accounts for the Prosper Company. The results of a job analysis indicate that Jim's job includes four principal activities. A summary of Jim's superior's ratings of the activities and Jim's performance of each of them is shown here.

---

[4]A 90 percent confidence interval for the mean may be calculated by the following formula: $\overline{X} \pm 1.64\ SD/\sqrt{N}$. The interpretation of the result is: if we were to repeat the above procedure often, each time selecting a different sample from the same population, then, on the average, 90 out of every 100 similar intervals obtained would contain the true value of the population mean.

Principal activity	Time/ frequency	Importance	Consequence of error	Level of difficulty	Performance rating (points)
1	30	3	5	3	1.00
2	20	5	3	5	2.00
3	40	2	1	2	0.50
4	10	7	6	4	1.00

Assuming Jim is paid $30,000 per year, use CREPID to estimate the overall economic value of Jim's job performance.

References

BROGDEN, H. E., and TAYLOR, E. K. "The Dollar Criterion—Applying the Cost Accounting Concept to Criterion Construction." *Personnel Psychology*, 1950, 3:133–154.

CRONBACH, L. J., and GLESER, G. C., eds. *Psychological Tests and Personnel Decisions*. Urbana: University of Illinois Press, 1965.

HORNGREN, C. T. *Cost Accounting: A Managerial Emphasis*. 3rd ed. Englewood Cliffs, N.J.: Prentice-Hall, 1972

HOWARD, R. A., ed. *Proceedings of the Fourth International Conference on Operational Research*. New York: John Wiley & Sons, 1966.

HOWARD, R. A., MATHESON, J. E., and NORTH, D. W. "The Decision to Seed Hurricanes." *Science*, 1972, 176:1191–1202.

MATHESON, J. E. "Decision Analysis Practice: Examples and Insights." *Proceedings of the Fifth International Conference on Operational Research* (OR 69). London: Tavistock, 1969.

ROCHE, W. J., JR. "The Cronbach-Gleser Utility Function in Fixed Treatment Employee Selection." (Doctoral dissertation, Southern Illinois University, 1961.) *Dissertation Abstracts International*, 1961–1962, 22:4413. (University Microfilms No. 62–1570.) Portions reproduced in L. J. Cronbach & G. C. Gleser, eds., *Psychological Tests and Personnel Decisions*. Urbana: University of Illinois Press, 1965.

SCHMIDT, F. L., HUNTER, J. E., MCKENZIE, R. C., and MULDROW, T. W. "Impact of Valid Selection Procedures on Work-Force Productivity." *Journal of Applied Psychology*, 1979, 64:609–626.

STEVENS, S. S. "Issues in Psychophysical Measurement." *Psychological Review*, 1971, 78:426–450.

9

Valid Selection
Procedures Can Pay Off

In Chapters 7 and 8 we introduced the concept of utility analysis, described the assumptions and data requirements of alternative utility models, and presented methods for estimating the economic value of each employee's job performance. Our objective in this chapter is to tie these ideas together to demonstrate how they can and have been applied in work settings. We will show how valid selection (or promotion) procedures can save organizations nationwide millions of dollars annually. The gains that can be realized have not yet been recognized because utility analysis has not been widely used. However, as the pressure increases on personnel executives to justify new or continuing personnel programs in the face of budgetary constraints and escalating personnel costs, one might expect that those programs that can be justified economically will be most likely to be retained. As examples of the savings to be expected from valid selection procedures, we will present results from three studies previously mentioned: the Roche (1961) study of radial drill operators; the Schmidt, Hunter, McKenzie, and Muldrow (1979) study of computer programmers in ten federal agencies; and the Cascio and Silbey (1979) study of the assessment center in a sales organization.

The Utility of a Selection Test for Radial Drill Operators

As we noted in Chapter 8, the average payoff of a radial drill operator (RDO-1) was calculated as the hourly profit at standard production ($5.51 in 1961 dollars) multiplied by his or her corrected performance ratio (the burden adjustment). The standard deviation of this distribution (SD_e) was $0.585 in 1961 dollars.

Calculation of Savings

Determination of the Validity of Test Performance (r_{ye}) Validities were determined by computing the Pearson product-moment correlations between payoff-values and scores on the following predictors: The Personnel Test (Wonderlic, Form F), the Test of Mechanical Comprehension (Bennett, Form AA), the Cornell Word Form, and the Cornell Selectee Index. These tests comprised the basic battery used in the selection of factory personnel by the company. Among the test-payoff correlations, only the correlation with the Test of Mechanical Comprehension was significant ($r = 0.313$). Thus utility was computed only for this variable.

Determination of the Ordinate Corresponding to the Selection Ratio Used $\lambda(y')$ To determine the cutoff point at and above which selection is made, company records were checked for the ten years preceding the study. During this time the company's average selection ratio for factory personnel was 0.33. The ordinate was therefore set at the point corresponding to this selection ratio. (To verify this, consult a table of areas of the normal curve, find 0.33 under "area in the smaller portion," and read the ordinate corresponding to this area.) In other words, it was assumed that RDO-1s are taken at random from the highest third of the test-score distribution of applicants. Assuming a normal distribution, $\lambda(y')$ is therefore 0.366.

Determination of the Cost of Testing (c_y) Only the actual cost of the tests used in the employment battery was considered in the determination of c_y, since some of the pertinent cost elements were already included in the burden factor (for example, management personnel salaries, rental of office space, heat, light, and taxes). The cost of each test was taken from the most recent publisher's catalogue. Since the element SD_e is expressed in dollars per hour it was necessary to express the cost of testing in comparable units. Cost of testing must be distributed over the period of time that an employee can be expected to work as a radial drill operator. For purposes of the study it was assumed that an employee will work in this classification for one year, or 2,080 hours. (This estimate is very conservative, since company records indicate that most RDO-1 employees remain in that job for more than one year.) In determining c_y, the cost of those not selected must also be included in the cost of those selected. The cost of testing per employee selected, in dollars per hour, is arrived at by multiplying the cost of one battery of tests by three (three persons are tested for each one hired), and dividing by 2,080 (hours per year). The total cost of the test battery per applicant in 1961 was $0.117. The cost of testing per employee selected is therefore: (.117 × 3)/2,080 or approximately $0.0002 per hour.

Computation of ΔU For the Mechanical Comprehension Test (the only significant predictor), the gain in utility per person selected (ΔU) was computed by substituting into the following equation:

$$\Delta U = SD_e r_{ye} \frac{\lambda(y')}{\phi(y')} - \frac{c_y}{\phi(y')}$$

where ΔU is the net gain in utility; SD_e is the standard deviation of the payoff; r_{ye} is the correlation of the predictor with the evaluated payoff; $\lambda(y')$ is the ordinate of the normal curve at the cutting score on the test; $\phi(y')$ is the area (upper tail) corresponding to the cutting score; and c_y is the cost of testing. The actual values included were:

$$\Delta U = (\$0.585)\,(0.313)\,\frac{(0.366)}{(0.326)} - \frac{(\$0.0002)}{(0.326)} = \$0.205$$

Therefore, when the company selects a radial drill operator on the basis of the test score rather than by a random process, the company can expect an average gain of 20 cents per hour (65 cents per hour in 1981 dollars) for the duration of his or her employment. This represents a potential gain in profit per hour of 3.7 percent at standard production (0.203 ÷ $5.51). Hence, for each RDO-1 who remains in that classification for three years (6,240 hours), the company would realize an average gain in profit of $4,056 (in 1981 dollars) by selecting RDO-1s on the basis of test scores rather than randomly. If only half of the 291 RDO-1s employed by the company remained RDO-1s for three years, the company would still save over half a million dollars ($588,120).

Discussion

Roche's (1961) study is important for three reasons. First, it demonstrates that the economic value of job performance (the dollar criterion) *can* be developed and then applied in the Brogden-Cronbach-Gleser utility model. Second, the results also demonstrate that a test of relatively low validity has appreciable practical value, as had been argued on theoretical grounds. In this case, selection with the aid of a test having a validity of 0.313 made possible an increase in earnings (before taxes and fixed charges) of 3 or 4 percent on the operation in question. Benefits of this magnitude are by no means unimportant to management. Finally, and perhaps most importantly, Roche (1961) showed that the dollar criterion can be determined even where employees in a job classification are working on different tasks, where the tasks assigned a particular employee vary from week to week, and where the tasks vary in profitability.

On the other hand, a number of questions were raised about the accuracy of the cost accounting procedures themselves. Consider the cost of testing. The analysis took into account only the cost of the tests themselves. Factors classified by the cost accountants as overhead, such as management personnel salaries, cost of utilities, and rent, were included in the determination of payoff rather than in c_y. The employment division of the company offered the figure of \$105.00 (\$366 in 1981 dollars) as a conservative estimate of the cost of placing a factory employee on the job. This figure includes the cost of recruiting, interviewing, and physical examination. It can be argued that a c_y that includes only the cost of tests is sufficient, because most other employment procedure costs would be constant values if tests were not used. These other costs need not be added to the determination of c_y. There are other factors recognized as important in the determination of c_y, such as the salary paid the person who administers and scores the tests, the cost of utilities for the operation of the placement testing office, and a portion of the supervising psychologist's salary. It would be impossible to extract these costs from SD_e and then add them to c_y. The chief reason for wishing to transfer these costs to c_y is that they are now treated as a charge against profits that would arise even if there were no selection testing. Cost analysts could offer no solution to this problem, and therefore these costs were left within the burden factor used in the determination of SD_e.

Secondly, Roche (1961) based his calculations on an assumed joint normal distribution of test and payoff, but as Cronbach (1965) later commented, it would have been preferable to use the *actual* joint distribution. If data are available for the total applicant population, complete information on skewness and curvature is taken into account. Roche's payoffs have a marked skew, since few workers performed far above standard. If the available data come only from workers screened by a test or by on-the-job observations, extrapolation to the total applicant population is required; even so, it might be better to compare the actual mean payoff in the selected population with that estimated for the unselected population. This estimate would depend on the regression line but would not entail an assumption of normality.

In summary, it is clear that the dollar payoff resulting from an employee's work is an elusive concept. It is also clear, as the costs of selection errors continue to grow, that the economic implications of alternative selection procedures must be examined more closely. We cannot ignore the problem of cost-benefit analysis of personnel programs. Rather we must deal directly with this issue, using the most current techniques research makes available. In our next section we will consider a more recent approach to the analysis of the utility of a selection program.

The Utility of a Selection Test for Computer Programmers

The purpose of the Schmidt et al. (1979) study of computer programmers in the federal government was to examine the productivity (economic utility) implications of a valid selection procedure (the Programmer Aptitude Test), as we pointed out in Chapter 8. A global estimation procedure was used to estimate the standard deviation of job performance in dollars (SD_e). The average SD_e estimated was $10,413 per year. The Programmer Aptitude Test (PAT) was selected for consideration because previous research had demonstrated that the total PAT score validity is high for predicting performance of computer programmers (the estimated true validity is 0.76) and that this validity is essentially constant across situations (organizations). Thus it is possible to estimate PAT payoffs in the federal government as well as in the economy as a whole. The estimated cost of the PAT per examinee is $10. The study focused on the selection of federal government computer programmers at the GS-5 through GS-9 levels. GS-5 is the lowest level in this occupational series. Beyond GS-9, it is unlikely that an aptitude test like the PAT would be used in selection: applicants for higher level programmer positions are required to have considerable expertise in programming and are selected on the basis of achievement and experience rather than directly on aptitude. The majority of programmers hired at the GS-9 level are promoted to GS-11 after one year. Similarly, all but a minority hired at the GS-5 level advance to GS-7 in one year and to GS-9 the following year. Therefore, the SD_e estimates were obtained for the GS-9 through GS-11 levels. The average yearly selection rate of GS-5 through GS-9 programmers is 618, and their average tenure is 9.69 years. On the basis of 1970 U.S. census data it was also estimated that over all, 10,210 computer programmers could be hired each year in the U.S. economy using the PAT. In view of the current rapid expansion of this occupation, it is likely that this number is a substantial underestimate.

Since it was not possible to determine the prevailing selection ratio (SR) for computer programmers either in the general economy or in the federal government, utilities were calculated for SRs of 0.05 and intervals of 0.10 from 0.10 to 0.80. The gains in utility or productivity are those that result when a valid procedure is introduced where previously no procedure or a totally invalid procedure has been used. The assumption that the true validity of the previous procedure is essentially zero may be valid in some cases, but in other situations the PAT would, if introduced, replace a procedure with lower but nonzero true validity. Hence, utilities were calculated assuming previous procedure true validities of 0.20, 0.30, 0.40, and 0.50, as well as zero.

To estimate the impact of the PAT on productivity, utilities that would result from one year's use of the PAT for selection of new programmers in the federal government and the economy as a whole were computed for each of the combinations of SR and previous procedure validity given above. When the previous procedure was assumed to have zero validity, its associated testing cost was also assumed to be zero; that is, it was assumed that no procedure was used and that otherwise prescreened applicants were hired randomly. When the previous procedure was assumed to have a nonzero validity, its associated cost was assumed to be the same as that of the PAT, that is, $10 per applicant. As mentioned above, average tenure for government programmers was found to be 9.69 years; in the absence of other information, this tenure figure was also assumed for the private sector. The average gain in utility per selectee per year was multiplied by 9.69 to give a total average gain in utility per selectee. Cost of testing was charged only to the first year. The Brogden-Cronbach-Gleser general utility equation was then modified in order to obtain the equation actually used in computing the utilities:

$$\Delta U = tN_s(r_1 - r_2)SD_e\lambda/\phi - N_s(c_1 - c_2)/\phi \qquad (1)$$

where ΔU = the gain in productivity in dollars from using the new selection procedure for one year; t = tenure in years of the average selectee (here 9.69); N_s = number selected in a given year (this figure was 618 for the federal government and 10,210 for the U.S. economy); r_1 = validity of the new procedure, here the PAT (r_1 = 0.76); r_2 = validity of the previous procedure (r_2 ranges from 0 to 0.50); c_1 = the cost per applicant of the new procedure, here $10; and c_2 = the cost per applicant of the previous procedure, here zero or $10. The terms SD_e, ϕ and λ are as defined previously. The figure for SD_e was the average of the two estimates obtained by using the global estimation procedure. Note that although this equation gives the productivity gain that results from substituting for one year the new (more valid) selection procedure for the previous procedure, these gains are not all realized the first year. They are spread out over the tenure of the new employees.

Results

Exhibit 9.1 shows the gains in productivity in millions of dollars that would result from one year's use of the PAT to select computer programmers in the federal government for different combinations of SR and previous procedure validity. As expected, these gains increase as SR decreases and as the validity of the previous procedure decreases. When SR is 0.05 and the previous procedure has no validity, use of the PAT for one year produces an aggregate productivity gain of $97.2 million. At the other extreme, if SR is 0.80 and the procedure the PAT replaces has a validity of 0.50, the gain is only $5.6 million.

To illustrate how entries for Exhibit 9.1 were derived, let us assume that the SR = 0.20 and the previous procedure has a validity of 0.30. All other terms are as defined above.

$$\Delta U = 9.69(618)(0.76 - 0.30)(10,413)(0.2789 \div 0.20)$$
$$- 618(10 - 10)/0.20$$
$$\Delta U = 9.69(618)(0.46)(10,413)(1.3945) - 0$$
$$\Delta U = 40,000,412$$

Exhibit 9.1   Estimated Productivity Increase From One Year's Use of the Programmer Aptitude Test to Select Computer Programmers in the Federal Government (in Millions of Dollars)

Selection Ratio	True Validity of Previous Procedure				
	0.00	*0.20*	*0.30*	*0.40*	*0.50*
0.05	97.2	71.7	58.9	46.1	33.3
0.10	82.8	60.1	50.1	39.2	28.3
0.20	66.0	48.6	40.0	31.3	22.6
0.30	54.7	40.3	33.1	25.9	18.7
0.40	45.6	34.6	27.6	21.6	15.6
0.50	37.6	27.7	22.8	17.8	12.9
0.60	30.4	22.4	18.4	14.4	10.4
0.70	23.4	17.2	14.1	11.1	8.0
0.80	16.5	12.2	10.0	7.8	5.6

Source: F. L. Schmidt, J. E. Hunter, R. C. McKenzie, and T. W. Muldrow. "Impact of Valid Selection Procedures on Work Force Productivity." *Journal of Applied Psychology*, 1979, 64:622.

To be sure, the figures in Exhibit 9.1 are larger than most of us would have expected; however, these figures are for total utility. The gain per selectee for any cell in the table can be obtained by dividing the cell entry by 618, the assumed yearly number of selectees. When this is done for our example above (40,000,412 ÷ 618), the gain per selectee is $64,725.59. This figure is still quite high, but remember that the gains shown in Exhibit 9.1 are produced by one year's use of the PAT. As we pointed out earlier, these gains are not all realized during the first year. They are spread out over the tenure of the new employees. Gains per year per selectee for any cell in Exhibit 9.1 can be obtained by dividing the cell entry first by 618 and then by 9.69, the average tenure of computer programmers. In our example, this produces a per year gain of $6,679.63 per selectee, or to carry it even further, a $3.21 gain per hour per year per selectee (assuming 2080 hours per work year). As might be expected, estimated productivity gains resulting from use of the PAT in the economy as a whole are even greater, exceeding $1 billion in several cells.

In addition to the assumptions of linearity of the predictor-criterion relationship and normality of dollar outcomes of job performance, the productivity gains in Exhibit 9.1 are based on two more assumptions.

The first is the assumption that selection proceeds from top-scoring applicants down until the SR has been reached. That is, these analyses assume that selection procedures are used optimally. Because of the linearity of the relation between test score and job performance, any other use of a valid test would result in lower mean productivity levels among selectees. For example, if a cutoff score were set at a point lower than that corresponding to the SR and if applicants scoring above this minimum score were then selected randomly (or selected using other nonvalid procedures or considerations), productivity gains, while still substantial, would be considerably lower than those shown in Exhibit 9.1.

The second assumption is that all applicants who are offered jobs accept and are hired. This is often not the case, and the effect of rejection of job offers by applicants is to increase the SR and thus to lower the productivity gains from selection. For example, if a SR of 0.20 would yield the needed number of new employees given no rejections by applicants and if half of all job offers are rejected, the SR must be increased to 0.40 to yield the desired number of selectees. If the validity of the previous procedure were zero, Exhibit 9.1 shows that rejection by applicants would reduce productivity gains from $66.0 to $45.6 million, a reduction of $20.4 million. If the validity of the previous procedure were not zero, job rejection by applicants would reduce both its utility and the utility of the new test. However, since the utility function is multiplicative, the utility of the more valid procedure would be reduced by a greater amount. Therefore, the utility advantage of the more valid procedure over the less valid procedure would be reduced. For example, Exhibit 9.1 shows that if the validity of the previous procedure were 0.30, the productivity advantage of the more valid test would be $40 million if the needed workers could be hired using a selection ratio of 0.20. But if half of the applicants rejected job offers, we would have to use a SR of 0.40, and the advantage of the more valid test would drop by almost 45 percent to $27.6 million. To some extent, these utility losses caused by job offer rejection can be offset by additional recruiting efforts that increase the size of the applicant pool and, therefore, restore use of smaller SRs. For more on this see Hogarth and Einhorn (1976).

Thus far we have been proceeding on the assumption that a new, more valid selection procedure is simply substituted for an older, less valid one. But work force productivity will often be optimized by combining the existing procedure and the new procedure to obtain validity higher than either procedure can provide individually. This possibility should be investigated whenever utility analysis is done.

Finally, Schmidt et al. (1979) caution that productivity gains in individual jobs from improved selection cannot be extrapolated directly to productivity gains in the composite of all jobs making up the national economy. To illustrate, if the potential gain economywide in the computer programmer occupation is \$10.78 billion and if there is a total of N jobs in the economy (that is, programmers and all other jobs), the gain to be expected from use of improved selection procedures in all N jobs will not in general be as great as N times \$10.78 billion. Since the total talent pool is not unlimited, gains due to selection in one job are partially offset by losses in other jobs. The size of the net gain for the economy depends on such factors as the number of jobs, the correlation between jobs of predicted success composites, and differences between jobs in SD_e. Nevertheless, potential net gains for the economy as a whole are large.

Evidence presented in this study, along with that of Roche (1961) and the study to be described next, leads inescapably to the conclusion that it does make a difference, an important, practical difference, how people are selected. The implications of valid selection procedures for work force productivity are clearly much greater than most of us might have suspected.

The Utility of an Assessment Center as a Selection Device

Ever since the pioneering studies by Bray (1964) at American Telephone and Telegraph in the 1950s, the assessment center approach to personnel selection has been an extremely popular technique. The attractiveness of the method is not surprising, for it is firmly rooted in sound psychometric principles. By using multiple assessment techniques, by standardizing methods of making inferences from such techniques, and by pooling the judgments of multiple assessors in rating each candidate's behavior, it is felt that the likelihood of successfully predicting performance is enhanced considerably. Reviews of the predictive validity of assessment center ratings and subsequent job performance have consistently been positive (Bray, Campbell, and Grant, 1974; Cohen, Moses, and Byham, 1974; Howard, 1974; Huck, 1973; Mitchell, 1975). Assessment centers do predict performance, and they do it well, with predictive validities in the 0.50s and 0.60s not uncommon.

In short, the assessment center has easily met the psychometric requirements of the classical validity approach to selection. Emphasis has been placed on measurement and prediction, and the primary objective has been to maximize the correlation (simple or multiple) between predicted and actual criterion scores.

Regardless of how many validity studies are conducted, however, the overall worth of the assessment center as a selection device in a particular organization or across organizations cannot definitively be established in the absence of utility analyses. The objective of the study by Cascio and Silbey (1979) is to use examples to make the utility model a more meaningful tool for those who must interpret the data from the assessment center method. The utility analysis was accomplished by means of the Brogden-Cronbach-Gleser continuous variable utility model.

Six parameters were varied systematically: the validity and cost of the assessment center, the validity of the ordinary selection procedure, the selection ratio, the standard deviation of the criterion in dollars, and the number of assessment centers. The payoff of the assessment center was then compared to an ordinary selection procedure and to random selection. By expressly including the estimated costs of recruiting, inducting, selecting, and training a sufficient number of persons to meet a quota of personnel, this model enables decision makers to evaluate the costs of alternative selection strategies in terms of their system-wide implications.

Input and Cost Assumptions

The utility model was applied to the selection and placement of second-level managers in a hypothetical firm. Since both costs and benefits can be expected to vary considerably from firm to firm, a representative range of values was used to calculate the outcomes. The impact of each parameter was determined by holding all other parameters constant while one parameter was varied. It was assumed that selection for promotion ranged from first- to second-level management; promotion from within was company policy; there was a fixed quota of fifty managers; and that half of all (within-company) candidates came from out of town. Costs for the selection and placement process included the cost of recruitment, induction and processing, training, and the selection procedure itself (either ordinary selection or selection by assessment center). Only the cost of the selection procedure differed when ordinary selection (or random selection) was compared to the assessment center procedure. However, to illustrate the systemic nature of the selection process, all costs were included in the analysis.

The following cost estimates were used: Recruitment costs consisted of $100 for in-house advertising and $200 for each of the out-of-town candidates. The number of persons recruited was determined by dividing the quota for selection (50) by the selection ratio. For example, when the selection ratio was 0.5, 100 persons would have to be recruited to meet the quota. Hence, recruitment costs were determined by the selection ratio. When the selection ratio was allowed to vary, model values ranged from 0.1 to 0.9 in steps of 0.1. When other parameters were varied, the selection ratio was set at 0.5. This value was chosen because in a typical assessment center only about half of those assessed are rated acceptable.

The cost of induction and processing was assumed to be minimal ($10 per candidate), since all candidates were current employees. This cost was held constant throughout the analysis, and its total changed only as the number of candidates changed.

Training costs were assumed to be $450 per person selected. Since a fixed quota of 50 managers was assumed, the total training cost for all selected persons was $22,500. The cost of selection was different for the ordinary procedure and for the assessment center. The overall cost of the ordinary selection procedure (a series of three interviews with third-level managers, spread over a two-day period) was estimated at $290 per candidate.

The validity of the ordinary selection procedure was another parameter varied in the model. When the validity of ordinary selection was varied, it ranged from 0.05 to 0.95 in steps of 0.05. A validity of 0.25 for the ordinary selection procedure (i.e., multiple interviews) was assumed when other parameters were varied.

Assessment center costs fell into three categories: costs of establishing the assessment center, costs of the assessors, and costs of the candidates (assessees). The costs of establishing the assessment center were estimated at $3,200; each of six assessors was estimated to cost $361 during the three days over which each assessment center was conducted (for a total of $2,166); and total candidate costs were estimated at $198 per candidate.

The number of assessment centers to be conducted was determined by the assessor-to-assessee ratio and by the number of candidates to be assessed. For the utility model a range of ratios from 1:1.5 to 1:2.5 was used. Therefore, each assessment center evaluated from 9 to 15 candidates per session. When other parameters were being varied, the number of candidates per assessment center was assumed to be approximately 12. For example, with 100 candidates, eight assessment centers (four with 12 and four with 13 candidates) would be required.

The total cost per candidate of the assessment center could not be calculated beforehand, since that cost was determined by the number of assessment centers to be conducted. Instead, costs per candidate were calculated by spreading the costs of the assessment center procedure (start-up of $3,200, assessor costs of $2,166 × the number of assessment centers, and candidate costs of $198 × the number of candidates) over all of the candidates in a particular run of the utility model.

Regardless of which other parameters were being varied, the validity of the assessment center always varied from 0.05 to 0.95. However, for comparisons, a validity of 0.35 was used. Most studies in the literature yield validities within this range (Cohen et al., 1974). The rationale underlying each of the input and cost assumptions described above is developed more fully in Cascio and Silbey, 1979.

For benefit calculations, the mean and standard deviation of the criterion distribution were determined by the global estimation procedure (Schmidt et al., 1979) outlined in Chapter 8. Average yearly dollar values for the second-level managers were about $30,000, with a standard deviation of approximately $9,500 in this firm.

This figure provides an estimate of each second-level manager's yearly value of sales to the company. For purposes of the model, we assumed that all second-level managers made approximately equal contributions to the firm. Admittedly, this is a questionable assumption, and for this reason a range of criterion standard deviations was examined. The SD_e values varied from $1,000 to $20,000 in the first year in steps of $1,000. These SD_e values center about the $9,500 value that was used as a constant when other parameters were varied.

It is important to point out that this figure is pertinent for one year only. Assuming that the average tenure of second-level managers is five years and that the average stability of performance is 0.7 from year to year, then the criterion standard deviation (SD_e) for a five-year period can be calculated using the formula for the standard deviation of a sum (Guilford, 1965, p. 542):

$$\left[SD_{(e_1 + e_2 + \ldots + e_n)}\right]^2 = S_1^2 + S_2^2 + \ldots + S_n^2 + 2r_{12}SD_1SD_2 + 2r_{13}SD_1SD_3$$

$$+ \ldots + 2r_{1n}SD_1SD_n + \ldots + 2r_{(n-1)n}SD_{(n-1)}SD_n$$

Taking the square root of both sides and substituting in our assumed values:

$$SD_e = \sqrt{5(9,500^2) + 0.7(20)(9,500)(9,500)}$$

$$SD_e = \$41,409.54$$

Output Explanation

An example of assessment center utility analysis output is presented in Exhibit 9.2. In this example there is a quota of 50 successful managers; the selection ratio is 0.5; and therefore 100 persons must be recruited. Costs per candidate are as follows: $101 for recruitment; $10 for induction and processing; $290 for ordinary selection; $403.28 for assessment center; and $450 for training. The standard deviation of the criterion distribution is $9,500 in the first year and $41,409.54 over the five-year period. The validity of the ordinary selection procedure is 0.25. Separate utility analyses are presented for the ordinary selection procedure and the assessment center.

The column labeled *incremental gain* represents the product of $NSD_e r_{ye} \lambda(_y')$, the left-hand term in the general utility equation. In this expression $SD_e r_{ye}$ is the slope of the payoff function relating expected payoff to performance on the selection measure. As can be seen, an increase in validity leads to an increase in slope, but slope also depends on the dispersion of criterion scores, a fact we shall discuss further in a following section.

The column labeled *total cost* represents the product of Nc_y, the right-hand term in the general utility equation, and the column labeled *gain in utility* represents the difference between incremental gain and total cost. It is the net gain over random selection. In the example shown in Exhibit 9.2, the total cost of selecting 50 managers using the ordinary selection procedure represents a savings of $350,356.62 over random selection, given our assumptions.

In the assessment center's utility analysis, a range of validities, varying from 0.05 to 0.95 in steps of 0.05, was examined. For each validity the incremental gain, the total cost of the assessment center procedure, and the gain in utility were computed. The gain in utility over random selection by means of the assessment center was then compared to the gain in utility using the ordinary selection procedure. The difference between these values represents the net assessment center payoff, in dollars, over the

Exhibit 9.2 Sample Utility Analysis Output

Type of Cost	Per Candidate	Total
Recruitment	$ 101.00	$10,100.00
Processing and induction	$ 10.00	$ 1,000.00
Ordinary selection	$ 290.00	$29,000.00
Assessment center	$ 403.28	$40,328.00
Training	$ 450.00	$22,500.00
	1st year	5-year total
Criterion SD	$9,500.00	$41,409.54

Ordinary Selection

Validity	Incremental gain	Total cost	Gain in utility
0.25	$412,956.62	$62,600.00	$350,356.62

Assessment Center[a]

Validity	Incremental gain	Gain in utility	Per selectee A.C. payoff[b]	Total A.C. payoff
0.05	$82,591.33	$8,663.33	$ -6,833.87	$ -341,693.30
0.10	$165,182.65	$91,254.65	$ -5,182.04	$ -259,101.98
0.15	$247,773.97	$173,845.97	$ -3,530.21	$ -176,510.65
0.20	$330,365.30	$256,437.30	$ -1,878.39	$ -93,919.32
0.25	$412,956.62	$339,028.62	$ -226.56	$ -11,328.00
0.30	$495,547.95	$421,619.95	$1,425.27	$71,263.32
0.35	$578,139.27	$504,211.27	$3,077.09	$153,854.65
0.40	$660,730.60	$586,802.60	$4,728.92	$236,445.98

0.45	$743,321.92	$669,393.92	$6,380.75	$319,037.30
0.50	$825,913.25	$751,985.25	$8,032.57	$401,628.62
0.55	$908,504.56	$834,576.56	$9,684.40	$484,219.94
0.60	$991,095.89	$917,167.89	$11,336.23	$566,811.27
0.65	$1,073,687.20	$999,759.20	$12,988.05	$649,402.58
0.70	$1,156,278.55	$1,082,350.55	$14,639.88	$731,993.92
0.75	$1,238,869.86	$1,164,941.86	$16,291.70	$814,585.23
0.80	$1,321,461.20	$1,247,533.20	$17,943.53	$897,176.58
0.85	$1,404,052.52	$1,330,124.52	$19,595.36	$979,767.89
0.90	$1,486,643.84	$1,412,715.84	$21,247.18	$1,062,359.22
0.95	$1,569,235.17	$1,495,307.17	$22,899.01	$1,144,950.55

Note. Quota for selection = 50. Selection ratio = 0.50. Ordinate at selection ratio = 0.399. Number recruited = 100. Number of assessment centers = 8.

[a]Total cost = $73,928.00

[b]A.C. = assessment center.

Source: W. F. Cascio and V. Silbey. "Utility of the Assessment Center as a Selection Device." *Journal of Applied Psychology,* 1979, 61:111.

ordinary selection procedure. This is shown both for the group as a whole (total assessment center payoff) and per selectee (per selectee assessment center payoff).

Results

The impact of each parameter was evaluated in terms of assessment center payoff per selectee. Payoff refers to the dollar amount of incremental gain (or loss if negative) accruing to a firm that uses the assessment center instead of the ordinary selection procedure. The utility analysis output shown in Exhibit 9.2 served as the basis for all calculations.

Neither variations in the number of assessment centers nor variations in the cost of the assessment center exerted any significant effects on payoffs. However, variations in selection ratio and criterion standard deviation clearly did have a major impact on payoffs. For example, consider Exhibit 9.3, which shows the effect of changes in the criterion standard deviation on the assessment center payoff per selectee. The lines from top to bottom represent five-year criterion standard deviations of $87,178, $65,389, $43,589, $21,794, and $4,359. These values correspond to first-year standard deviations of $20,000, $15,000, $10,000, $5,000, and $1,000.

All lines radiate from a point located at an assessment center validity of 0.25 and an assessment center payoff per selectee of $226.56. At this point the validity of the assessment center is equal to the validity of the ordinary selection procedure used in the utility analysis (0.25), and the assessment center payoff is equal to the difference in cost between the assessment center and the ordinary selection procedure.

As can be seen from Exhibit 9.3, the larger the criterion standard deviation, the larger the payoff of the assessment center, assuming, of course, that assessment center validity exceeds the validity of the ordinary selection procedure.

Variations in the validity of the ordinary selection procedure and the validity of the assessment center also had a major impact on payoffs. Since the impact on payoff of increasing the ordinary selection procedure's validity is equivalent to lowering the assessment center's validity, the discussion of these changes can be combined. Ordinary selection procedure validities varied from 0.05 to 0.95 and resulted in assessment center payoffs at an assessment center validity of 0.35 ranging from $9,684 to −$20,048. To put the magnitude of these changes in perspective, consider that the slope of the regression line relating payoff to validity (33,036.53) indicates

Exhibit 9.3   Effect of Variations in Criterion Standard Deviation (σ_e) and Assessment Center Validity on Assessment Center Payoff

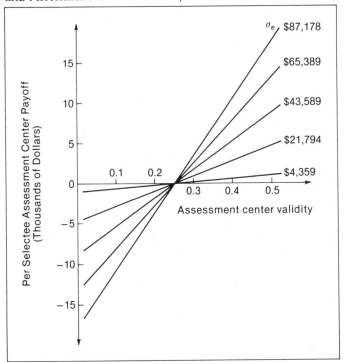

Source: W. F. Cascio and V. Silbey. "Utility of the Assessment Center as a Selection Device." *Journal of Applied Psychology,* 1979, 64, 113.

that for every change of 0.01 in validity, the payoff would change by $330.37. The only difference is that when the change means an increase in validity for the ordinary selection procedure, then assessment center payoff decreases; and when the change means an increase in assessment center validity, then the assessment center payoff increases.

Conclusion

One of the most significant impacts on assessment center payoff appears to come from the size of the criterion standard deviation. It is in this respect that the assessment center can make a major contribution to a selection program—when individual differences in criterion performance are large and significant—yet the classical validity approach to selection ignores this fact. In fact, even when the standard deviation of the criterion distribution is as low as $5,000 in the first year, assessment centers with validities of only 0.1 still show positive gains in utility over random selection. It should also be noted, however, that since the ordinary selection procedure is cheaper, it demonstrates positive utility over random selection at even lower criterion standard deviations. This study also demonstrated when Brogden pointed out in 1949: since gains in utility depend on the product $r_{ye}SD_e$ and since a large SD_e indicates that individual differences in criterion performance have large practical importance, predictors with low validity may still yield considerable benefit if SD_e is large. Conversely, procedures with high validity may be less useful if individual differences in payoff are small. These results demonstrate that validities must be considered not in isolation but in comparison to other parameters.

The cost of the assessment center played a relatively minor role in determining payoffs. At first glance this may seem surprising, but when one stops to consider that for many jobs the standard deviation of criterion outcomes can be as high as $15,000 to $20,000 in the first year (and $65,000 to $87,000 over five years), the increased cost of a more valid selection procedure may be a small price to pay for the long-term payoff that the procedure may provide.

This completes our three-chapter look at utility analysis. Although the theory itself is fairly well developed, many more practical applications are needed to enhance our understanding of the actual gains to be derived from valid selection procedures. The term *selection procedures* is intended to be broad. Just like the legal definition of a test, a selection procedure refers to any basis for an employment decision. This may include, for example, a written test, an assessment center, a polygraph examination, or a training program. As long as results from the procedure can be quantified and correlated with dollar-valued job performance, the general utility equation can be used. Indeed, even when the general utility equation cannot be used, the model on which it is based should still guide decisions that are made. In this sense utility analysis is more than an equation or series of equations: it is a stimulating way of thinking.

Exercises

1. You are given the following information regarding the CAP test for clerical personnel (clerk-2s) at the Berol Corporation:

average tenure as a clerk-2: 7.26 years

number selected per year: 120

validity of the CAP test: 0.61

validity of previously used test: 0.18

cost per applicant of CAP: $8

cost per applicant of old test: $5

SR: 0.50

ordinate at SR: 0.399

SD_e in first year: $3,000

Determine (a) the total utility of the CAP test; (b) utility per selectee; (c) per year gain in utility per selectee.

2. The Top Dollar Co. is trying to decide whether to use an assessment center to select middle managers for its consumer products operations. The following information has been determined:

recruitment cost: $500

induction and processing cost: $100

ordinary selection procedure cost: $500

assessment center cost: $2,000

training cost: $3,000

first year criterion SD: $25,000

validity of ordinary selection procedure: 0.20

validity of assessment center: 0.50

quota for selection: 75

selection ratio: 0.20

ordinate at SR: 0.2789

average tenure as a middle manager: 8 years

average stability of performance across years: 0.70

Should management adopt the assessment center to select middle managers? Why? What payoffs can be expected (a) in total, (b) per selectee, and (c) per selectee in the first year?

3. In problem 2, suppose that Top Dollar, upon closer investigation, learns the following:

The first year criterion SD is only $10,000.

The validity of the assessment center is really 0.30.

Should management still use the assessment center to select middle managers? Based on the new information, what has been the *change* in total payoff, payoff per selectee, and first year payoff per selectee?

References

BRAY, D. W. "The Management Progress Study." *American Psychologist,* 1964, 19:419–420.

BRAY, D. W., CAMPBELL, R. J., and GRANT, D. C. *Formative Years in Business: A Long-Term AT&T Study of Managerial Lives.* New York: Wiley, 1974.

BROGDEN, H. E. "When Testing Pays Off." *Personnel Psychology,* 1949, 2:171–183.

CASCIO, W. F., and SILBEY, V. "Utility of the Assessment Center as a Selection Device." *Journal of Applied Psychology,* 1979, 64:107–118.

COHEN, B. M., MOSES, J. L., and BYHAM, W. C. *The Validity of Assessment Centers: A Literature Review* (Monograph 2). Pittsburgh, Pa.: Development Dimensions Press, 1974.

CRONBACH, L. J. Comments on "A Dollar Criterion in Fixed-Treatment Employee Selection." In L. J. CRONBACH, G. C. GLESER, eds., *Psychological Tests and Personnel Deicisions.* 2nd ed. Urbana: University of Illinois Press, 1965.

GUILFORD, J. P. *Fundamental Statistics in Psychology and Education,* 4th ed. New York: McGraw-Hill, 1965.

HOGARTH, R. M., and EINHORN, H. J. "Optimal Strategies for Personnel Selection When Candidates Can Reject Offers." *Journal of Business,* 1976, 49:478–495.

HOWARD, A. "An Assessment of Assessment Centers." *Academy of Management Journal,* 1974, 17:115–134.

HUCK, J. R. "Assessment Centers: A Review of the External and Internal Validities." *Personnel Psychology,* 1973, 26:191–212.

MITCHELL, J. O. "Assessment Center Validity: A Longitudinal Study." *Journal of Applied Psychology,* 1975, 60:573–579.

ROCHE, W. J., Jr. "The Cronbach-Gleser Utility Function in Fixed Treatment Employee Selection." (Doctoral dissertation, Southern Illinois University, 1961.) *Dissertation Abstracts International,* 1961–1962, 22:4413. (University Microfilms No. 62–1570.) Portions reproduced in L. J. CRONBACH and G. C. GLESER, eds., *Psychological Tests and Personnel Decisions.* Urbana: University of Illinois Press, 1965.

SCHMIDT, F. L., HUNTER, J. E., MCKENZIE, R. C., and MULDROW, T. W. "Impact of Valid Selection Procedures on Work-Force Productivity." *Journal of Applied Psychology,* 1979, 64:609–626.

10

Estimating the Costs and Benefits of Human Resource Development Programs

Organizations in the United States spend at least $137 billion each year for training (McKeon, 1981). This astonishingly high figure reflects (1) the aggregate cost of keeping abreast of technological and social changes, (2) the extent of managerial commitment to achieving a competent, productive work force, and (3) the broad array of opportunities available for individuals to improve their productive and social skills. Mills (1975) coined the term *human resource development* (HRD) to represent the wide range of behavioral science and management technologies intended to improve both the operating effectiveness of a firm and the quality of working life experienced by its employees. The technologies range from basic skills training to job enrichment and training in interpersonal skills, team building, and decision making (see Goldstein, 1980 for a thorough review). Unfortunately, while $137 billion may be spent providing training and development programs, little is spent assessing the social and financial outcomes of these activities. As a result, there is little comparative evidence by which to evaluate the impact and generalizability of the various technologies (Kahn, 1974). Decision makers thus remain unguided by systematic evaluations of past experiments and uninformed about the costs and benefits of alternative HRD programs when considering training efforts in their own organizations. "Millions for training, but not one cent for evaluation" is an exaggerated, but not altogether untrue, characterization of present training practice in many organizations.

Our intent in this chapter is not to present true experimental or quasi-experimentral designs for evaluating HRD programs (see Cascio, 1982, Chap. 15; also Cook and Campbell, 1979). Rather, it is to illustrate how the economic consequences of HRD programs can be expressed. To do so we present three very different examples of efforts to assess the financial impact of specific programs. Let us begin by considering how to determine the true cost of off-site meetings.

Example 1: Determining Off-Site Meeting Costs

Off-site meetings, those conducted away from organizational property, are becoming increasingly popular for a variety of purposes: for conducting HRD programs, for communicating information, for strategic planning, and for decision making. In many cases, however, the true dollar costs of an off-site meeting remain unknown as long as attendee costs are not included in the final tally along with the direct and obvious expenses. The method described here enables planners to compute actual off-site meeting costs and in addition offers two advantages: the identification and the evaluation of the dollars invested in each type of activity included in the program.

The method for costing off-site meetings was developed by McKeon (1981). We make the following assumptions about a hypothetical firm, Valco Ltd. The firm has five hundred employees, including one hundred first-line supervisors and management personnel. A total of ten days of off-site meetings per year (either training sessions or various types of meetings for managers) are held under the general planning and direction of Valco's training department (one manager and one secretary). Outside speakers and consultants are engaged to develop and conduct the meetings. On the average, twenty managers attend each meeting, and the typical meeting lasts two full days. Costs shown in Exhibit 10.1 are based on these figures.

These estimates are broad averages intended only to create a model for purposes of comparison. Note that no attempt is made to place a dollar

Exhibit 10.1 Cost Breakdown for an Off-Site Management Meeting

Cost Elements	Total Costs	Cost Per Participant Per Day
A. Development of programs (figured on an annual basis)		
1. Training department overhead		
2. Training staff salaries		
3. Use of outside consultants		
4. Equipment and materials for meeting (films, supplies, workbooks)	$100,000	$100[1]
B. Participant cost (figured on an annual basis)		
1. Salaries and benefits of participants (figured for average participant)	$20,000	
2. Capital investment in participants (based on an average of various industries from *Fortune* magazine)	$25,000	
	$ 45,000	190.68[2]
C. Delivery of one meeting for 20 persons		
1. Facility costs		
a. Sleeping rooms	1,000	
b. Three meals daily	800	
c. Coffee breaks	60	
d. Misc. tips, telephone	200	
e. Reception	200	
	2,260	56.50[3]

Exhibit 10.1 (continued)

2. Meeting charges
   a. Room rental
   b. A/V rental
   c. Secretarial services
3. Transportation to the meeting   2,500   62.50[4]

Summary: Total Per Day Per Person Cost

A. Development of programs	$ 100
B. Participant cost	190
C. Delivery of one meeting (hotel and transportation)	119
Total	$ 409

Note: Meeting duration: two full days. Number of attendees: 20 people. These costs do not reflect a figure for the productive time lost of the people in the program. If that cost were added—and it would be realistic to do so—the above cost would increase dramatically.

[1]To determine per day cost, divide $100,000 by number of meeting days held per year (10). Then divide answer ($10,000) by total number of management people (100) attending all programs = $100 per day of a meeting.

[2]To determine per day cost, divide total of $45,000 by 236 (average number of working days in a year) = $190.68 per day of work year.

[3]To determine per day, per person cost, divide group total ($2,260) by number of participants (20) and then divide resulting figure ($113) by number of meeting days (2) = $56.50 per day.

[4]To determine per day, per person cost, divide group total ($2,500) by number of people and then divide resulting figure ($125) by number of meeting days (2) = $62.50 per day.

Source: Adapted from W. J. McKeon. "How to Determine Off-Site Meeting Costs." *Training and Development Journal,* May 1981, p. 117.

value on the loss of productive time from the job, although such costs are realistic and could also be figured into the calculations. As with the illustrations in other chapters, we have attempted to make the numbers as realistic as possible, but primary concern should be with the methodology rather than with the numbers.

As can be seen in Exhibit 10.1, the per day, per person cost of Valco's meeting comes to $409. This figure is probably far higher than most of us would have suspected. But before the decision is made simply to stop holding off-site meetings because of the expense involved, perhaps managers should first answer the following questions:

1. Are we spending the hours in our meeting day—and the dollars that they cost—so that we produce maximum benefits for participants and our organization? Surveys by the National Conference Center indicate that for a typical two-day meeting (with an overnight stay) attended by 15–30 people, approximately 15 learning-related hours are available in a 24-hour day (McKeon, 1981). Typically these hours are divided as follows:

1. presentation and discussion in principal meeting room	5.25 hours
2. assigned work in small groups	2.25
3. coffee breaks	0.67
4. three meals	3.00
5. cocktail party	0.75
6. other socializing with participants	0.75
7. participation in outdoor or indoor recreation (possibly learning related)	1.00
8. individual reading or other work related to program	1.33
	15.00 hours

Training managers should ask how meeting days in their organization compare to these figures.

2. How can we schedule, design, and pace our meeting day (and the learning environment within it) to maximize the impact of our fifteen learning hours? To be sure, much of the increasing cost of training (from an overall estimated bill of $100 billion in 1976 to $137 billion in 1981)

is beyond the training manager's ability to control: the spiraling costs of wages, benefits, overhead, and capital investment per employee. What the training manager can control is subject matter, methods, and what is being given greater attention—the environment in which the meeting takes place.

The influence of the environment on training is the chief reason cited for selecting an outside facility for a meeting. Not only can a professionally designed and operated meeting facility make a meeting more productive, it can also make that meeting more enjoyable. The task for decision makers is to consider whether facility costs as a percentage of the total—that is, the total of the true meeting costs identified—will or will not be offset by a corresponding increase in learning effectiveness. In the example shown in Exhibit 10.1, the cost per person, per day was $409. If an additional $10, $20, or even $30 was added per day to hold the meeting in a superior facility, the extra cost would be 5 to 7 percent. However, if learning effectiveness were increased by a factor of greater than 10 percent—and over 20 percent is a realistic possibility—the desirability of the tradeoff is obvious. In short, it is only by considering all of the factors that have an impact on learning effectiveness—program planning and administration, trainer, program delivery, and environment in which the learning takes place—that the time and dollars spent on training can yield the greatest return on this substantial investment in people.

Example 2: The Value of Structured Versus Unstructured Training in Basic Skills

In broad terms, industrial training may be characterized as structured or unstructured. The term *structure* implies a systematically developed educational program designed to train a new worker in a logical progression from no job competency to a specified mastery of the job. The trainee is the focal point of the training effort. Unstructured training, on the other hand, implies on-the-job training of a new worker, without a specific program, by an experienced worker who simultaneously continues to perform his or her regular duties. Ongoing production output is the focal point of the worker-trainer instead of the training experience of the trainee, and mastery is not defined.

Structured job skills training is widely *assumed* to be more effective than unstructured training, although little controlled research has been done (Cullen, Sawzin, Sisson, and Swanson, 1976). To some extent this is understandable since the variables in ongoing plant operations are so complex. Controlling them in a simulation is, in itself, very difficult. Nevertheless, failure to conduct controlled studies is perhaps the most serious shortcoming of industrial training programs, many of which are, in fact, extremely well done, for there is no empirical linkage of the results of training to improved productivity. In the absence of such a connection, it should come as no surprise that training activities are often the first to go when profits tumble. This need not always be the case, as a fourteen-month study by Cullen et al. (1976) in a university industrial manufacturing laboratory indicates. The origins of the study and its financial support came from the Johns-Manville Corporation.

The Experiment

The purpose of the study was to conduct an experimental comparison of the structured versus unstructured training of semiskilled production workers. The job studied was the Rainville plastics extruder. This job was selected because it was representative of Johns-Manville (J-M) operations and because of its general difficulty of operation. The job involves processing raw materials into quality plastic pipe from a plastic extrusion machine.

There were six major steps in the development of the extruder operator structured-training program:

1. job and task analysis
2. general training-design decisions
3. specific training-design decisions
4. production of the training program
5. pilot test
6. training-program revision

Subjects responded to recruitment methods either by telephoning about the position or by applying in person. As part of the selection procedure subjects were asked to complete an application form and the Bennett Mechanical Comprehension Test. Forty subjects were selected, matched on characteristics such as age, education, community background, and test scores (to help ensure pre-experimental equivalence), and then randomly assigned to the structured and unstructured groups (twenty in each group). Measures of product quantity and quality, worker competence, cost effectiveness, and worker attitudes were as follows.

Measures of Quantity and Quality   Quantity was measured by count and weight. The quality of pipe production was based on visual and dimensional criteria. To aid visual judgments, samples of defective pipe were used as standards. The dimensional criteria of pipe roundness and concentricity required the development and validation of a mechanical test device.

Worker Competence   Worker competence was defined as the ability to start up production, to develop quality pipe, and to recover from two production problems (remotely manipulated machine variables) without a loss of production rate. A concealed closed-circuit television system was set up to monitor the extruder operator's work area and was broadcast to the project office some one-hundred feet away. In addition, all production rates and observation logs were systematically time-referenced.

Cost Effectiveness   Inputs to a cost-effectiveness model for the two industrial training methods were handled in a very practical manner: actual expenditures were used. Simply stated, the hourly rate of the research assistant performing as the industrial trainer was used, as were all the project costs, even to the point of costing out the paper on which the job analysis was written.

Worker Attitudes   A worker attitude inventory was developed to assess the attitudes of trainees toward their training and job. Content validity was established through the development of questions about attitudes toward the job, the training, the trainer, and the equipment.

Subjects in both groups were trained individually since most new workers at a J-M plant enter singly, to replace workers who have left, and not in groups. Data collecting and recording methods depended on the type of data needed. The times a trainee reported for work and ended work, the hours a subject was a trainee, and the hours a subject was a worker-trainer were recorded in a log.

To compare the material efficiency of one group to another, data were collected on production rates, production weight, and material waste (scrap). Production rate was recorded as the number of acceptable pieces of pipe extruded per hour of work. At the end of each hour the researcher collected and counted the production. The production count and weight were then recorded in the log.

The plastic determined as scrap was collected, weighed, and recorded at the end of each hour by the researcher. Scrap was defined as plastic extruded not as pipe and pipe not meeting the dimensional and visual standards. Comparisons were made between production weight and scrap weight per training group.

The attitudes of the subjects were recorded by a questionnaire completed individually at the end of the employment period.

Study Results

Time to Achieve Competence   Mean training time for individuals in the unstructured group was 16.3 hours, compared to an average of 4.6 hours for those in the structured group. This difference is statistically significant ($p < 0.005$) and indicates a 72 percent savings in training time using the structured method.

Level of Job Competence   Subjects in the structured training group achieved significantly higher ($p < 0.01$) job competence after four hours of training. Though statistically significant differences were not found at eight- and twelve-hour intervals, there were still substantial differences in training times. Certainly statistical power[1] would have been greater with a larger sample size.

Costs of Training   The $56.25 average cost to train a group of 20 extruder operators by the structured method was not significantly different ($p > 0.05$) from the $57.25 average to train an identical-size group by the unstructured method. Such a conclusion is probably an artifact of group size in this study. Normally an industrial training program would be used to train considerably more than twenty workers. As the number of trainees increases under a structured-training program, the average cost per trainee is reduced because the cost to develop a structured program is fixed while the number of trainees increases. In an unstructured approach, however, the entire cost varies directly with the number of trainees. Exhibit 10.2

---

[1]Statistical power is the probability of detecting a significant effect, given that it is indeed present.

Exhibit 10.2   Cost Comparisons Between the Unstructured and Structured Training of 1–20 Semiskilled Workers

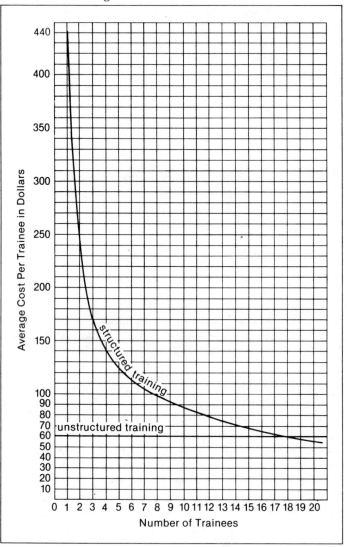

Source: J. G. Cullen, S. A. Sawzin, G. R. Sisson, and R. A. Swanson. "Training: What's It Worth?" *Training and Development Journal,* 1976, 30:17.

illustrates this break-even concept. For the extruder operator experiment, break-even was about eighteen people.

Production Losses   As might be expected, training under both the structured and unstructured methods resulted in reductions from standard minimum-production rates. The average 2.91 pounds of production loss resulting from structured training was significantly less ($p < 0.01$) than the average 9.35 pounds of production loss resulting from the unstructured training. This represents approximately a 70 percent difference in production losses between unstructured and structured training. Such a comparison can be useful in projecting the potential returns for very specific training programs.

Resolution of Production Problems   The 80 percent of success in production troubleshooting by the structured program trainees was significantly higher ($p < 0.025$) than the 33 percent rate of success by unstructured program trainees. This represents a 130 percent increase in solved production problems when structured training is used. Industrial situations characterized by expensive production downtime or difficult start-up procedures would make the reported differences of even greater concern.

Job attitudes   There was no significant difference ($p > 0.8$) in attitudes toward the pipe-extrusion job between structured and unstructured trainees.

The Economics of Training: A Cost Effectiveness Model

To estimate accurately the resources that should be allocated to industrial training, management must know the expected gains of that training. Controversy over training is often fueled by inadequate knowledge of its economic returns. At face value, training costs appear to be an economic burden that reduces company profits. However, since some form of training is necessary to maintain worker productivity, a cost-effectiveness model is needed to determine the relative economic returns of alternative training strategies.

Evaluation of training costs may be divided into two major categories: cost benefit and cost effectiveness. *Cost benefit* (CB) is the analysis of training costs in monetary units as compared to benefits derived from training in nonmonetary terms. Examples of nonmonetary benefits are trainee attitudes, health, and safety. *Cost effectiveness* (CE) is the analysis of training costs in monetary units as compared to benefits derived from training in monetary terms. Monetary benefits such as production increases, production waste, scrap savings, and production downtime savings, are considered (Cullen, Sawzin, Sisson, and Swanson, 1978).

At the most basic level, the lesson from the comparison of structured to unstructured training is that money spent for structured training will be returned many times over. Training can therefore be viewed as an investment by the company to further its objectives. Gains or losses derived from training are considered returns, and the comparison of returns to investment results in the subsequent cost benefits or cost effectiveness of the training.

A cost-effectiveness model developed by Cullen et al. (1978) for assessing the outcomes of industrial training programs is presented in Exhibit 10.3. To illustrate how the model works, let us use as an example the comparison of structured versus unstructured training for plastic extruder operators that we just described.

Training Costs   For this model the costs for training are classified as either fixed or variable. Fixed costs are costs that do not vary with numbers of trainees, training time, or training program development. Variable costs are costs that change as the number of trainees, training time, and training program development vary. For example, if regular production equipment (which is a fixed cost for production) is used for training, the losses in production are considered a variable cost.

Training costs in the left-most column of Exhibit 10.3 include the following elements:

1. Training development
   a. analysis time: total people hours to analyze the job
   b. design time: total people hours to design the training program
   c. material costs: all material costs incurred from onset through completion of one training program, including supplies to facilitate training-program development (secretarial, graphics work, travel, duplicating, display boards, training aids, and so on)

Exhibit 10.3   Industrial Training Cost-Effectiveness Model

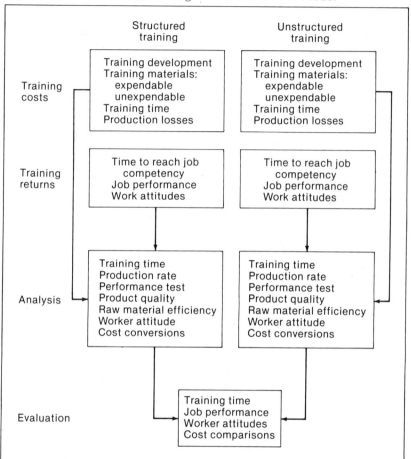

	Structured training	Unstructured training

Training costs	Training development
	Training materials:
	  expendable
	  unexpendable
	Training time
	Production losses
		Training development
		Training materials:
		  expendable
		  unexpendable
		Training time
		Production losses

Training returns	Time to reach job
	  competency
	Job performance
	Work attitudes
		Time to reach job
		  competency
		Job performance
		Work attitudes

Analysis	Training time Production rate Performance test Product quality Raw material efficiency Worker attitude Cost conversions	Training time Production rate Performance test Product quality Raw material efficiency Worker attitude Cost conversions
Evaluation	Training time Job performance Worker attitudes Cost comparisons	

Source: J. G. Cullen, S. A. Sawzin, G. R. Sisson, and R. A. Swanson. "Cost-Effectiveness: A Model for Assessing the Training Investment." *Training and Development Journal,* 1978, 32:27.

2. Training materials (expendable): cost of reproducing copies of developed training program
3. training materials (unexpendable)
   a. instructional hardware: shelf items purchased for the training

program (such as production machine to be used just for training, filmstrip projector, or tape recorder)

b. instructional software: shelf items of instructional content purchased for the training program (such as manufacturer's operating manual, filmstrips, or transparencies)

4. training time

a. trainee time: total hours, and resulting salary, incurred for
trainee to reach competency

b. trainer time: total hours, and resulting salary, incurred for
trainee to reach competency

5. production losses resulting from training

a. production rate losses

b. material losses

Training Returns   The return of the training program, either structured
or unstructured, is a competent production worker. To evaluate a competent production worker, one must specify the competencies required in
each situation. The sum of the components then determines the total
evaluation. For the plastic extruder operator training program, production
task performance included the following components:

1. Trainee can successfully perform job startup.

2. Trainee can maintain set standard of plastic tubing.

3. Trainee can successfully perform in production malfunction performance tests.

4. Trainee can successfully perform job shutdown.

Analyses of Training Returns   Measurements of actual task performance,
for purposes of assessing training returns, included:

1. Measurement of task performance

a. time: to reach competency, to deal successfully with deliber-
ately-induced machine malfunctions, to follow startup procedures

b. production rate: number of three-foot lengths of acceptable
pipe per hour of production

c. performance test: reaction to induction of machine malfunctions via performance test (downtime, loss of tubing, time of

malfunction injection versus time to respond to malfunction, time to correct malfunction)

d. product quality: measured by visual and dimensional criteria (comparison to samples of defective and non-defective pipe)

e. raw material usage: weight of raw material supplied to the machine versus weight of scrap and amount of acceptable product produced (weight raw material supplied, scrap, and hour bundles of acceptable tubing)

2. measurement of trainee attitudes toward training and the job: measured by the worker attitude inventory described earlier in the chapter

3. monetary value of returns

   a. convert trainee performance data to a monetary value

   b. total returns of structured training program and unstructured training program

Evaluation   The final phase of assessing cost effectiveness is known as evaluation. As Exhibit 10.3 demonstrates, the structured and unstructured training methods should be compared on all the points just mentioned. Each variable under training costs and training returns should be quantified. For those that are expressed in nonmonetary indexes (for example, time), monetary equivalents should be calculated whenever possible. As we have shown in Chapter 5, the financial impact of employee attitudes can also be estimated. These figures can then be used for the analysis and evaluation stage.

The general approach to cost-effectiveness comparison of alternative training strategies is to analyze the training variables, to convert them to monetary equivalents, and then to compare costs. If desired, individual variables such as "time taken to reach competency" can also be compared and reported as separate indexes of effectiveness.

The cost-effectiveness model we have just described has been used successfully in several industrial training situations. To be sure, there are some types of HRD programs (such as programs to change attitudes or improve decision-making skills) for which the components of the model may be inappropriate. The general model or approach to cost effectiveness should still guide evaluation in these circumstances. While evaluation isn't always easy, failure to establish empirically the links between HRD and improvements in productivity will ensure that training will continue to be viewed as a cost rather than as an investment in many organizations.

Example 3: Estimating the Cost Effectiveness of Proposed Personnel Programs

As is true of all functional areas of business that have to operate within budgetary limits, the key question personnel decision makers must answer is, How can we best allocate our scarce resources toward the most cost-effective undertakings? Faced with a bewildering array of alternatives, decision makers must select the programs that will improve productivity and profits. They then must continuously allocate staff resources only to those programs. The Xerox Corporation has developed such an approach to resource allocation and uses it to develop operating budgets for selected human resource management units throughout the organization (Cheek, 1973). The overall aim of the method is to apply well-known systems concepts and program management techniques to personnel operations. The method involves four steps.

1. Define each HRD program (proposed or ongoing) in a distinct package. Working as a team, human resource managers and staff specialists specify in as much detail as possible each program's objectives, target population, implementation schedule, human resource levels required, salaries, productivity, costs, and benefits. An example of such an analysis for a proposed job enrichment program is shown in Exhibit 10.4.

2. Identify legal requirements. Many of the resources of a personnel staff must be allocated to legally required programs, for example, pension plans, minority hiring, labor relations, and safety. Therefore these are treated separately from all other proposals and assigned highest priority.

3. Evaluate the feasibility of each program. This is the heart of the process and its most challenging aspect. Four distinct issues are considered. First, determine the state of the art requirements. Are the necessary skills available within the personnel department? If data processing support is necessary, how complex is the required programming? Is equipment available? The state of the art can be rated high, medium, or low (see Exhibit 10.4).

Second, determine the ease of implementation. Will line management support and implement the program? This is the most critical stage of the feasibility evaluation. If line management's attitudes and styles along with

Exhibit 10.4 Cost Effectiveness Analysis of Proposed Job Enrichment Program

	Program Name: Service Force Job Enrichment Program			Program No. 16
1. Define and describe the program. 2. Identify and segregate legally required efforts.	Description (objectives, target population, implementation schedule) To extend the job enrichment program for the service force—as piloted in Spring Falls, Avon Hills, and Maplewood branches—to all branches between 1972 and 1976. Is program legally required? ☐ Yes ☒ No			
3. Evaluate feasibility: a. state-of-the-art implications	State of the Art	☒ High	☐ Medium	☐ Low
	Ease of Implementation	☐ High	☐ Medium	☒ Low
b. ease of implementation	Economic Benefits	☒ High	☐ Medium	☐ Low

c. net economic benefits		Potential revenue impact	Probability of occurrence	Probable gross benefit (cost)
	Identifiable benefits: Reduction in service force turnover of 1 point	$ 450,000	0.2	$ 90,000
	Extension of 1.2 points reduction in absenteeism, as demonstrated in pilot project.	$ 2,132,500	0.8	$1,706,000
	Extension of 5% increase in service force productivity, as demonstrated in initial efforts.	$85,500,000	0.1	$8,550,000
	Total benefits	$88,082,500	0.12	$10,346,000

Tangible costs to Xerox of acting
Group personnel staff time to develop program, and line management time to implement program in all branches. | ($ 472,950) | 0.9 | $ 425,655

| Total costs | ($ 472,950) | 0.9 | $ 425,655 |

Probable net benefits (cost) $9,920,345

d. and intangibles

Intangible benefits

Increased morale in service force, with improved customer service and satisfaction. "Contagious effect" of job enrichment to other groups, e.g., sales and clericals.

Improved service manager development with concurrent sharpening of their motivational skills. As an extreme example, one manager at Avon Hills increased his team's productivity 70%.

e. Economic risks

Economic Risks
Possible consequences of not acting
Continued escalation of service costs as a percent of revenue.

☒ High   ☐ Medium   ☐ Low

Assumptions and Other Considerations

Cost estimates assume 4.4 man years of group staff time, .26 man years of branch manager time, and 15.8 man years of service manager time to implement program in a population of 1,053 service managers.

Benefit estimates assume elimination of 3 days absenteeism per month for each of 1,053 service teams, favourable productivity, and that turnover experience in pilot branches can be cascaded to all branches.

Source: From Logan M. Cheek, "Cost Effectiveness Comes to the Personnel Function," *Harvard Business Review,* May-June 1973, p. 99. Copyright © 1973 by the President and Fellows of Harvard College; all rights reserved.

the organization's policies, structure, and operating environment must be changed substantially (as they often must in programs of job enrichment, assessment centers, and organization development), then the ease of program implementation must be considered low (see Exhibit 10.4). Under these circumstances the program would be justified only if the risks identified in this stage were offset by exceptionally high evaluations in other stages.

Third, determine the economic benefits. Will the program be cost effective? In the job enrichment program proposal shown in Exhibit 10.4, a pilot program had been conducted and from this results could be projected to other locations. This made it possible to identify benefits and to estimate their probability and cost. In the absence of pilot data personnel managers can either contrast the cost of a present program to the cost of a proposed program (for example, hiring managers through executive search firms versus through the company's own efforts) and thereby estimate benefits, or at least identify target benefits.

Finally, determine the economic risks. Can the organization afford not to act? Although relative risks will vary by type of organization, the failure to increase productivity could increase costs, or the continued use of less valid selection procedures (which decreases the overall quality of those hired) could represent substantial opportunity costs for the firm.

4. Rank all programs and allocate and deploy staff resources accordingly. After each program has been evaluated separately, its overall feasibility must be determined. This can be done by designing a decision table structured so that a high rating on any factor will not automatically decide in favor of the program, but a low rating on any factor could eliminate it from further consideration. Each program can then be classified as very desirable, moderately desirable, marginally desirable, or not worthwhile. When all programs have been so classified, they are ranked in an overall program priorities schedule (with all legally required programs listed first). This schedule then becomes the basic guide for allocating staff resources (see Exhibit 10.5).

To be successful, this evaluation procedure must be viewed as dynamic and ongoing. New programs must continually be integrated into the program priorities schedule, existing programs must be reevaluated periodically, and the execution of each program must be monitored continually. Perhaps the method's main advantage is the discipline it instills in the human resource management staff. Although it is by no means perfect, "it can guide management to the gains in profit and productivity that come from personnel programs targeted on results" (Cheek, 1973, p. 105).

Exhibit 10.5   Program Priorities Schedule

ACTION PROGRAM	Priority	Timing 1972	1973	1974	1975	1976	1977	Net annual dollar benefit	Cost/benefit ratio (l:n)
LEGALLY REQUIRED PROGRAMS									
Labor Relations Strategy	x							($ 619)	n/a
Protect Right to Select Employees	x							($ 86)	n/a
Continue Validation of Selection Tests	x							$35,000	78.17
Redesign Personnel Data System	x							$ 273	1.78
Develop Part-Time Female Employment Approaches	x	III						$ 227	4.16
VERY DESIRABLE PROGRAMS									
Restructuring Service Force	1							$14,608	9.6
Service College Coop Program	2	III III						$ 4,490	2.74
MODERATELY DESIRABLE PROGRAMS									
Service Job Enrichment	3							$ 9,920	24.3
Assessment Center	4	III III						$ 4,946	15.40
Education & Training Center	5							$ 4,780	3.57
Clerical Selection Program	6	III III						$ 1,799	19.94
Develop College Campus as Primary Employment Source	7							$ 834	2.06
Interfunctional Moves & Fast Track Program	8	III						$ 679	7.54
Selection Standards for New Sales/Tech. Rep. Types	9	III						$ 520	11.6
Improve Economics of Field Employment Operations	10							$ 472	1.42
Build Better Technical Recruiting/Selection Capability	11	III						$ 222	2.48
Monitor Sales & Tech. Rep. Selection Tests	12							$ 211	9.05
MARGINAL BUT DESIRABLE PROGRAMS									
Implement Executive Search Function	13	III						$ 177	1.67
Refine Career Path Guides	14							$ 110	1.75
Continue National Trend Attitude Surveys	15							$ 107	1.33
Reevaluate Overall Organization Approach	16							$ 93	2.37
NOT WORTHWHILE									
Executive Retreat	x							($ 450)	n/a
Corporate Jet	x							($ 769)	n/a
Savings Plan	x	III III						($ 75)	n/a

Marginal notes (left column):

1. Legally required efforts come first
2. ...then, other programs are ranked by overall feasibility category
3. ...and within feasibility category by net benefits
4. Priorities are indicated here
5. Starting from the lowest priority program, marginal efforts may be trimmed as required by the budget
6. In any case, these programs are eliminated

IIIIIIII Program and design development
▬ Program Implementation

One of the important lessons to be learned from the material presented in this chapter is that methods are available *now* for estimating the cost effectiveness of HRD programs, proposed, ongoing, or completed. Instead of depending on the power of persuasion to convince decision makers of the value of HRD programs, human resource professionals can, by the use of cost-effectiveness models, join with the other functional areas of business in justifying the allocation of scarce organizational resources on the basis of evidence, rather than on that of beliefs.

Exercises

1. Pilgrim Industries, a 2,000-employee firm with 400 management personnel, holds 40 days of off-site meetings per year. Outside consultants develop and conduct the meetings, and on the average 20 managers attend each meeting. The typical meeting lasts two full days. Last year, total program development costs consumed $200,000. The average attendee's salary was $25,000, and Pilgrim's capital investment in each attendee was, on the average, an additional $25,000. To deliver each two-day meeting for 20 people, sleeping accommodations, food, telephone, and a cocktail reception cost $3,000. In addition, transportation, secretarial services, room, and audio-visual equipment rental totaled another $3,200. Determine the total per day per person cost of one off-site meeting.

2. Soclear, Inc., a janitorial service firm, wants to conduct a controlled study of structured versus unstructured training for window washers of office buildings. How would you design the structured and unstructured training programs? In order to use the cost effectiveness model shown in Exhibit 10.3 what criteria of job performance might you use? How will data be collected and recorded? How can cost comparisons be made?

3. For some time now you have been wanting to computerize your company's (1,800 employees) personnel data system. However, in order to convince top management to allocate resources (time, staff, money) to this project you must demonstrate the expected cost effectiveness of the effort. Make whatever assumptions are necessary (but document them), and, using as an outline the model shown in Exhibit 10.4, estimate the probable net benefits (tangible and intangible) of computerizing the company's personnel data system.

References

Cascio, W. F. *Applied Psychology in Personnel Management*. 2nd ed. Reston, Va.: Reston, 1982.

CHEEK, L. M. "Cost Effectiveness Comes to the Personnel Function." *Harvard Business Review*, 1973 (May-June), 96–105.

COOK, T. D., and CAMPBELL, D. T. *Quasi-Experimentation: Design and Analysis Issues for Field Settings*. Chicago: Rand-McNally, 1979.

CULLEN, J. G., SAWZIN, S. A., SISSON, G. R., and SWANSON, R. A. "Training: What's It Worth?" *Training and Development Journal*, 1976, 30 (8), 12–20.

CULLEN, J. G., SAWZIN, S. A., SISSON, G. R., and SWANSON, R. A. "Cost Effectiveness: A Model for Assessing the Training Investment." *Training and Development Journal*, 1978, 32 (1), 24–29.

GOLDSTEIN, I. L. "Training in Work Organizations." *Annual Review of Psychology*, 1980, 31:229–279.

KAHN, R. L. "Organizational Development: Some Problems and Proposals." *Journal of Applied Behavioral Science*, 1974, 10:485–502.

McKEON, W. J. "How to Determine Off-Site Meeting Costs." *Training and Development Journal*, 1981 (May), 35:116–122.

MILLS, T. "Human Resources—Why the New Concern?" *Harvard Business Review*, 1975 (March-April), 120–134.

Appendix A
The Taylor-Russell Tables

$\mathbf{T}$ ables of the Proportion who will be Satisfactory among those Selected (Success Ratio) for Given Values of the Proportion of Present Employees Considered Satisfactory (Base Rate), the Selection Ratio, and r

Proportion of Employees Considered Satisfactory = 0.05
Selection Ratio

r	0.05	0.10	0.20	0.30	0.40	0.50	0.60	0.70	0.80	0.90	0.95
0.00	0.05	0.05	0.05	0.05	0.05	0.05	0.05	0.05	0.05	0.05	0.05
0.05	0.06	0.06	0.06	0.06	0.06	0.05	0.05	0.05	0.05	0.05	0.05
0.10	0.07	0.07	0.07	0.06	0.06	0.06	0.06	0.05	0.05	0.05	0.05
0.15	0.09	0.08	0.07	0.07	0.07	0.06	0.06	0.06	0.05	0.05	0.05
0.20	0.11	0.09	0.08	0.08	0.07	0.07	0.06	0.06	0.06	0.05	0.05

Source: H. C. Taylor and J. T. Russell. "The Relationship of Validity Coefficients to the Practical Effectiveness of Tests in Selection: Discussion and Tables." *Journal of Applied Psychology,* 1939, *23,* 565–578.

Proportion of Employees Considered Satisfactory = 0.05 (cont.)
Selection Ratio

r	0.05	0.10	0.20	0.30	0.40	0.50	0.60	0.70	0.80	0.90	0.95
0.25	0.12	0.11	0.09	0.08	0.08	0.07	0.07	0.06	0.06	0.05	0.05
0.30	0.14	0.12	0.10	0.09	0.08	0.07	0.07	0.06	0.06	0.05	0.05
0.35	0.17	0.14	0.11	0.10	0.09	0.08	0.07	0.06	0.06	0.05	0.05
0.40	0.19	0.16	0.12	0.10	0.09	0.08	0.07	0.07	0.06	0.05	0.05
0.45	0.22	0.17	0.13	0.11	0.10	0.08	0.08	0.07	0.06	0.06	0.05
0.50	0.24	0.19	0.15	0.12	0.10	0.09	0.08	0.07	0.06	0.06	0.05
0.55	0.28	0.22	0.16	0.13	0.11	0.09	0.08	0.07	0.06	0.06	0.05
0.60	0.31	0.24	0.17	0.13	0.11	0.09	0.08	0.07	0.06	0.06	0.05
0.65	0.35	0.26	0.18	0.14	0.11	0.10	0.08	0.07	0.06	0.06	0.05
0.70	0.39	0.29	0.20	0.15	0.12	0.10	0.08	0.07	0.06	0.06	0.05
0.75	0.44	0.32	0.21	0.15	0.12	0.10	0.08	0.07	0.06	0.06	0.05
0.80	0.50	0.35	0.22	0.16	0.12	0.10	0.08	0.07	0.06	0.06	0.05
0.85	0.56	0.39	0.23	0.16	0.12	0.10	0.08	0.07	0.06	0.06	0.05
0.90	0.64	0.43	0.24	0.17	0.13	0.10	0.08	0.07	0.06	0.06	0.05
0.95	0.73	0.47	0.25	0.17	0.13	0.10	0.08	0.07	0.06	0.06	0.05
1.00	1.00	0.50	0.25	0.17	0.13	0.10	0.08	0.07	0.06	0.06	0.05

Proportion of Employees Considered Satisfactory = 0.10
Selection Ratio

r	0.05	0.10	0.20	0.30	0.40	0.50	0.60	0.70	0.80	0.90	0.95
0.00	0.10	0.10	0.10	0.10	0.10	0.10	0.10	0.10	0.10	0.10	0.10
0.05	0.12	0.12	0.11	0.11	0.11	0.11	0.11	0.10	0.10	0.10	0.10
0.10	0.14	0.13	0.13	0.12	0.12	0.11	0.11	0.11	0.11	0.10	0.10
0.15	0.16	0.15	0.14	0.13	0.13	0.12	0.12	0.11	0.11	0.10	0.10
0.20	0.19	0.17	0.15	0.14	0.14	0.13	0.12	0.12	0.11	0.11	0.10
0.25	0.22	0.19	0.17	0.16	0.14	0.13	0.13	0.12	0.11	0.11	0.10
0.30	0.25	0.22	0.19	0.17	0.15	0.14	0.13	0.12	0.12	0.11	0.10
0.35	0.28	0.24	0.20	0.18	0.16	0.15	0.14	0.13	0.12	0.11	0.10
0.40	0.31	0.27	0.22	0.19	0.17	0.16	0.14	0.13	0.12	0.11	0.10
0.45	0.35	0.29	0.24	0.20	0.18	0.16	0.15	0.13	0.12	0.11	0.10
0.50	0.39	0.32	0.26	0.22	0.19	0.17	0.15	0.13	0.12	0.11	0.11
0.55	0.43	0.36	0.28	0.23	0.20	0.17	0.15	0.14	0.12	0.11	0.11
0.60	0.48	0.39	0.30	0.25	0.21	0.18	0.16	0.14	0.12	0.11	0.11
0.65	0.53	0.43	0.32	0.26	0.22	0.18	0.16	0.14	0.12	0.11	0.11

Proportion of Employees Considered Satisfactory = 0.10 (cont.)
Selection Ratio

r	0.05	0.10	0.20	0.30	0.40	0.50	0.60	0.70	0.80	0.90	0.95
0.70	0.58	0.47	0.35	0.27	0.22	0.19	0.16	0.14	0.12	0.11	0.11
0.75	0.64	0.51	0.37	0.29	0.23	0.19	0.16	0.14	0.12	0.11	0.11
0.80	0.71	0.56	0.40	0.30	0.24	0.20	0.17	0.14	0.12	0.11	0.11
0.85	0.78	0.62	0.43	0.31	0.25	0.20	0.17	0.14	0.12	0.11	0.11
0.90	0.86	0.69	0.46	0.33	0.25	0.20	0.17	0.14	0.12	0.11	0.11
0.95	0.95	0.78	0.49	0.33	0.25	0.20	0.17	0.14	0.12	0.11	0.11
1.00	1.00	1.00	0.50	0.33	0.25	0.20	0.17	0.14	0.13	0.11	0.11

Proportion of Employees Considered Satisfactory = 0.20
Selection Ratio

r	0.05	0.10	0.20	0.30	0.40	0.50	0.60	0.70	0.80	0.90	0.95
0.00	0.20	0.20	0.20	0.20	0.20	0.20	0.20	0.20	0.20	0.20	0.20
0.05	0.23	0.23	0.22	0.22	0.21	0.21	0.21	0.21	0.20	0.20	0.20
0.10	0.26	0.25	0.24	0.23	0.23	0.22	0.22	0.21	0.21	0.21	0.20
0.15	0.30	0.28	0.26	0.25	0.24	0.23	0.23	0.22	0.21	0.21	0.20
0.20	0.33	0.31	0.28	0.27	0.26	0.25	0.24	0.23	0.22	0.21	0.21
0.25	0.37	0.34	0.31	0.29	0.27	0.26	0.24	0.23	0.22	0.21	0.21
0.30	0.41	0.37	0.33	0.30	0.28	0.27	0.25	0.24	0.23	0.21	0.21
0.35	0.45	0.41	0.36	0.32	0.30	0.28	0.26	0.24	0.23	0.22	0.21
0.40	0.49	0.44	0.38	0.34	0.31	0.29	0.27	0.25	0.23	0.22	0.21
0.45	0.54	0.48	0.41	0.36	0.33	0.30	0.28	0.26	0.24	0.22	0.21
0.50	0.59	0.52	0.44	0.38	0.35	0.31	0.29	0.26	0.24	0.22	0.21
0.55	0.63	0.56	0.47	0.41	0.36	0.32	0.29	0.27	0.24	0.22	0.21
0.60	0.68	0.60	0.50	0.43	0.38	0.34	0.30	0.27	0.24	0.22	0.21
0.65	0.73	0.64	0.53	0.45	0.39	0.35	0.31	0.27	0.25	0.22	0.21
0.70	0.79	0.69	0.56	0.48	0.41	0.36	0.31	0.28	0.25	0.22	0.21
0.75	0.84	0.74	0.60	0.50	0.43	0.37	0.32	0.28	0.25	0.22	0.21
0.80	0.89	0.79	0.64	0.53	0.45	0.38	0.33	0.28	0.25	0.22	0.21
0.85	0.94	0.85	0.69	0.56	0.47	0.39	0.33	0.28	0.25	0.22	0.21
0.90	0.98	0.91	0.75	0.60	0.48	0.40	0.33	0.29	0.25	0.22	0.21
0.95	1.00	0.97	0.82	0.64	0.50	0.40	0.33	0.29	0.25	0.22	0.21
1.00	1.00	1.00	1.00	0.67	0.50	0.40	0.33	0.29	0.25	0.22	0.21

Proportion of Employees Considered Satisfactory = 0.30
Selection Ratio

r	0.05	0.10	0.20	0.30	0.40	0.50	0.60	0.70	0.80	0.90	0.95
0.00	0.30	0.30	0.30	0.30	0.30	0.30	0.30	0.30	0.30	0.30	0.30
0.05	0.34	0.33	0.33	0.32	0.32	0.31	0.31	0.31	0.31	0.30	0.30
0.10	0.38	0.36	0.35	0.34	0.33	0.33	0.32	0.32	0.31	0.31	0.30
0.15	0.42	0.40	0.38	0.36	0.35	0.34	0.33	0.33	0.32	0.31	0.31
0.20	0.46	0.43	0.40	0.38	0.37	0.36	0.34	0.33	0.32	0.31	0.31
0.25	0.50	0.47	0.43	0.41	0.39	0.37	0.36	0.34	0.33	0.32	0.31
0.30	0.54	0.50	0.46	0.43	0.40	0.38	0.37	0.35	0.33	0.32	0.31
0.35	0.58	0.54	0.49	0.45	0.42	0.40	0.38	0.36	0.34	0.32	0.31
0.40	0.63	0.58	0.51	0.47	0.44	0.41	0.39	0.37	0.34	0.32	0.31
0.45	0.67	0.61	0.55	0.50	0.46	0.43	0.40	0.37	0.35	0.32	0.31
0.50	0.72	0.65	0.58	0.52	0.48	0.44	0.41	0.38	0.35	0.33	0.31
0.55	0.76	0.69	0.61	0.55	0.50	0.46	0.42	0.39	0.36	0.33	0.31
0.60	0.81	0.74	0.64	0.58	0.52	0.47	0.43	0.40	0.36	0.33	0.31
0.65	0.85	0.78	0.68	0.60	0.54	0.49	0.44	0.40	0.37	0.33	0.32
0.70	0.89	0.82	0.72	0.63	0.57	0.51	0.46	0.41	0.37	0.33	0.32
0.75	0.93	0.86	0.76	0.67	0.59	0.52	0.47	0.42	0.37	0.33	0.32
0.80	0.96	0.90	0.80	0.70	0.62	0.54	0.48	0.42	0.37	0.33	0.32
0.85	0.99	0.94	0.85	0.74	0.65	0.56	0.49	0.43	0.37	0.33	0.32
0.90	1.00	0.98	0.90	0.79	0.68	0.58	0.49	0.43	0.37	0.33	0.32
0.95	1.00	1.00	0.96	0.85	0.72	0.60	0.50	0.43	0.37	0.33	0.32
1.00	1.00	1.00	1.00	1.00	0.75	0.60	0.50	0.43	0.38	0.33	0.32

Proportion of Employees Considered Satisfactory = 0.40
Selection Ratio

r	0.05	0.10	0.20	0.30	0.40	0.50	0.60	0.70	0.80	0.90	0.95
0.00	0.40	0.40	0.40	0.40	0.40	0.40	0.40	0.40	0.40	0.40	0.40
0.05	0.44	0.43	0.43	0.42	0.42	0.42	0.41	0.41	0.41	0.40	0.40
0.10	0.48	0.47	0.46	0.45	0.44	0.43	0.42	0.42	0.41	0.41	0.40
0.15	0.52	0.50	0.48	0.47	0.46	0.45	0.44	0.43	0.42	0.41	0.41
0.20	0.57	0.54	0.51	0.49	0.48	0.46	0.45	0.44	0.43	0.41	0.41
0.25	0.61	0.58	0.54	0.51	0.49	0.48	0.46	0.45	0.43	0.42	0.41
0.30	0.65	0.61	0.57	0.54	0.51	0.49	0.47	0.46	0.44	0.42	0.41
0.35	0.69	0.65	0.60	0.56	0.53	0.51	0.49	0.47	0.45	0.42	0.41
0.40	0.73	0.69	0.63	0.59	0.56	0.53	0.50	0.48	0.45	0.43	0.41

Proportion of Employees Considered Satisfactory = 0.40 (cont.)
Selection Ratio

r	0.05	0.10	0.20	0.30	0.40	0.50	0.60	0.70	0.80	0.90	0.95
0.45	0.77	0.72	0.66	0.61	0.58	0.54	0.51	0.49	0.46	0.43	0.42
0.50	0.81	0.76	0.69	0.64	0.60	0.56	0.53	0.49	0.46	0.43	0.42
0.55	0.85	0.79	0.72	0.67	0.62	0.58	0.54	0.50	0.47	0.44	0.42
0.60	0.89	0.83	0.75	0.69	0.64	0.60	0.55	0.51	0.48	0.44	0.42
0.65	0.92	0.87	0.79	0.72	0.67	0.62	0.57	0.52	0.48	0.44	0.42
0.70	0.95	0.90	0.82	0.76	0.69	0.64	0.58	0.53	0.49	0.44	0.42
0.75	0.97	0.93	0.86	0.79	0.72	0.66	0.60	0.54	0.49	0.44	0.42
0.80	0.99	0.96	0.89	0.82	0.75	0.68	0.61	0.55	0.49	0.44	0.42
0.85	1.00	0.98	0.93	0.86	0.79	0.71	0.63	0.56	0.50	0.44	0.42
0.90	1.00	1.00	0.97	0.91	0.82	0.74	0.65	0.57	0.50	0.44	0.42
0.95	1.00	1.00	0.99	0.96	0.87	0.77	0.66	0.57	0.50	0.44	0.42
1.00	1.00	1.00	1.00	1.00	1.00	0.80	0.67	0.57	0.50	0.44	0.42

Proportion of Employees Considered Satisfactory = 0.50
Selection Ratio

r	0.05	0.10	0.20	0.30	0.40	0.50	0.60	0.70	0.80	0.90	0.95
0.00	0.50	0.50	0.50	0.50	0.50	0.50	0.50	0.50	0.50	0.50	0.50
0.05	0.54	0.54	0.53	0.52	0.52	0.52	0.51	0.51	0.51	0.50	0.50
0.10	0.58	0.57	0.56	0.55	0.54	0.53	0.53	0.52	0.51	0.51	0.50
0.15	0.63	0.61	0.58	0.57	0.56	0.55	0.54	0.53	0.52	0.51	0.51
0.20	0.67	0.64	0.61	0.59	0.58	0.56	0.55	0.54	0.53	0.52	0.51
0.25	0.70	0.67	0.64	0.62	0.60	0.58	0.56	0.55	0.54	0.52	0.51
0.30	0.74	0.71	0.67	0.64	0.62	0.60	0.58	0.56	0.54	0.52	0.51
0.35	0.78	0.74	0.70	0.66	0.64	0.61	0.59	0.57	0.55	0.53	0.51
0.40	0.82	0.78	0.73	0.69	0.66	0.63	0.61	0.58	0.56	0.53	0.52
0.45	0.85	0.81	0.75	0.71	0.68	0.65	0.62	0.59	0.56	0.53	0.52
0.50	0.88	0.84	0.78	0.74	0.70	0.67	0.63	0.60	0.57	0.54	0.52
0.55	0.91	0.87	0.81	0.76	0.72	0.69	0.65	0.61	0.58	0.54	0.52
0.60	0.94	0.90	0.84	0.79	0.75	0.70	0.66	0.62	0.59	0.54	0.52
0.65	0.96	0.92	0.87	0.82	0.77	0.73	0.68	0.64	0.59	0.55	0.52
0.70	0.98	0.95	0.90	0.85	0.80	0.75	0.70	0.65	0.60	0.55	0.53
0.75	0.99	0.97	0.92	0.87	0.82	0.77	0.72	0.66	0.61	0.55	0.53

Proportion of Employees Considered Satisfactory = 0.50 (cont.)
Selection Ratio

r	0.05	0.10	0.20	0.30	0.40	0.50	0.60	0.70	0.80	0.90	0.95
0.80	1.00	0.99	0.95	0.90	0.85	0.80	0.73	0.67	0.61	0.55	0.53
0.85	1.00	0.99	0.97	0.94	0.88	0.82	0.76	0.69	0.62	0.55	0.53
0.90	1.00	1.00	0.99	0.97	0.92	0.86	0.78	0.70	0.62	0.56	0.53
0.95	1.00	1.00	1.00	0.99	0.96	0.90	0.81	0.71	0.63	0.56	0.53
1.00	1.00	1.00	1.00	1.00	1.00	1.00	0.83	0.71	0.63	0.56	0.53

Proportion of Employees Considered Satisfactory = 0.60
Selection Ratio

r	0.05	0.10	0.20	0.30	0.40	0.50	0.60	0.70	0.80	0.90	0.95
0.00	0.60	0.60	0.60	0.60	0.60	0.60	0.60	0.60	0.60	0.60	0.60
0.05	0.64	0.63	0.63	0.62	0.62	0.62	0.61	0.61	0.61	0.60	0.60
0.10	0.68	0.67	0.65	0.64	0.64	0.63	0.63	0.62	0.61	0.61	0.60
0.15	0.71	0.70	0.68	0.67	0.66	0.65	0.64	0.63	0.62	0.61	0.61
0.20	0.75	0.73	0.71	0.69	0.67	0.66	0.65	0.64	0.63	0.62	0.61
0.25	0.78	0.76	0.73	0.71	0.69	0.68	0.66	0.65	0.63	0.62	0.61
0.30	0.82	0.79	0.76	0.73	0.71	0.69	0.68	0.66	0.64	0.62	0.61
0.35	0.85	0.82	0.78	0.75	0.73	0.71	0.69	0.67	0.65	0.63	0.62
0.40	0.88	0.85	0.81	0.78	0.75	0.73	0.70	0.68	0.66	0.63	0.62
0.45	0.90	0.87	0.83	0.80	0.77	0.74	0.72	0.69	0.66	0.64	0.62
0.50	0.93	0.90	0.86	0.82	0.79	0.76	0.73	0.70	0.67	0.64	0.62
0.55	0.95	0.92	0.88	0.84	0.81	0.78	0.75	0.71	0.68	0.64	0.62
0.60	0.96	0.94	0.90	0.87	0.83	0.80	0.76	0.73	0.69	0.65	0.63
0.65	0.98	0.96	0.92	0.89	0.85	0.82	0.78	0.74	0.70	0.65	0.63
0.70	0.99	0.97	0.94	0.91	0.87	0.84	0.80	0.75	0.71	0.66	0.63
0.75	0.99	0.99	0.96	0.93	0.90	0.86	0.81	0.77	0.71	0.66	0.63
0.80	1.00	0.99	0.98	0.95	0.92	0.88	0.83	0.78	0.72	0.66	0.63
0.85	1.00	1.00	0.99	0.97	0.95	0.91	0.86	0.80	0.73	0.66	0.63
0.90	1.00	1.00	1.00	0.99	0.97	0.94	0.88	0.82	0.74	0.67	0.63
0.95	1.00	1.00	1.00	1.00	0.99	0.97	0.92	0.84	0.75	0.67	0.63
1.00	1.00	1.00	1.00	1.00	1.00	1.00	1.00	0.86	0.75	0.67	0.63

Proportion of Employees Considered Satisfactory = 0.70

Selection Ratio

r	0.05	0.10	0.20	0.30	0.40	0.50	0.60	0.70	0.80	0.90	0.95
0.00	0.70	0.70	0.70	0.70	0.70	0.70	0.70	0.70	0.70	0.70	0.70
0.05	0.73	0.73	0.72	0.72	0.72	0.71	0.71	0.71	0.71	0.70	0.70
0.10	0.77	0.76	0.75	0.74	0.73	0.73	0.72	0.72	0.71	0.71	0.70
0.15	0.80	0.79	0.77	0.76	0.75	0.74	0.73	0.73	0.72	0.71	0.71
0.20	0.83	0.81	0.79	0.78	0.77	0.76	0.75	0.74	0.73	0.71	0.71
0.25	0.86	0.84	0.81	0.80	0.78	0.77	0.76	0.75	0.73	0.72	0.71
0.30	0.88	0.86	0.84	0.82	0.80	0.78	0.77	0.75	0.74	0.72	0.71
0.35	0.91	0.89	0.86	0.83	0.82	0.80	0.78	0.76	0.75	0.73	0.71
0.40	0.93	0.91	0.88	0.85	0.83	0.81	0.79	0.77	0.75	0.73	0.72
0.45	0.94	0.93	0.90	0.87	0.85	0.83	0.81	0.78	0.76	0.73	0.72
0.50	0.96	0.94	0.91	0.89	0.87	0.84	0.82	0.80	0.77	0.74	0.72
0.55	0.97	0.96	0.93	0.91	0.88	0.86	0.83	0.81	0.78	0.74	0.72
0.60	0.98	0.97	0.95	0.92	0.90	0.87	0.85	0.82	0.79	0.75	0.73
0.65	0.99	0.98	0.96	0.94	0.92	0.89	0.86	0.83	0.80	0.75	0.73
0.70	1.00	0.99	0.97	0.96	0.93	0.91	0.88	0.84	0.80	0.76	0.73
0.75	1.00	1.00	0.98	0.97	0.95	0.92	0.89	0.86	0.81	0.76	0.73
0.80	1.00	1.00	0.99	0.98	0.97	0.94	0.91	0.87	0.82	0.77	0.73
0.85	1.00	1.00	1.00	0.99	0.98	0.96	0.93	0.89	0.84	0.77	0.74
0.90	1.00	1.00	1.00	1.00	0.99	0.98	0.95	0.91	0.85	0.78	0.74
0.95	1.00	1.00	1.00	1.00	1.00	0.99	0.98	0.94	0.86	0.78	0.74
1.00	1.00	1.00	1.00	1.00	1.00	1.00	1.00	1.00	0.88	0.78	0.74

Proportion of Employees Considered Satisfactory = 0.80

Selection Ratio

r	0.05	0.10	0.20	0.30	0.40	0.50	0.60	0.70	0.80	0.90	0.95
0.00	0.80	0.80	0.80	0.80	0.80	0.80	0.80	0.80	0.80	0.80	0.80
0.05	0.83	0.82	0.82	0.82	0.81	0.81	0.81	0.81	0.81	0.80	0.80
0.10	0.85	0.85	0.84	0.83	0.83	0.82	0.82	0.81	0.81	0.81	0.80
0.15	0.88	0.87	0.86	0.85	0.84	0.83	0.83	0.82	0.82	0.81	0.81
0.20	0.90	0.89	0.87	0.86	0.85	0.84	0.84	0.83	0.82	0.81	0.81
0.25	0.92	0.91	0.89	0.88	0.87	0.86	0.85	0.84	0.83	0.82	0.81
0.30	0.94	0.92	0.90	0.89	0.88	0.87	0.86	0.84	0.83	0.82	0.81
0.35	0.95	0.94	0.92	0.90	0.89	0.89	0.87	0.85	0.84	0.82	0.81
0.40	0.96	0.95	0.93	0.92	0.90	0.89	0.88	0.86	0.85	0.83	0.82

Proportion of Employees Considered Satisfactory = 0.80 (cont.)
Selection Ratio

r	0.05	0.10	0.20	0.30	0.40	0.50	0.60	0.70	0.80	0.90	0.95
0.45	0.97	0.96	0.95	0.93	0.92	0.90	0.89	0.87	0.85	0.83	0.82
0.50	0.98	0.97	0.96	0.94	0.93	0.91	0.90	0.88	0.86	0.84	0.82
0.55	0.99	0.98	0.97	0.95	0.94	0.92	0.91	0.89	0.87	0.84	0.82
0.60	0.99	0.99	0.98	0.96	0.95	0.94	0.92	0.90	0.87	0.84	0.83
0.65	1.00	0.99	0.98	0.97	0.96	0.95	0.93	0.91	0.88	0.85	0.83
0.70	1.00	1.00	0.99	0.98	0.97	0.96	0.94	0.92	0.89	0.85	0.83
0.75	1.00	1.00	1.00	0.99	0.98	0.97	0.95	0.93	0.90	0.86	0.83
0.80	1.00	1.00	1.00	1.00	0.99	0.98	0.96	0.94	0.91	0.87	0.84
0.85	1.00	1.00	1.00	1.00	1.00	0.99	0.98	0.96	0.92	0.87	0.84
0.90	1.00	1.00	1.00	1.00	1.00	1.00	0.99	0.97	0.94	0.88	0.84
0.95	1.00	1.00	1.00	1.00	1.00	1.00	1.00	0.99	0.96	0.89	0.84
1.00	1.00	1.00	1.00	1.00	1.00	1.00	1.00	1.00	1.00	0.89	0.84

Proportion of Employees Considered Satisfactory = 0.90
Selection Ratio

r	0.05	0.10	0.20	0.30	0.40	0.50	0.60	0.70	0.80	0.90	0.95
0.00	0.90	0.90	0.90	0.90	0.90	0.90	0.90	0.90	0.90	0.90	0.90
0.05	0.92	0.91	0.91	0.91	0.91	0.91	0.91	0.90	0.90	0.90	0.90
0.10	0.93	0.93	0.92	0.92	0.92	0.91	0.91	0.91	0.91	0.90	0.90
0.15	0.95	0.94	0.93	0.93	0.92	0.92	0.92	0.91	0.91	0.91	0.90
0.20	0.96	0.95	0.94	0.94	0.93	0.93	0.92	0.92	0.91	0.91	0.90
0.25	0.97	0.96	0.95	0.95	0.94	0.93	0.93	0.92	0.92	0.91	0.91
0.30	0.98	0.97	0.96	0.95	0.95	0.94	0.94	0.93	0.92	0.91	0.91
0.35	0.98	0.98	0.97	0.96	0.95	0.95	0.94	0.93	0.93	0.92	0.91
0.40	0.99	0.98	0.98	0.97	0.96	0.95	0.95	0.94	0.93	0.92	0.91
0.45	0.99	0.99	0.98	0.98	0.97	0.96	0.95	0.94	0.93	0.92	0.91
0.50	1.00	0.99	0.99	0.98	0.97	0.97	0.96	0.95	0.94	0.92	0.92
0.55	1.00	1.00	0.99	0.99	0.98	0.97	0.97	0.96	0.94	0.93	0.92
0.60	1.00	1.00	0.99	0.99	0.99	0.98	0.97	0.96	0.95	0.93	0.92
0.65	1.00	1.00	1.00	0.99	0.99	0.98	0.98	0.97	0.96	0.94	0.92
0.70	1.00	1.00	1.00	1.00	0.99	0.99	0.98	0.97	0.96	0.94	0.93
0.75	1.00	1.00	1.00	1.00	1.00	0.99	0.99	0.98	0.97	0.95	0.93
0.80	1.00	1.00	1.00	1.00	1.00	1.00	0.99	0.99	0.97	0.95	0.93

Proportion of Employees Considered Satisfactory = 0.90 (cont.)
Selection Ratio

r	0.05	0.10	0.20	0.30	0.40	0.50	0.60	0.70	0.80	0.90	0.95
0.85	1.00	1.00	1.00	1.00	1.00	1.00	1.00	0.99	0.98	0.96	0.94
0.90	1.00	1.00	1.00	1.00	1.00	1.00	1.00	1.00	0.99	0.97	0.94
0.95	1.00	1.00	1.00	1.00	1.00	1.00	1.00	1.00	1.00	0.98	0.94
1.00	1.00	1.00	1.00	1.00	1.00	1.00	1.00	1.00	1.00	1.00	0.95

Appendix B
The Naylor-Shine Table for Determining the Increase in Mean Criterion Score Obtained by Using a Selection Device

Using the Table

The following definitions are used in the table:

r_{xy} = validity coefficient

Z_{xi} = cutoff point (score) on the predictor in standard score units

ϕ_i = selection ratio

$\overline{Z}_{yi}$ = mean criterion score (in standard score units) of all cases above cutoff

λ_i = ordinate of normal distribution at Z_{xi}

and the table is based upon the following equation:

$$\overline{Z}_{yi} = r_{xy} \frac{\lambda_i}{\phi_i}$$

Note: The use of the table may differ slightly in the case where r_{xy} is really a multiple regression coefficient. The major difference occurs in the Z_{xi} column. With a single predictor there is no difficulty in expressing a cutoff score in terms of a particular value of X, the predictor variable (thus we use Z_{xi}). However, in the case of multiple predictors it is no longer feasible to do so, since there are several X variables. The easiest procedure, therefore, is conceptually to reduce the multivariate case to the bivariate case by treating the multiple correlation coefficient as the correlation coefficient between the observed criterion scores (Z_y) and the predicted criterion scores (Z'_y). Thus it becomes possible to talk about cutoff values for the multiple predictor case, but these cutoff scores are expressed in terms of Z'_{yi} values, rather than Z_{xi} values. The only difficulty this creates is that $s^2_{z'y} \neq 1$, but will always be equal to R^2_{xy}, the squared multiple correlation coefficient. Thus, in order to use the tables when r_{xy} is actually a multiple correlation coefficient it is necessary to transform Z'_{yi} values by

$$Z_{xi} = \frac{Z'_{yi}}{R_{xy}}$$

Source: J. C. Naylor and L. C. Shine. "A Table for Determining the Increase in Mean Criterion Score Obtained by Using a Selection Device." *Journal of Industrial Psychology*, 1965, 3, 33–42. Used by permission.

A Table for Computing the Mean Criterion Score (Z_{yi}) for the Group Falling Above Some Cutoff Score (Z_{xi})[1]

ϕ_i	Z_{xi}	λ_i	λ_i/ϕ_i	ϕ_i	Z_{xi}	λ_i	λ_i/ϕ_i	ϕ_i	Z_{xi}	λ_i	λ_i/ϕ_i
0.9987	-3.00	0.0044	0.00	0.9974	-2.79	0.0081	0.01	0.9951	-2.58	0.0143	0.01
0.9986	-2.99	0.0046	0.00	0.9973	-2.78	0.0084	0.01	0.9949	-2.57	0.0147	0.01
0.9986	-2.98	0.0047	0.00	0.9972	-2.77	0.0086	0.01	0.9948	-2.56	0.0151	0.02
0.9985	-2.97	0.0048	0.00	0.9971	-2.76	0.0088	0.01	0.9946	-2.55	0.0154	0.02
0.9985	-2.96	0.0050	0.01	0.9970	-2.75	0.0091	0.01	0.9945	-2.54	0.0158	0.02
0.9984	-2.95	0.0051	0.01	0.9969	-2.74	0.0093	0.01	0.9943	-2.53	0.0163	0.02
0.9984	-2.94	0.0053	0.01	0.9968	-2.73	0.0096	0.01	0.9941	-2.52	0.0167	0.02
0.9983	-2.93	0.0055	0.01	0.9967	-2.72	0.0099	0.01	0.9940	-2.51	0.0171	0.02
0.9982	-2.92	0.0056	0.01	0.9966	-2.71	0.0101	0.01	0.9938	-2.50	0.0175	0.02
0.9982	-2.91	0.0058	0.01	0.9965	-2.70	0.0104	0.01	0.9936	-2.49	0.0180	0.02
0.9981	-2.90	0.0060	0.01	0.9964	-2.69	0.0107	0.01	0.9934	-2.48	0.0184	0.02
0.9981	-2.89	0.0061	0.01	0.9963	-2.68	0.0110	0.01	0.9932	-2.47	0.0189	0.02
0.9980	-2.88	0.0063	0.01	0.9962	-2.67	0.0113	0.01	0.9931	-2.46	0.0194	0.02
0.9979	-2.87	0.0065	0.01	0.9961	-2.66	0.0116	0.01	0.9929	-2.45	0.0198	0.02
0.9979	-2.86	0.0067	0.01	0.9960	-2.65	0.0119	0.01	0.9927	-2.44	0.0203	0.02
0.9978	-2.85	0.0069	0.01	0.9959	-2.64	0.0122	0.01	0.9925	-2.43	0.0208	0.02
0.9977	-2.84	0.0071	0.01	0.9957	-2.63	0.0126	0.01	0.9922	-2.42	0.0213	0.02
0.9977	-2.83	0.0073	0.01	0.9956	-2.62	0.0129	0.01	0.9920	-2.41	0.0219	0.02
0.9976	-2.82	0.0075	0.01	0.9955	-2.61	0.0132	0.01	0.9918	-2.40	0.0224	0.02
0.9975	-2.81	0.0077	0.01	0.9953	-2.60	0.0136	0.01	0.9916	-2.39	0.0229	0.02
0.9974	-2.80	0.0079	0.01	0.9952	-2.59	0.0139	0.01	0.9913	-2.38	0.0235	0.02

[1]ϕ_i = proportion above cutoff (selection ratio)

Z_{xi} = predictor cutoff value in standard score form

λ_i = normal curve ordinate at Z_{xi}

A Table for Computing the Mean Criterion Score (Z_{yi}) for the Group Falling Above Some Cutoff Score (Z_{xi})[1]

ϕ_i	Z_{xi}	λ_i	λ_i/ϕ_i	ϕ_i	Z_{xi}	λ_i	λ_i/ϕ_i	ϕ_i	Z_{xi}	λ_i	λ_i/ϕ_i
0.9911	−2.37	0.0241	0.02	0.9834	−2.13	0.0413	0.04	0.9706	−1.89	0.0669	0.07
0.9909	−2.36	0.0246	0.02	0.9830	−2.12	0.0422	0.04	0.9699	−1.88	0.0681	0.07
0.9906	−2.35	0.0252	0.03	0.9826	−2.11	0.0431	0.04	0.9693	−1.87	0.0694	0.07
0.9904	−2.34	0.0258	0.03	0.9821	−2.10	0.0440	0.04	0.9686	−1.86	0.0707	0.07
0.9901	−2.33	0.0264	0.03	0.9817	−2.09	0.0449	0.05	0.9678	−1.85	0.0721	0.07
0.9898	−2.32	0.0270	0.03	0.9812	−2.08	0.0459	0.05	0.9671	−1.84	0.0734	0.07
0.9896	−2.31	0.0277	0.03	0.9808	−2.07	0.0468	0.05	0.9664	−1.83	0.0748	0.08
0.9893	−2.30	0.0283	0.03	0.9803	−2.06	0.0478	0.05	0.9656	−1.82	0.0761	0.08
0.9890	−2.29	0.0290	0.03	0.9798	−2.05	0.0488	0.05	0.9649	−1.81	0.0775	0.08
0.9887	−2.28	0.0297	0.03	0.9793	−2.04	0.0498	0.05	0.9641	−1.80	0.0790	0.08
0.9884	−2.27	0.0303	0.03	0.9788	−2.03	0.0508	0.05	0.9633	−1.79	0.0804	0.08
0.9881	−2.26	0.0310	0.03	0.9783	−2.02	0.0519	0.05	0.9625	−1.78	0.0818	0.08
0.9878	−2.25	0.0317	0.03	0.9778	−2.01	0.0529	0.05	0.9616	−1.77	0.0833	0.09
0.9875	−2.24	0.0325	0.03	0.9772	−2.00	0.0540	0.06	0.9608	−1.76	0.0848	0.09
0.9871	−2.23	0.0332	0.03	0.9767	−1.99	0.0551	0.06	0.9599	−1.75	0.0863	0.09
0.9868	−2.22	0.0339	0.03	0.9761	−1.98	0.0562	0.06	0.9591	−1.74	0.0878	0.09
0.9864	−2.21	0.0347	0.04	0.9756	−1.97	0.0573	0.06	0.9582	−1.73	0.0893	0.09
0.9861	−2.20	0.0355	0.04	0.9750	−1.96	0.0584	0.06	0.9573	−1.72	0.0909	0.09
0.9857	−2.19	0.0363	0.04	0.9744	−1.95	0.0596	0.06	0.9564	−1.71	0.0925	0.10
0.9854	−2.18	0.0371	0.04	0.9738	−1.94	0.0608	0.06	0.9554	−1.70	0.0940	0.10
0.9850	−2.17	0.0379	0.04	0.9732	−1.93	0.0620	0.06	0.9545	−1.69	0.0957	0.10
0.9846	−2.16	0.0387	0.04	0.9726	−1.92	0.0632	0.06	0.9535	−1.68	0.0973	0.10
0.9842	−2.15	0.0396	0.04	0.9719	−1.91	0.0644	0.07	0.9525	−1.67	0.0989	0.10
0.9838	−2.14	0.0404	0.04	0.9713	−1.90	0.0656	0.07	0.9515	−1.66	0.1006	0.11

ϕ_i	Z_{xi}	λ_i	
0.9505	−1.65	0.1023	0.11
0.9495	−1.64	0.1040	0.11
0.9484	−1.63	0.1057	0.11
0.9474	−1.62	0.1074	0.11
0.9463	−1.61	0.1092	0.12
0.9452	−1.60	0.1109	0.12
0.9441	−1.59	0.1127	0.12
0.9429	−1.58	0.1145	0.12
0.9418	−1.57	0.1163	0.12
0.9406	−1.56	0.1182	0.13
0.9394	−1.55	0.1200	0.13
0.9382	−1.54	0.1219	0.13
0.9370	−1.53	0.1238	0.13
0.9357	−1.52	0.1257	0.13
0.9345	−1.51	0.1276	0.14
0.9332	−1.50	0.1295	0.14
0.9319	−1.49	0.1315	0.14
0.9306	−1.48	0.1334	0.14
0.9292	−1.47	0.1354	0.15
0.9279	−1.46	0.1374	0.15
0.9265	−1.45	0.1394	0.15
0.9251	−1.44	0.1415	0.15
0.9236	−1.43	0.1435	0.16
0.9222	−1.42	0.1456	0.16
0.9207	−1.41	0.1476	0.16
0.9192	−1.40	0.1497	0.16
0.9177	−1.39	0.1518	0.17
0.9162	−1.38	0.1539	0.17
0.9147	−1.37	0.1561	0.17
0.9131	−1.36	0.1582	0.17
0.9115	−1.35	0.1604	0.18
0.9099	−1.34	0.1626	0.18
0.9082	−1.33	0.1647	0.18
0.9066	−1.32	0.1669	0.18
0.9049	−1.31	0.1691	0.19
0.9032	−1.30	0.1714	0.19
0.9015	−1.29	0.1736	0.19
0.8997	−1.28	0.1758	0.20
0.8980	−1.27	0.1781	0.20
0.8962	−1.26	0.1804	0.20
0.8944	−1.25	0.1826	0.20
0.8925	−1.24	0.1849	0.21
0.8907	−1.23	0.1872	0.21
0.8888	−1.22	0.1895	0.21
0.8869	−1.21	0.1919	0.22
0.8849	−1.20	0.1942	0.22
0.8830	−1.19	0.1965	0.22
0.8810	−1.18	0.1989	0.23
0.8790	−1.17	0.2012	0.23
0.8770	−1.16	0.2036	0.23
0.8749	−1.15	0.2059	0.24
0.8729	−1.14	0.2083	0.24
0.8708	−1.13	0.2107	0.24
0.8686	−1.12	0.2131	0.25
0.8665	−1.11	0.2155	0.25
0.8643	−1.10	0.2179	0.25
0.8621	−1.09	0.2203	0.26
0.8599	−1.08	0.2227	0.26
0.8577	−1.07	0.2251	0.26
0.8554	−1.06	0.2275	0.27
0.8531	−1.05	0.2299	0.27
0.8508	−1.04	0.2323	0.27
0.8485	−1.03	0.2347	0.28
0.8461	−1.02	0.2371	0.28
0.8438	−1.01	0.2396	0.28
0.8413	−1.00	0.2420	0.29
0.8389	−0.99	0.2444	0.29
0.8365	−0.98	0.2468	0.30
0.8340	−0.97	0.2492	0.30
0.8315	−0.96	0.2516	0.30
0.8289	−0.95	0.2541	0.31
0.8264	−0.94	0.2565	0.31
0.8238	−0.93	0.2589	0.31
0.8212	−0.92	0.2613	0.32
0.8186	−0.91	0.2637	0.32

ϕ_i = proportion above cutoff (selection ratio)
Z_{xi} = predictor cutoff value in standard score form
λ_i = normal curve ordinate at Z_{xi}

A Table for Computing the Mean Criterion Score (Z_{yi}) for the Group Falling Above Some Cutoff Score (Z_{xi})[1]

ϕ_i	Z_{xi}	λ_i	λ_i/ϕ_i	ϕ_i	Z_{xi}	λ_i	λ_i/ϕ_i	ϕ_i	Z_{xi}	λ_i	λ_i/ϕ_i
0.8159	-0.90	0.2661	0.33	0.7454	-0.66	0.3209	0.43	0.6628	-0.42	0.3653	0.55
0.8133	-0.89	0.2685	0.33	0.7422	-0.65	0.3230	0.44	0.6591	-0.41	0.3668	0.56
0.8106	-0.88	0.2709	0.33	0.7389	-0.64	0.3251	0.44	0.6554	-0.40	0.3683	0.56
0.8078	-0.87	0.2732	0.34	0.7357	-0.63	0.3271	0.44	0.6517	-0.39	0.3697	0.57
0.8051	-0.86	0.2756	0.34	0.7324	-0.62	0.3292	0.45	0.6480	-0.38	0.3712	0.57
0.8023	-0.85	0.2780	0.35	0.7291	-0.61	0.3312	0.45	0.6443	-0.37	0.3725	0.58
0.7995	-0.84	0.2803	0.35	0.7257	-0.60	0.3332	0.46	0.6406	-0.36	0.3739	0.58
0.7967	-0.83	0.2827	0.35	0.7224	-0.59	0.3352	0.46	0.6368	-0.35	0.3752	0.59
0.7939	-0.82	0.2850	0.36	0.7190	-0.58	0.3372	0.47	0.6331	-0.34	0.3765	0.59
0.7910	-0.81	0.2874	0.36	0.7157	-0.57	0.3391	0.47	0.6293	-0.33	0.3778	0.60
0.7881	-0.80	0.2897	0.37	0.7123	-0.56	0.3410	0.48	0.6255	-0.32	0.3790	0.61
0.7852	-0.79	0.2920	0.37	0.7088	-0.55	0.3429	0.48	0.6217	-0.31	0.3802	0.61
0.7823	-0.78	0.2943	0.38	0.7054	-0.54	0.3448	0.49	0.6179	-0.30	0.3814	0.62
0.7794	-0.77	0.2966	0.38	0.7019	-0.53	0.3467	0.49	0.6141	-0.29	0.3825	0.62
0.7764	-0.76	0.2989	0.38	0.6985	-0.52	0.3485	0.50	0.6103	-0.28	0.3836	0.63
0.7734	-0.75	0.3011	0.39	0.6950	-0.51	0.3503	0.50	0.6064	-0.27	0.3847	0.64
0.7704	-0.74	0.3034	0.39	0.6915	-0.50	0.3521	0.51	0.6026	-0.26	0.3857	0.64
0.7673	-0.73	0.3056	0.40	0.6879	-0.49	0.3538	0.51	0.5987	-0.25	0.3867	0.65
0.7642	-0.72	0.3079	0.40	0.6844	-0.48	0.3555	0.52	0.5948	-0.24	0.3876	0.65
0.7611	-0.71	0.3101	0.41	0.6808	-0.47	0.3572	0.52	0.5910	-0.23	0.3885	0.66
0.7580	-0.70	0.3123	0.41	0.6772	-0.46	0.3589	0.53	0.5871	-0.22	0.3894	0.66
0.7549	-0.69	0.3144	0.42	0.6736	-0.45	0.3605	0.54	0.5832	-0.21	0.3902	0.67
0.7517	-0.68	0.3166	0.42	0.6700	-0.44	0.3621	0.54	0.5793	-0.20	0.3910	0.67
0.7486	-0.67	0.3187	0.43	0.6664	-0.43	0.3637	0.55	0.5753	-0.19	0.3918	0.68

ϕ_1	Z_{xi}	λ_i	ϕ_1	Z_{xi}	λ_i	ϕ_1	Z_{xi}	λ_i	Z_{xi}	Z_{xi}	Z_{xi}
0.5714	−0.18	0.3925	0.4721	0.07	0.3980	0.3745	0.32	0.3790	0.69	0.84	1.01
0.5675	−0.17	0.3932	0.4681	0.08	0.3977	0.3707	0.33	0.3778	0.69	0.85	1.02
0.5636	−0.16	0.3939	0.4641	0.09	0.3973	0.3669	0.34	0.3765	0.70	0.86	1.03
0.5596	−0.15	0.3945	0.4602	0.10	0.3970	0.3632	0.35	0.3752	0.70	0.86	1.03
0.5557	−0.14	0.3951	0.4562	0.11	0.3965	0.3594	0.36	0.3739	0.71	0.87	1.04
0.5517	−0.13	0.3956	0.4522	0.12	0.3961	0.3557	0.37	0.3725	0.72	0.88	1.05
0.5478	−0.12	0.3961	0.4483	0.13	0.3956	0.3520	0.38	0.3712	0.72	0.88	1.05
0.5438	−0.11	0.3965	0.4443	0.14	0.3951	0.3483	0.39	0.3697	0.73	0.89	1.06
0.5398	−0.10	0.3970	0.4404	0.15	0.3945	0.3446	0.40	0.3683	0.74	0.90	1.07
0.5359	−0.09	0.3973	0.4364	0.16	0.3939	0.3409	0.41	0.3668	0.74	0.90	1.08
0.5319	−0.08	0.3977	0.4325	0.17	0.3932	0.3372	0.42	0.3653	0.75	0.91	1.08
0.5279	−0.07	0.3980	0.4286	0.18	0.3925	0.3336	0.43	0.3637	0.75	0.92	1.09
0.5239	−0.06	0.3982	0.4247	0.19	0.3918	0.3300	0.44	0.3621	0.76	0.92	1.10
0.5199	−0.05	0.3984	0.4207	0.20	0.3910	0.3264	0.45	0.3605	0.77	0.93	1.10
0.5160	−0.04	0.3986	0.4168	0.21	0.3902	0.3228	0.46	0.3589	0.77	0.94	1.11
0.5120	−0.03	0.3988	0.4129	0.22	0.3894	0.3192	0.47	0.3572	0.78	0.94	1.12
0.5080	−0.02	0.3989	0.4090	0.23	0.3885	0.3156	0.48	0.3555	0.79	0.95	1.13
0.5040	−0.01	0.3989	0.4052	0.24	0.3876	0.3121	0.49	0.3538	0.79	0.96	1.13
0.5000	0.00	0.3989	0.4013	0.25	0.3867	0.3085	0.50	0.3521	0.80	0.96	1.14
0.4960	0.01	0.3989	0.3974	0.26	0.3857	0.3050	0.51	0.3503	0.80	0.97	1.15
0.4920	0.02	0.3989	0.3936	0.27	0.3847	0.3015	0.52	0.3485	0.81	0.98	1.16
0.4880	0.03	0.3988	0.3897	0.28	0.3836	0.2981	0.53	0.3467	0.82	0.98	1.16
0.4840	0.04	0.3986	0.3859	0.29	0.3825	0.2946	0.54	0.3448	0.82	0.99	1.17
0.4801	0.05	0.3984	0.3821	0.30	0.3814	0.2912	0.55	0.3429	0.83	1.00	1.18
0.4761	0.06	0.3982	0.3783	0.31	0.3802	0.2877	0.56	0.3410	0.84	1.01	1.19

ϕ_1 = proportion above cutoff (selection ratio)
Z_{xi} = predictor cutoff value in standard score form
λ_i = normal curve ordinate at Z_{xi}

A Table for Computing the Mean Criterion Score (Z_{yi}) for the Group Falling Above Some Cutoff Score (Z_{xi})[1]

ϕ_i	Z_{xi}	λ_i	λ_i/ϕ_i	ϕ_i	Z_{xi}	λ_i	λ_i/ϕ_i	ϕ_i	Z_{xi}	λ_i	λ_i/ϕ_i
0.2843	0.57	0.3391	1.19	0.2090	0.81	0.2874	1.38	0.1469	1.05	0.2299	1.57
0.2810	0.58	0.3372	1.20	0.2061	0.82	0.2850	1.38	0.1446	1.06	0.2275	1.57
0.2776	0.59	0.3352	1.21	0.2033	0.83	0.2827	1.39	0.1423	1.07	0.2251	1.58
0.2743	0.60	0.3332	1.21	0.2005	0.84	0.2803	1.40	0.1401	1.08	0.2227	1.59
0.2709	0.61	0.3312	1.22	0.1977	0.85	0.2780	1.41	0.1379	1.09	0.2203	1.60
0.2676	0.62	0.3292	1.23	0.1949	0.86	0.2756	1.41	0.1357	1.10	0.2179	1.61
0.2643	0.63	0.3271	1.24	0.1922	0.87	0.2732	1.42	0.1335	1.11	0.2155	1.61
0.2611	0.64	0.3251	1.25	0.1894	0.88	0.2709	1.43	0.1314	1.12	0.2131	1.62
0.2578	0.65	0.3230	1.25	0.1867	0.89	0.2685	1.44	0.1292	1.13	0.2107	1.63
0.2546	0.66	0.3209	1.26	0.1841	0.90	0.2661	1.45	0.1271	1.14	0.2083	1.64
0.2514	0.67	0.3187	1.27	0.1814	0.91	0.2637	1.45	0.1251	1.15	0.2059	1.65
0.2483	0.68	0.3166	1.28	0.1788	0.92	0.2613	1.46	0.1230	1.16	0.2036	1.66
0.2451	0.69	0.3144	1.28	0.1762	0.93	0.2589	1.47	0.1210	1.17	0.2012	1.66
0.2420	0.70	0.3123	1.29	0.1736	0.94	0.2565	1.48	0.1190	1.18	0.1989	1.67
0.2389	0.71	0.3101	1.30	0.1711	0.95	0.2541	1.49	0.1170	1.19	0.1965	1.68
0.2358	0.72	0.3079	1.31	0.1685	0.96	0.2516	1.49	0.1151	1.20	0.1942	1.69
0.2327	0.73	0.3056	1.31	0.1660	0.97	0.2492	1.50	0.1131	1.21	0.1919	1.70
0.2296	0.74	0.3034	1.32	0.1635	0.98	0.2468	1.51	0.1112	1.22	0.1895	1.70
0.2266	0.75	0.3011	1.33	0.1611	0.99	0.2444	1.52	0.1093	1.23	0.1872	1.71
0.2236	0.76	0.2989	1.34	0.1587	1.00	0.2420	1.52	0.1075	1.24	0.1849	1.72
0.2206	0.77	0.2966	1.34	0.1562	1.01	0.2396	1.53	0.1056	1.25	0.1826	1.73
0.2177	0.78	0.2943	1.35	0.1539	1.02	0.2371	1.54	0.1038	1.26	0.1804	1.74
0.2148	0.79	0.2920	1.36	0.1515	1.03	0.2347	1.55	0.1020	1.27	0.1781	1.75
0.2119	0.80	0.2897	1.37	0.1492	1.04	0.2323	1.56	0.1003	1.28	0.1758	1.75

ϕ_i	Z_{xi}	λ_i	
0.0985	1.29	0.1736	1.76
0.0968	1.30	0.1714	1.77
0.0951	1.31	0.1691	1.78
0.0934	1.32	0.1669	1.79
0.0918	1.33	0.1647	1.79
0.0901	1.34	0.1626	1.80
0.0885	1.35	0.1604	1.81
0.0869	1.36	0.1582	1.82
0.0853	1.37	0.1561	1.83
0.0838	1.38	0.1539	1.84
0.0823	1.39	0.1518	1.84
0.0808	1.40	0.1497	1.85
0.0793	1.41	0.1476	1.86
0.0778	1.42	0.1456	1.87
0.0764	1.43	0.1435	1.88
0.0749	1.44	0.1415	1.89
0.0735	1.45	0.1394	1.90
0.0721	1.46	0.1374	1.91
0.0708	1.47	0.1354	1.91
0.0694	1.48	0.1334	1.92
0.0681	1.49	0.1315	1.93
0.0668	1.50	0.1295	1.94
0.0655	1.51	0.1276	1.95
0.0643	1.52	0.1257	1.95
0.0630	1.53	0.1238	1.97
0.0618	1.54	0.1219	1.97
0.0606	1.55	0.1200	1.98
0.0594	1.56	0.1182	1.99
0.0582	1.57	0.1163	2.00
0.0571	1.58	0.1145	2.01
0.0559	1.59	0.1127	2.02
0.0548	1.60	0.1109	2.02
0.0537	1.61	0.1092	2.03
0.0526	1.62	0.1074	2.04
0.0516	1.63	0.1057	2.05
0.0505	1.64	0.1040	2.06
0.0495	1.65	0.1023	2.07
0.0485	1.66	0.1006	2.07
0.0475	1.67	0.0989	2.08
0.0465	1.68	0.0973	2.09
0.0455	1.69	0.0957	2.10
0.0446	1.70	0.0940	2.11
0.0436	1.71	0.0925	2.12
0.0427	1.72	0.0909	2.13
0.0418	1.73	0.0893	2.14
0.0409	1.74	0.0878	2.15
0.0401	1.75	0.0863	2.15
0.0392	1.76	0.0848	2.16
0.0384	1.77	0.0833	2.17
0.0375	1.78	0.0818	2.18
0.0367	1.79	0.0804	2.19
0.0359	1.80	0.0790	2.20
0.0351	1.81	0.0775	2.21
0.0344	1.82	0.0761	2.21
0.0336	1.83	0.0748	2.23
0.0329	1.84	0.0734	2.23
0.0322	1.85	0.0721	2.24
0.0314	1.86	0.0707	2.25
0.0307	1.87	0.0694	2.26
0.0301	1.88	0.0681	2.26
0.0294	1.89	0.0669	2.28
0.0287	1.90	0.0656	2.29
0.0281	1.91	0.0644	2.29
0.0274	1.92	0.0632	2.31
0.0268	1.93	0.0620	2.31
0.0262	1.94	0.0608	2.32
0.0256	1.95	0.0596	2.33
0.0250	1.96	0.0584	2.34
0.0244	1.97	0.0573	2.35
0.0239	1.98	0.0562	2.35
0.0233	1.99	0.0551	2.36
0.0228	2.00	0.0540	2.37
0.0222	2.01	0.0529	2.38
0.0217	2.02	0.0519	2.39
0.0212	2.03	0.0508	2.40

ϕ_i = proportion above cutoff (selection ratio)

Z_{xi} = predictor cutoff value in standard score form

λ_i = normal curve ordinate at Z_{xi}

A Table for Computing the Mean Criterion Score (Z_{yi}) for the Group Falling Above Some Cutoff Score (Z_{xi})[1]

ϕ_i	Z_{xi}	λ_i	λ_i/ϕ_i	ϕ_i	Z_{xi}	λ_i	λ_i/ϕ_i	ϕ_i	Z_{xi}	λ_i	λ_i/ϕ_i
0.0207	2.04	0.0498	2.41	0.0113	2.28	0.0297	2.63	0.0059	2.52	0.0167	2.84
0.0202	2.05	0.0488	2.42	0.0110	2.29	0.0290	2.64	0.0057	2.53	0.0163	2.85
0.0197	2.06	0.0478	2.43	0.0107	2.30	0.0283	2.64	0.0055	2.54	0.0158	2.86
0.0192	2.07	0.0468	2.44	0.0104	2.31	0.0277	2.65	0.0054	2.55	0.0154	2.87
0.0188	2.08	0.0459	2.44	0.0102	2.32	0.0270	2.66	0.0052	2.56	0.0151	2.88
0.0183	2.09	0.0449	2.45	0.0099	2.33	0.0264	2.67	0.0051	2.57	0.0147	2.89
0.0179	2.10	0.0440	2.46	0.0096	2.34	0.0258	2.68	0.0049	2.58	0.0143	2.90
0.0174	2.11	0.0431	2.48	0.0094	2.35	0.0252	2.68	0.0048	2.59	0.0139	2.90
0.0170	2.12	0.0422	2.48	0.0091	2.36	0.0246	2.69	0.0047	2.60	0.0136	2.91
0.0166	2.13	0.0413	2.49	0.0089	2.37	0.0241	2.71	0.0045	2.61	0.0132	2.92
0.0162	2.14	0.0404	2.49	0.0087	2.38	0.0235	2.71	0.0044	2.62	0.0129	2.93
0.0158	2.15	0.0396	2.51	0.0084	2.39	0.0229	2.72	0.0043	2.63	0.0126	2.94
0.0154	2.16	0.0387	2.51	0.0082	2.40	0.0224	2.73	0.0041	2.64	0.0122	2.95
0.0150	2.17	0.0379	2.53	0.0080	2.41	0.0219	2.74	0.0040	2.65	0.0119	2.96
0.0146	2.18	0.0371	2.54	0.0078	2.42	0.0213	2.74	0.0039	2.66	0.0116	2.97
0.0143	2.19	0.0363	2.54	0.0075	2.43	0.0208	2.76	0.0038	2.67	0.0113	2.98
0.0139	2.20	0.0355	2.55	0.0073	2.44	0.0203	2.76	0.0037	2.68	0.0110	2.99
0.0136	2.21	0.0347	2.55	0.0071	2.45	0.0198	2.77	0.0036	2.69	0.0107	3.00
0.0132	2.22	0.0339	2.57	0.0069	2.46	0.0194	2.79	0.0035	2.70	0.0104	3.01
0.0129	2.23	0.0332	2.57	0.0068	2.47	0.0189	2.80	0.0034	2.71	0.0101	3.01
0.0125	2.24	0.0325	2.60	0.0066	2.48	0.0184	2.80	0.0033	2.72	0.0099	3.02
0.0122	2.25	0.0317	2.60	0.0064	2.49	0.0180	2.82	0.0032	2.73	0.0096	3.03
0.0119	2.26	0.0310	2.61	0.0062	2.50	0.0175	2.82	0.0031	2.74	0.0093	3.04
0.0116	2.27	0.0303	2.61	0.0060	2.51	0.0171	2.83	0.0030	2.75	0.0091	3.05

ϕ_i	Z_{xi}	λ_i	
0.0029	2.76	0.0088	3.06
0.0028	2.77	0.0086	3.07
0.0027	2.78	0.0084	3.08
0.0026	2.79	0.0081	3.09
0.0026	2.80	0.0079	3.10
0.0025	2.81	0.0077	3.11
0.0024	2.82	0.0075	3.12
0.0023	2.83	0.0073	3.13
0.0023	2.84	0.0071	3.13
0.0022	2.85	0.0069	3.14
0.0021	2.86	0.0067	3.15
0.0021	2.87	0.0065	3.16
0.0020	2.88	0.0063	3.17
0.0019	2.89	0.0061	3.18
0.0019	2.90	0.0060	3.19
0.0018	2.91	0.0058	3.20
0.0018	2.92	0.0056	3.21
0.0017	2.93	0.0055	3.22
0.0016	2.94	0.0053	3.23
0.0016	2.95	0.0051	3.24
0.0015	2.96	0.0050	3.25
0.0015	2.97	0.0048	3.26
0.0014	2.98	0.0047	3.26
0.0014	2.99	0.0046	3.27
0.0013	3.00	0.0044	3.28

[1]ϕ_i = proportion above cutoff (selection ratio)
Z_{xi} = predictor cutoff value in standard score form
λ_i = normal curve ordinate at Z_{xi}

Index